The Blue Plate

A Food Lover's Guide to Climate Chaos

Mark J. Easter

patagonia®

The Blue Plate *A Food Lover's Guide to Climate Chaos*

Patagonia publishes a select list of titles on wilderness, wildlife, and outdoor sports that inspire and restore a connection to the natural world and encourage action to combat climate chaos.

Published by Patagonia Works.

Hardcover Edition.

Printed in Canada on Rolland Enviro 100 Satin FSC certified 100 percent postconsumer-waste paper.

Hardcover ISBN 978-1-952338-20-5
E-Book ISBN 978-1-952338-21-2
Library of Congress Control Number 2024941642

Editor - John Dutton
Photo Editor - Jane Sievert
Art Director/Designer - Christina Speed
Figures and Map - Christina Speed
Project Manager - Sonia Moore
Photo Production - Angelo Partemi
Production - Natausha Greenblott
Creative Director - Michael Leon
Publisher - Karla Olson

ENVIRONMENTAL BENEFITS STATEMENT

Patagonia Inc saved the following resources by printing the pages of this book on chlorine free paper made with 100% post-consumer waste.

TREES	WATER	ENERGY	SOLID WASTE	GREENHOUSE GASES
204	16,000	86	670	88,200
FULLY GROWN	GALLONS	MILLION BTUs	POUNDS	POUNDS

Environmental impact estimates were made using the Environmental Paper Network Paper Calculator 4.0. For more information visit www.papercalculator.org

FOR THE PLANET

MEMBER

FSC
www.fsc.org

MIX
Paper | Supporting responsible forestry

FSC® C016245

Cover and Chapter Title Artwork: Liam O'Farrell

Endpaper: A spring orchard full of blooming peach trees. *Vasilis Ververidis / Alamy*

Facing title page: Spring lunch. *Amy Kumler*

For the microbes.

Clam steamers with seasonal greens. *Remy Anthes / Hog Island Oyster Co.*

Is it still possible to face the gathering darkness and say to the physical Earth, and to all its creatures, including ourselves, fiercely and without embarrassment, I love you, and to embrace fearlessly the burning world? *Barry Lopez*

Foreword

From Nice Ingredients to Collective Economic Regeneration

Anthony Myint

My relationship to food systems has veered wildly, with many highs and lows, but ultimately the shift to regeneration has given my life hope and meaning.

I became a chef in an improbable way, to say the least. I was a line cook at a good restaurant and, on a lark, my wife and I made arrangements to sublet a Guatemalan snack cart. I prepared ingredients for a special kind of taco that we'd serve on a Thursday night—the cart was parked near the bars on Friday and Saturday—and we arranged to borrow it the next Thursday for $125.

This was the first of many instances of creating opportunities with limited resources. New media was just beginning, and this oddball food truck went viral (or the 2008 equivalent). There was a line before I set foot in the truck, and after a few fever-pitched Thursday nights, we made arrangements to move into a run-down Chinese restaurant a couple of blocks away. Journalists would later refer to this as a "pop-up."

Previous spread: Research Technician James Bowden tends a field of Kernza® at The Land Institute near Salina, Kansas. *Amy Kumler*

Mission Street Food felt like the start of an indie-restaurant movement with a new theme menu, new co-chef, and a new charitable beneficiary every Thursday and Saturday. My wife joked that it was like planning a wedding twice a week. We had lines down the block and were able to keep managing all the chaos for weeks. The *San Francisco Chronicle* referred to it as "The Most Influential Restaurant of the Past Decade."

While we were sending all the profits to a local food bank each week, and building community in the industry, I did not consider myself a food activist. We were having fun and were definitely sourcing more from the Asian market than the farmers market. Even as the restaurant evolved into a permanent pop-up called Mission Chinese Food, it was more about breaking down boundaries than raising the bar on the ingredients or focusing on social impact. After gaining traction in our Chinese restaurant within another Chinese restaurant in San Francisco, my cofounder, the great chef Danny Bowien, pushed us to open a location in Manhattan. We had only $55,000 saved up and signed a lease on a Thai takeout window attached to a plywood beer garden. Miraculously, Mission Chinese was named Restaurant of the Year by the *New York Times* for Szechuan-influenced dishes like Kung Pao Pastrami. But while the food was mashing up techniques across cuisines and price points and making a statement about class and cultural capital, it was just as disconnected from agriculture as most of the food economy.

That year, while Danny was working a hundred hours a week and becoming a celebrity chef, my wife and I celebrated the birth of our daughter, Aviva. Becoming parents really shifted our priorities and we dedicated ourselves to steering our industry toward climate solutions. We began to research both the scale of the climate impacts and the immense opportunity for the food system. A lot of the prevailing sentiment was around the opportunities from reducing waste and making plant-forward choices. But even those big shifts felt like merely delaying the inevitable.

So when we learned about regenerative agriculture, I knew immediately that it was the most important story in food. For starters, it was optimistic. But whereas the idea of ecosystem restoration seemed positive, I gained new clarity—massive amounts of emissions could be removed from the atmosphere and then actually restored as healthy soil! This changed everything. And unlike most climate solutions, nobody had to give up things they enjoy. We just needed to shift the growing practices. And bonus: improved nutrition and flavor. It seemed too good to be true!

We began to make connections and lay the groundwork for opening a restaurant to champion regenerative agriculture. The Perennial opened in 2015 with sourdough bread made with Kernza®, a new perennial grain developed by The Land Institute. We also boasted a whole-animal butchery program with beef from the innovative Marin Carbon Project compost pilot sites. Soil tests from the pastures analyzed by scientists at UC Berkeley showed that after only a few years, the carbon pulled from the atmosphere into the soil on just one-tenth of the ranch counteracted the burning of an extraordinary amount of gasoline! These kinds of ingredients represented literally world-saving potential if farms across the globe could shift from extractive to regenerative agriculture.

But even when a customer would listen to my spiel and get inspired, there was no way to take action. There was no supply of regenerative ingredients. And even though we paid great farmers a good price, it had no bearing on the next farm—in fact, it didn't even really help the regenerative farmer implement the next practice. Any real change was at someone else's discretion, if they cared enough, or had enough money. But often, getting the next farmer to practice on the next acre meant six-figure loans, so I began to doubt whether a chef paying an extra dollar was even making an impact. People having good intentions does not equate to action.

My optimism really tanked when I learned that even the whole organic movement, which has clear price premiums and broad market penetration, was still just 1 percent of the total acres farmed after fifty-plus years. In 2019 we closed The Perennial. We'd been named *Bon Appétit's* Most Sustainable Restaurant in America, but we'd also sunk our life savings and several years into a project that failed to truly make change.

They say hindsight is twenty-twenty, and of course it was now clear why we'd failed: Buying a nice ingredient didn't change how crops were grown on any acres. We'd accidentally established the pop-up movement, but despite our years of effort, chefs and customers hadn't jumped onto the regenerative bandwagon. Or if they did, it was just an idea, not a paradigm shift. Regenerative agriculture seemed to me like the biggest win-win available to society, and yet customers and farmers didn't have a way to team up and change acres.

But later that year, we began discussions with the California Department of Food and Agriculture and other state agencies about a new mechanism that could actually make transformative change possible. It's appropriate that this book is being published by Patagonia, because they've had clarity for decades and are themselves reinventing capitalism. Just as Mark and many other researchers have been creating scientific frameworks to unlock change in the field, Patagonia's 1% for the Planet program has been economically advancing environmental solutions for years. Research from Project Drawdown also finds that, globally, if society used just 1 percent of GDP per year on climate solutions, instead of slightly more than 0 percent, we'd not only reach net zero, but we'd lower temperatures by 2050.

My nonprofit, Zero Foodprint, is operationalizing that kind of regenerative economy by offering a focused solution that directly connects the next dollar to the adoption of regenerative practices on the next acre. For example, businesses ranging from a Michelin three-star restaurant to all five Subway sandwich shop locations in Boulder, Colorado, to wine companies, caterers, and even compost companies are sending 1 percent of their sales to regenerative practices. We collect what's typically a few cents from each purchase and then use the funds to team up with farms and ranches, economically, to switch from chemical fertilizer to compost, or to plant cover crops or perennials, or just to help a regenerative farmer extend their practices to more acres. This shift—from occasionally buying a regenerative ingredient to actively supporting regenerative farming—is the key.

This Table to Farm movement also makes customers feel great because every purchase is part of a local climate solution. And most businesses choose to make it optional, so any customer can opt out, though only about one out of a thousand actually do. Since 2020, we've already helped sixty-five farms and ranches implement projects that have sequestered as much carbon as not burning about four million gallons of gas. And we're just getting started.

My voyage of discovery was characterized by opportunism and strategic use of resources, and it has led me to collaborations with other like-minded leaders like Mark Easter, Dorn Cox, John Wick, Patagonia, Dr. Bronner's, and dozens of changemakers and regenerative farmers and ranchers, who are all finding ways to regenerate and create systems for regeneration.

Just to be as clear as possible: You can be part of the solution! And natural climate solutions create compounding, local benefits. In other words, society saving the planet can be as straightforward as each person just saving one little piece of Earth at a time.

Hopefully our stories can be part of your voyage of discovery. Welcome to the movement!

Anthony Myint with his wife Karen Leibowitz. Anthony is a chef turned climate activist. He is the executive director at Zero Foodprint, a non-profit working with state and regional government to scale regenerative agriculture. Anthony is also the cofounder of Mission Street Food, Mission Chinese Food, The Perennial, and Commonwealth restaurants. Photo: Alanna Hale

Introduction

Can we eat our way out of the climate crisis?

   That question came to a head for me one June afternoon when my colleague Amy Swan streamed into my office and corralled me at my desk.

   "Today is produce pickup day at my CSA [community supported agriculture]. You've really got to come meet the farmers Amy and Rod, who run the show there," she said. "You are going to love it."

   Amy had been nudging me to connect with these two farmer friends of hers for months. I looked at my watch. It was late in the afternoon, and despite the late hour, I felt the all-too-familiar pull of my professional obligations. Amy and I are ecologists at Colorado State University, working in a research group that studies the carbon footprint of food. It was no surprise she would pop into my office to drag me away to an event focused on food, because we study food for a living. In fact, I think about food all the time—not just in my own kitchen or at the dining room table, but also in the car when I see crops and livestock in farm fields and pastures

Previous spread: Kate Rutherford does some last-minute shopping before heading into the backcountry in Picos de Europa, Spain. *Ken Etzel*

rolling past my windshield. In bookstores I first locate the shelves holding cookbooks and food writing. While on shopping errands I dawdle in aisles that display kitchen appliances, wondering about the latest advances in efficiency. My yard is filled with fruit trees and garden vegetables in season, and whenever I am outdoors, the edible parts of the landscape capture my attention first.

I trusted Amy implicitly in all things involving both science and food, and was really curious about these farmers she was so enthusiastic about. Yet, I still had a pile of reports and data analysis to complete, and felt the ever-present weight of responsibility anchoring me to my chair. I glanced up at Amy, who stood, arms crossed across her chest, foot absentmindedly tapping, a little smile on her face.

"They'll have yummy treats," she added.

"Let's go," I replied. We practically raced for our bikes.

Minutes later we arrived at an urban subdivision near the college campus where we worked. Rows of tidy houses with neat yards lined the street. It was a familiar space, but I was confused. My work has taken me onto hundreds of farms around the world, and nearly all of them have consisted of a farmhouse in a yard surrounded by equipment, barns, grain bins, sorting sheds, and other buildings. Fields and pastures border the yard. Yet the Sunspot Urban Farm headquarters is in the garage of a home in the center of a city of 150,000 people. Friends I hadn't seen in a while waved and greeted me, and I wondered what they knew that I didn't, and why they had never told me about this place.

A smiling woman worked the crowd, handing out glasses of lemonade. "Jalapeño-basil," she told me as I peered at the shredded greens and wafer-thin slices of chilies floating on the surface. Amy and I each took a glass and raised it to our noses. The aroma carried fresh lemon, pungent herb, and a faintly spicy bite of the pepper. I started salivating immediately, and quickly took a long sip. Amy raised her glass to me, with a smile that said, "See what you've been missing, you knucklehead?"

Then I started to look around, and my food curiosity meter pegged in delighted astonishment. Neat lines of tomatoes, kale, squash, herbs, and other vegetables ran through the yards of the homes on either side of us. Carefully laid paths of wood chips separated the beds that stretched out under evenly spaced, half-circle hoops of row cover frames, each like a clean, white rib. Strips of black irrigation drip tape stretched down the rows, meting out water and nutrients to the roots of the vegetables-in-waiting. A cache of tools leaned against the side of the house. Chickens squawked from the backyard. This was obviously a farm, growing delicious-looking produce.

I let the portions of my brain dominated by what my friend and colleague Dorn Cox calls farmphilia, or "love of farms," take over: the settled, relaxed, and focused way that I feel when I'm out on the land with people who spend their days tending soil, raising food, and who love what they're doing. It is the way I feel in my own garden, even when hot summer sweat drips into my eyes or I'm racing to harvest the last of my produce before a fall storm buries the garden in snow.

I walked over to a row of vibrant green tomato plants, knelt down, and nestled a green-tinged fruit in my hand. It was still a little firm, perhaps a week from harvest. It gave off a promising ·

grassy-savory, spicy aroma. I felt the leathery tenderness of deep-green dinosaur kale in the adjoining row. I thought about this food's path to the table, and its legacy. Before long it would be nourishing the people standing in the driveway, who had come to collect the farm's bounty. Once each week Amy Yackel and Rod Adams and their employees and interns at Sunspot Urban Farm collect the harvest to distribute into portions for the people who bought shares in their CSA. Compared with most food grown in the United States, which travels at least a thousand miles over days or weeks before landing on a grocer's shelves, the path of the food from a typical CSA is a few miles at most, harvested in the morning and distributed to people's homes by dinnertime.

Part of that farmphilia moment was my own curiosity about the farm's "carbon footprint," the collective weight of the greenhouse gases produced on the farm and "upstream" from the farm in the factories that manufactured the equipment, chemicals, fertilizers, and fuels used on farms and ranches. Not just those emissions, but those that come from the farm's ecosystem— greenhouse gases generated by the plants and livestock, and most importantly, those gases cycling into and out of the soil itself. In my conversations that day and afterward with my colleague Amy, and with the two farmers running Sunspot Urban Farm, a clear line of innovations emerged that set them apart from their peers and dramatically lowered the food's carbon footprint. Amy and I and our team at CSU had studied the carbon footprint of food and fiber crops grown on every continent except Antarctica, but rarely worked in what was practically my own backyard, and never on an urban CSA.

Could farms like this help shield us from the looming threat of the climate crisis? Could transforming the way humanity grows, processes, ships, and serves its food, and deals with the leftovers, through what is becoming known to the world as "regenerative farming" and "carbon farming," offset the calamitous burden of more than a century of burning fossil fuels?

This question once overwhelmed me during a terrifying epiphany I experienced early in my career.

I recently retired from my job as an ecologist at Colorado State University, working in a research group studying the carbon footprint of food. We are essentially greenhouse gas accountants. We try to understand how greenhouse gases move into and out of soils and plants on farms and ranches. We aggregate the flow of gases onto balance sheets, much like financial accountants monitor cash flows, to estimate the total carbon footprint for the food and fiber on farms and ranches around the world.

One evening in a grocery store after work I selected a cucumber from the cool, misty shelves and stood for a while examining it. Earlier that day, I'd encountered new research describing the total collective carbon footprint of agriculture around the world. The numbers shocked me. The research reported that about a quarter of the greenhouse gas emissions in the world's collective carbon footprint came from growing, processing, distributing, and cooking food, and dealing with the leftovers.[1,2] It was a stunning revelation into what has since been described as agriculture's long shadow.

Strawberries at Sunspot Urban Farm. Fort Collins, Colorado.
Amy Yackel Adams

Beyond the cucumber were the other items there—milk for morning coffee, meat for an evening meal, bread for sandwiches, tortilla chips and salsa, eggs, salad greens. They contained the carbon dioxide from fossil fuels burned to plant, harvest, and ship crops, process them into foods, and to manufacture the fuels and farm chemicals used to grow them. More carbon dioxide came from organic matter decomposed by microbes in degraded soils. Powerful trace gases like nitrous oxide from the fertilizers applied to the fields. Potent methane from the stomachs of the cows and from lagoons full of manure accumulating at dairies. A myriad of other sources. I don't know how long I stood there blocking the aisle, but in those moments my view of food changed forever.

What formerly had been to me this pure, elemental thing, the product of evolutionary miracles, was suddenly tainted with the chemical stench of steel, diesel exhaust, and factory smokestacks. Not only that, but the individual whispers of microbes collected into a deafening roar of the powerful, climate-heating trace gases all of their tiny bodies emit. The sum total of it was enormous. For me, food transitioned from something soft and almost mythical into something entirely new—both cold and hard, with dimensions I'd never imagined.

Since that day, a question has haunted me: Can we transform agriculture from a system that literally consumes the planet to one that nurtures and respects this home that is all we will ever know? Can we cultivate from the Earth meals that nourish us, a Blue Plate of sorts, rather than the Earth being the meal itself?

Every meal now begins for me with some quick arithmetic about the climate impacts on the plate before me. It is a frightening algorithm, bordering on deadly, and it has motivated me and my family to dramatically change what and how we eat.

What astonishes me to this day is that the chain of actions that transform seed, soil, air, sun, and rain into a head of lettuce, a pound of wheat, a hamburger, or a gallon of milk are among the forces driving the climate into frightening new territory. That perspective, which has now frankly shocked many in the scientific community as well as the public, could only be gained from the mountain of information research scientists have accumulated since the Earth Summit held in Rio de Janeiro in 1992, which birthed the imperative that societies measure and inventory greenhouse gas emissions from human activities. A new family of scientific disciplines emerged to meet that need, focusing on the greenhouse gas emissions that come from the way we grow food, maintain livestock pastures, and manage forests. Extraordinary new scientific themes have come out of the work. In particular, four of these stories stand out the most to me:

- Emissions from agriculture have likely been warming the climate for thousands of years. The dawn of agriculture ten thousand years ago led humans to clear the native forests, shrublands, and grasslands of their homes to grow crops. Just three seemingly simple actions that remain fundamental to agriculture to this day appear to have added enough greenhouse gases to the atmosphere to prevent the Earth from sliding into what is now believed to be an overdue Ice Age. They are 1) clearing forests and grasslands to make room for agriculture; 2) raising domesticated livestock; and 3) plowing soil to grow crops. Said a little differently, the carbon footprint of food is not new to the industrial era. It has been a very big deal throughout the history of human civilization.

- Fossil fuels aren't the greatest source of greenhouse gas emissions in agriculture; however, their use on the field and in manufacturing of farm equipment and chemicals leads to enormous emissions from ecosystems. Contemporary agriculture has adopted fossil fuel energy to address virtually every limiting factor in agriculture. Consider the simple act of a tractor dragging a plow through a field. The carbon bled into the atmosphere from that radically disturbed soil far exceeds the greenhouse gases from the diesel fuel burned in that tractor engine. Energy-intensive manufacturing of nitrogen fertilizers leads to very large nitrous oxide emissions in farm fields after fertilizers are applied. Modern electrical grids and pumps make it possible for dairies, pig farms, and other confined livestock feeding operations to store trillions of gallons of liquid manure in open lakes (called lagoons). Emissions from these lagoons, however, rank in the top tier of global emissions. Fossil fuels make it possible to manufacture chemical fertilizers that, once applied to crops, spawn enormous emissions of climate-heating nitrogen compounds from the soil. Similarly, modern roads and trash trucks make

Combines harvest soybeans on a cleared Brazilian Cerrado forest. Brazil is the world's largest exporter of soybeans, most of which go to feed livestock in concentrated animal feeding operations. *George Steinmetz*

it possible for food waste, once a relative rarity, to accumulate at the rate of hundreds of millions of tons per year in the oxygen-depleted depths of town dumps. The methane emissions from those dumps far exceed those from the diesel fuel burned to transport and bury the food there in the first place. In addition, fossil fuel use shifts what is known as the "energy balance" in agriculture so that far more fossil fuel calories of energy are burned to grow a crop compared with the caloric energy of the harvested crops.[3] Additionally, fossil fuels' pervasive use distorts human culture's relationship to land, making it possible to live in places like Phoenix, Abu Dhabi, and Las Vegas, cities that are hundreds to thousands of miles from the food-producing regions that support them.

• The vast storehouses of carbon currently in the soil, in forests, and in the fossil fuel reserves must be left where they are. It is increasingly clear that there is now little margin for error in creating a zero-carbon-emission future. "Keep it in the ground" has become a mantra for agriculture. Humanity must stop clearing any remaining forests and grasslands to create fields or pastures to raise food. We must make do with the fields and pastures we currently have. We must also leverage the billions of acres of crops, forests, pastures, and rangeland to pull more carbon from the atmosphere into the soil and keep it there.

A beef processing facility with cattle about to be slaughtered visible at the bottom of the photograph. Amarillo, Texas. *George Steinmetz*

- Microbes are both at the root of food's carbon footprint and at the center of the solutions. Legions of uncountable creatures laboring in complex, poorly understood ecosystems in the soil, the guts of animals, manure lagoons, and the depths of town dumps throughout the planet collectively contribute billions of tons of carbon and nitrogen pollution every year to our already-overheated climate. Astonishingly, we can actually join league with the microbial community to reverse much of that carbon pollution, working with nature rather than against it to take a big bite out of the climate crisis. We just have to feed the microbes in the right places and avoid feeding them in the wrong places.

As an ecologist, I can wrap my head around the fascinating processes and relationships that bring these emissions about. The sheer size of the emissions, however, is a damning condemnation of "business as usual" in the food system.

But there is good news to share! Innovative, low-carbon ways to raise food are already being practiced on millions of acres of fields and pastures throughout the world.

> • ‹

This book is my attempt to distill the art and science of carbon farming into stories centered on the plates of food around which our daily lives orbit. It is largely focused geographically on agriculture supporting what is known as the "Western diet" adopted by much of the developed world, which relies on industrialized agriculture, with stories mostly from North and South America.

The story in each morsel reveals the causes and effects of greenhouse gas emissions, as well as paths to a low-carbon food future. Consider what might be a typical meal at an American weekend dinner party. Perhaps a seafood appetizer or cup of chowder opens the meal. A giant bowl of tossed salad with a savory vinaigrette circles the table. Fragrant dinner rolls and a butter plate quickly follow. The host carries out from the kitchen a magnificent roast or a generous chicken casserole with a side of potatoes. A succulent pie with ice cream topping closes the meal. Consider the stories behind these foods—the soil that grew the lettuce, the farmers and ranchers and orchardists stewarding the land, the dairy and farmworkers and grocers who labored to bring it to the table. The meal probably is delicious, and there are millions of stories like this every day.

But now, try to imagine the intricate, highly engineered system that makes meals like this possible, no matter the season. Behind the head of lettuce are fantastic concrete dams described as the greatest wonders of the world, guaranteeing irrigation water for millions of acres of what was formerly diverse desert grasslands, where lettuce and a plethora of other vegetables and fruits now grow. Gigantic, refrigerated warehouses allow fresh vegetables to be cooled, processed, and deployed within hours to markets hundreds or even thousands of miles away. Airlines carrying fresh-caught fish from oceans to fishmongers throughout the world made the appetizer possible. Farmed fish and shrimp, once a restaurateur's novelty, now meet nearly half the world's demand for seafood. Somewhat rare a half century ago, concentrated animal feeding operations (CAFOs) around the world now accumulate manure piles and lagoons at giant dairies and animal feedlots housing thousands of animals each. Synthetic fertilizers that have been widely available for only about three generations now make it possible to raise the vast quantities of grain and fodder necessary to feed dairy and meat animals inside the cramped CAFOs that define animal husbandry today, rather than the pastures where these animals evolved. These technologies have led to declining nutritional quality of the foods coming from these systems.[4]

Each of these innovations interacts with the unseen but ever-present microbial legions to dramatically alter the landscape of food. Novel new ecosystems created in the process amplify food's carbon footprint far beyond what it was just a few generations ago. Our ancestors would likely recognize many of agriculture's solutions to the current crisis as practical features common to the agriculture of years past. Growing cover crops to feed the soil, preventing erosion, feeding livestock on pastures integrated with food crops, composting food waste and livestock manure to cycle nutrients back onto fields and pastures, and purchasing from one's local "foodshed" all were common-sense aspects of agriculture in times past. Putting to practical use the biomass in the tree trunks left after replanting an orchard was more than common sense; it was simply necessary. Today's farmers and ranchers are rediscovering and re-innovating these practices back into technological agriculture in ways that fit into the jigsaw puzzle of twenty-first-century food culture. In the process, evidence shows that regenerative agriculture and similar organic agricultural systems increase the nutrient density of the foods produced.[5,6,7,8] These approaches and others illustrate the redemptive nature of food for the Earth's climate, going well beyond how food redeems us daily, one plate at a time.

The stories that follow focus on these solutions. They are stories of hard work, experimentation, failure, and ultimately, success.

> • <

How do we account for what those emissions actually are, or how much potential solutions can help ease the crisis? One of the dramatic scientific discoveries made since the Rio de Janeiro Earth Summit is the now-clear understanding that the Earth constantly exchanges carbon and nitrogen between soil, plants, lakes, rivers, oceans, and atmosphere in ways that impact the climate.

The quantities are mind-boggling! Tens of billions of tons of carbon move each year between the Earth's plants and the atmosphere. The work of greenhouse gas accountants is to tally that flow. Like with the flow of money in a business, the direction that carbon and nitrogen travels (into the earth versus into the atmosphere) has enormous consequences for the future of civilization. A business hemorrhaging capital is likely to collapse in relatively short order. Ecosystems hemorrhaging carbon and nitrogen are likely to collapse in a similar way, but with consequences more far-reaching and on a far longer timescale than the bankruptcy of even the largest bank. Greenhouse gas accountants add the flows onto a balance sheet, note where the losses into the atmosphere are greatest, connect the dots between the soil, livestock, fertilizer, and food waste, and identify steps that can and must be taken to keep the agricultural ecosystem—and ultimately human society—afloat.

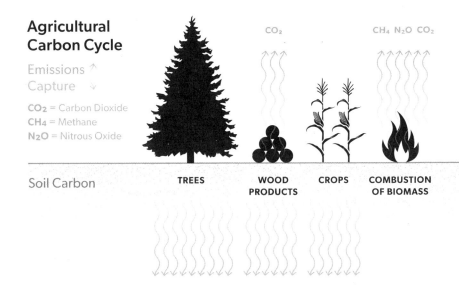

Agricultural Carbon Cycle

Emissions ⌃
Capture ⌄

CO₂ = Carbon Dioxide
CH₄ = Methane
N₂O = Nitrous Oxide

Soil Carbon

TREES   WOOD PRODUCTS   CROPS   COMBUSTION OF BIOMASS

The best work by the best people addressing this issue informs us that we must keep the climate from warming more than 1.5 to 2°C if we are to protect ourselves from devastating impacts to human civilization. Our best understanding today is that achieving that goal simply won't be possible unless agriculture and forestry play a major role. It is, in the words of scientists working in the Intergovernmental Panel on Climate Change (IPCC), the most authoritative body studying this issue,[9] "mandatory." We have to begin the process of what Dr. Chad Frischmann and his colleagues[10] coined as "drawdown": farming, ranching, and managing forests in a way that pulls more carbon dioxide out of the atmosphere, and leveraging ecosystems to provide the same services that we currently rely too much on fossil fuels and factories to do for us. Some argue that an agricultural revolution is needed

CH₄ N₂O CO₂

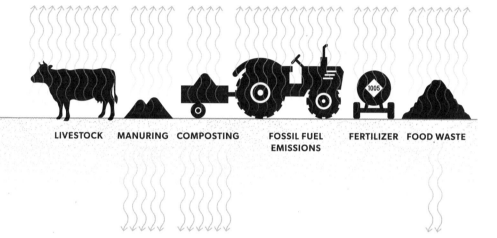

**LIVESTOCK   MANURING COMPOSTING   FOSSIL FUEL   FERTILIZER FOOD WASTE
                                        EMISSIONS**

to accomplish this, but the matter is too urgent to wait for a revolution to occur. We already have many of the tools at our disposal to begin the task, if taken to scale.

Here's why: Unlike in the energy and transportation sector, no new technological breakthroughs are required to begin the process of drawdown in agriculture. Good agricultural policy, accurate market pricing, and a simple commitment to efficient use

Carbon and nitrogen cycle continuously in agriculture between atmosphere, plants, and soil. Trees and crops capture atmospheric carbon dioxide through photosynthesis to produce wood and crop biomass, some of which becomes sequestered as soil carbon. Applying livestock manure and compost to fields and pastures helps sequester carbon in soil organic matter. All agricultural practices generate varying amounts of emissions of carbon dioxide, methane, and nitrous oxide.

33

of resources are what we need most today to extend the knowledge we have from the millions of acres where carbon farming is already practiced. The practices just need to be iterated upon at scale while new transformational technologies mature and become widely available.[11]

This knowledge helps me to sleep at night, and I hope it does for you as well.

The Agricultural Carbon Cycle

Agriculture produces three important greenhouse gases (see illustration on the previous page) that are the subject of this book.[12]

Carbon dioxide (CO_2) comes from burning fossil fuels; plowing soil; burning forests, pastures, and crops; and the chemical manufacturing of synthetic fertilizers. Carbon dioxide can be pulled from the atmosphere and stored in plants and soils through the process of photosynthesis and decomposition. This is known as "carbon sequestration" and is a major focus of this book. Carbon dioxide cycles slowly in the atmosphere, taking approximately one hundred years from the time it is emitted before it moves into another Earth carbon "sink" such as the ocean, forests, or soil. Scientists have assigned carbon dioxide a heat trapping effect of 1.

Methane (CH_4) is a powerful, short-lived greenhouse gas emitted from leaks in coal mines and oil and gas wells and distribution systems, landfills, livestock digestion, growing rice in wetland paddies, storing livestock manure in lagoons, and from managing manure, food waste, and agricultural waste. Methane cycles relatively quickly in the atmosphere and is transformed into carbon dioxide and water within about twelve years. No significant methane "sinks" have been identified in agriculture that can remove it from the atmosphere once emitted. One metric ton (about 10 percent larger than an English or short ton of two thousand pounds) of methane has the same global warming potential as approximately eighty metric tons of carbon dioxide over a twenty-year climate period, or eighty metric tons of CO_2e.

Nitrous oxide (N_2O) is a very powerful, long-lived greenhouse gas emitted from manufacturing and applying fertilizers, managing livestock manure, and when food and agricultural waste decompose. Nitrous oxide cycles slowly in the atmosphere, taking approximately 109 years after it is emitted to cycle into oxygen (O_2) and nitrogen (N_2) gas. No significant nitrous oxide "sinks" have been identified in agriculture that can remove it from the atmosphere once emitted. One metric ton of nitrous oxide has the same global warming potential as approximately 273 metric tons of carbon dioxide, or 273 metric tons of CO_2e.

These three gases can be compared in terms of carbon dioxide equivalents (CO_2e), a way of expressing the different impacts of different greenhouse gases on the atmosphere against carbon dioxide, the largest contributor to the climate crisis, and considered to be the common currency of greenhouse gases.

The Excited Skin of the Planet

Our family knew her simply as Neva.

It was February of 1935, in the depths of the Dust Bowl and the Great Depression. Just two weeks earlier the legal description for her farm outside Wray, Colorado, had appeared in the tax delinquency list in the *Wray Gazette*. I can picture her scissoring out the newspaper article that doomed her farm, underlining those fateful words, and mailing it to her son and daughter-in-law living in southwest Nebraska, along with a flannel onesie she had sewn for their infant daughter. Desperate, perhaps she included a note asking, "Is there anything at all that I can do? Are you able to help?" Her taciturn son Guy may have simply written back, "Dear Mother, I will come to be there with you on that day."

This woman, Ruth Geneva Lathrop Heilman, was my great-grandmother, her son Guy and daughter-in-law Helen were my grandparents, and their infant daughter, Jo Ann, was my mother. I picture Neva and Guy navigating the dirty snowdrifts with the

Previous spread: Bread loaves cooling on baker's racks. *Sarah Flotard*

cold chapping their cheeks to climb the stone steps into the Yuma County courthouse in Wray, the county seat. Perhaps they found a place in the back of the room, standing in solidarity with others there in silent protest to witness the loss of their homes and farms. I can imagine this attempt in the final hour to preserve some sense of dignity when their eastern Colorado farm was put on the auction block. As I believe she bitterly understood at the time, her loss paralleled the story of her soil. And, as scientists are beginning to understand, more than eighty years later, my great-grandmother Neva's story is as old as agriculture itself.

› • ‹

At courthouse tax lien auctions, the people with the money sat or stood near the front. During the Dust Bowl they would have been investors or agents for investment groups from Denver and Cheyenne, perhaps even from Chicago. It was a gallows moment when a piece of people's lives went on the block, and some without a direct stake in the auction gathered there just for the perverse entertainment value of seeing how pitifully low other people's lives would sell for. Simply paying the taxes was beyond the reach of many people who owned farms and homes during a time when money barely circulated.

The auction began with the undeveloped lots and elm- and cottonwood-shaded clapboard and brick homes in the Colorado towns of Wray and Yuma. The land and buildings lay dusty and empty, their occupants gone to California, back East, to the grave, or simply vanished. Some sold, but most property went into the stack to be offered up at the next auction. Eventually the auctioneer turned to the delinquent taxes on farmland, and the agents and buyers readied themselves. Agriculture had once been financially strong in the region. Investors still remembered the spectacular profits people had made growing wheat during and after the WWI years. Where should they invest their money? Stocks had become unmentionable horrors. Banks had failed throughout the country. Anybody with cash flow invested in farmland.

I imagine the tightening in Neva's throat, the anger and frustration and sheer hopelessness making her head pound as the clerk read the legal description for her 160 dryland acres southwest of town. The numbers for township and range, section and quarter echoed through the space, and then the bidding began. It was brief. The tax lien sold to a man from Denver.

She would have to sell to pay off the lien. Her farm was gone.

My family and I have pieced together from county land records, newspaper archives, interviews with county clerks and recorder staff, and family memories how Neva lost her farm during the Dust Bowl, the story of which Timothy Egan cataloged in his epic history *The Worst Hard Time*. My grandparents shared little about that bitter period in their lives, and so we are left to speculate on some of the details. However we account for it, my great-grandmother Neva had a very rough go of it. She moved to town to make her living as a seamstress and was never the same.

Neva died a few years before I was born, so we never knew each other. I imagine her standing amidst the greening wheat on a dewy spring morning, the song of nesting meadowlarks in her ears and a cup of strong coffee in her hands. I can see her calculating that if hail didn't thresh the wheat into the ground, grasshoppers didn't devour the field, and errant prairie fires didn't burn the wheat as it cured in the midsummer sun, she could harvest her grain and make a profit.

I also imagine her distraught and staggering through her field during a late-October dust storm—a scarf covering her nose and mouth, wind-driven sand pelting her eyes, the omnipresent taste of dust invading everything. Before her eyes the gale stripped from her any optimism she once had as it raked the soil from around the hapless germinating wheat seedlings in one

Heilman family photo, shot in 1914, Red Oak, Iowa. In the photo are (L to R) Neva, Guy (standing), Edward, and Elva. *Courtesy of Janet Heilman Hood and Elaine Perkins Hollen*

half of her field, and simultaneously buried the seedlings in the other half.

> • <

This is a story about my great-grandmother Neva, and it's a story about the soil under her wheat field on the dry western edge of the Great Plains. It is also a story about bread and the ecosystem legacy of the Great Plains, which has been a breadbasket for much of the world for more than a century. Like so many stories about the carbon footprint of food, the sheer deliciousness on our plates and in our mouths obscures wheat's heavy carbon burden. I don't believe Neva could have known this, but she and other farmers growing grain during her generation on the Great Plains released one of the greatest pulses of carbon emissions in recorded history.

And yet, emerging from the dry dust of tragedy are beautiful stories of hope and renewal. Fortunately, the same ecosystem legacy that led to that carbon pulse now holds promise for a new vanguard of farmers working to claw some of that carbon back. This is their story as well. Fine threads connect everything we eat back to the soil, and bread provides one of the cleanest lines.

> • <

Think of all the foods made with grains that we eat in our lives: bread, tortillas, crackers, noodles, pretzels, cooked grains, baked desserts, the list goes on. Humans devote more land to growing grains for these foods than any other class of crops.[13] A complex logistical umbilical cord connects them to the food factories supplying us. Bakeries are everywhere. In some cities, every neighborhood has at least one bakery. Most extended families have at least one home baker in their midst making cookies, cakes, loaves, or what have you.

I've experienced the magic of baking nearly everywhere I've traveled. In Guatemala City I came across a tortilleria cranking out tortillas and pupusas to a waiting, happy mob. In Nagpur, India, a tiny shop with an impatient crowd outside produced dangerously hot stacks of freshly baked naan smeared with ghee and a smattering of herbs. In Frankfurt, I once stood under an umbrella outside a bakery during a freezing downpour, the tangy perfume of baking rye somehow cutting through the weather and holding me and two dozen others in place as the line crept forward. At a university in Ethiopia, I came across a fragrant metal-sided kitchen filled with bakers devoted to producing piles and piles of pancake-like, spicy-sour injera for the students' next meal, with lines of student workers carrying the rolled pancakes in baskets to the dining hall next door.

The scent of cooking grains holds a unique magic, whether toasted or baked, steamed or boiled, and I wonder what the moment was like the first time one of our ancestors gathered ripe grains from a field of grasses, ground them into a powder, mixed in some water, and cooked the dough on a hot rock next to a fire. What I would give to have witnessed the olfactory moment humans first experienced the aroma of baking bread! It must have been glorious.

Such is the influence that grains have in our lives. Cultures across the world domesticated indigenous grains wherever they could be grown. There may be as many recipes for them as there are cultures and grains and cooking methods. Whether the grain is rice, wheat, teff, amaranth, oats, rye, barley, maize, sorghum, millet, quinoa, or some other fantastic and local crop—all are dietary staples where they are grown. Outside of the marine fish-and-mammal-eating cultures and livestock-herding cultures, humans consume more calories from grains than any other class of foods.[14] Domesticating grains appears to have changed us—our bodies, our minds, our culture—and archaeological evidence hints that it was the process of domesticating grains that led to the invention of agriculture. Through it, humans changed the world.

The clearest example of this for me is my home. I am a child of the Great Plains. From my work, I've come to learn that through agriculture, humans transformed the North American Great Plains perhaps more than any other great ecosystem in recent history.[15] In that nearly total transformation, farming and ranching acted independently to warm the climate through the seemingly wholesome act of growing food. How we choose to grow food in the future—and what we choose to eat—starts for me with understanding my great-grandmother's farm and the story of her soil.

And though bread and grains have some of the lowest carbon footprints on average of any food—about a pound and a half of CO_2e for every pound of bread, pasta, or tortillas[16]—the fact is that humans eat more of it than any other food. Under the guidelines of today's carbon accounting practices, bread's carbon footprint does not account for the centuries-long legacy of depleted soils and soil carbon loss. These impacts aren't unique to growing grains but dominate grain-producing regions more than perhaps

A seed mix known as Hanfetz is a mixture of wheat and barley grown in the Kutaber woreda, Ethiopian Highlands. Seed mixes increase yields and reduce climate risk, but have largely been replaced by monoculture agriculture. *Alex McAlvay*

any other crop. If those soil carbon losses are included, bread's carbon footprint would be much higher.

Ironically, farmers and scientists have shown that we can grow grains on depleted soils in a way that can be carbon negative—drawing more carbon from the atmosphere to rebuild soil carbon stocks than are emitted as trace gases in other parts of the growing process—and reverse some of the effects of climate change. More than anything having to do with bread, this simple fact makes Neva's story even more compelling.

> • ‹

All terrestrial life begins with soil; however, all soil was rock before plants and microbes biochemically transformed said rock into what the scientist C. C. Nikiforoff[17] called "the excited skin of the planet." Neva's farm lay in an area that was covered with tiny, glacially ground and windblown rock fragments left over from when the ice sheet that covered the Rocky Mountains melted about ten thousand years ago. During the last glacial maximum, long tongues of ice spilling out of the frozen heights of the Rocky Mountains to the west had bulldozed their way through thousands of cubic miles of rock. The ice pulverized the depths into everything from house-sized boulders down to the finest grains of sand and silt. As the ice melted, mile upon cubic mile of this landscape became exposed. During summer months the melting ice sent sand- and silt-laden rivers downstream, carrying and depositing their waterborne load in gooseneck meanders throughout the plains and leaving them exposed to the sky when the river flows dropped. Frigid air pooling on the high, ice-covered plateaus periodically descended into those tongues of glacial ice, with both gravity and the prevailing winds driving them faster and faster until they broke out of the canyons and raced across the open country east of the Rockies. The winds collected sand and silt from the glacial deposits into dust storms that far exceeded those in the Dust Bowl, lifting the material far out onto the landscape we now know as the Great Plains.

The height of land and ice, the geology upwind, and the landforms downwind determined what would fly and where material would fall. Enormous expanses became covered in glacial silt, known as "loess," caking the land in layers dozens of feet thick.[18] Mountains of sand more than a thousand feet high piled up downwind and eventually became the largest field of stabilized, grass-covered dunes in the world, the Sandhills of west-central Nebraska.[19] In other places, the silt fell more lightly, gradually layering into the existing soil across the prairie. Scattered along what would become the dry border of eastern Colorado, western Nebraska, and western Kansas, complexes of smaller dune fields formed, dozens of feet thick, covering hundreds of square miles. After the ice sheets finished melting and weather patterns stabilized somewhat, the long process of transforming what once was rock into soil could begin. In that process, photosynthesis and microbial decomposition combined in a tightly knit ecological collaboration between plants, tiny invertebrate animals, and microbes in the soil. Layers of glacially pulverized rock fragments gradually accumulated tons and tons of carbon and nitrogen from the air, transforming from simple rock into soil laced with organic matter.

The Sandhills of Garfield County, Nebraska, are the Earth's largest formation of stabilized sand dunes, and remain the largest intact, undeveloped grassland in North America. *Cheryl-Samantha Owen / Nature Picture Library / Alamy*

How does that huge amount of carbon and nitrogen make it into the soil? Consider Neva's farm. It lay on a level patch of land that at one time was part of a field of shallow sand dunes. If we could travel ten thousand years back in time to her farm, we'd find layers of sand with pockets of plants dotting the dunes here and there. Plants and windblown sand had battled each other for decades; however, a time arrived when the winds abated enough that plants filled in the bare spaces and covered the ground completely. Then the work of soil building really began.

It might have begun in one particular patch when a thunderstorm washed a wind-deposited seed into a depression and covered it lightly with sand and some windblown silt. Winter came and went, and the following spring the seed absorbed enough moisture to expand and burst from its coat, germinating into the damp sand, and began growing.

The plant gathered light through photosynthesis, growing larger while developing a complex network of roots a few feet underground. The root systems formed a dense network of fine roots, called root hairs, so many that if the roots and root hairs underneath a square foot of prairie soil were laid end to end, they would run for miles. Microbes and fungi live in very tight quarters with these root hairs. They gather nutrients from water in the soil and shuttle them to plants through the root hairs in exchange for food the plants manufacture in their leaves, transport to the roots, and weep into the soil in a mucus-like material called exudates.

The microbes and fungi consumed the exudates and the root hairs and larger roots as they died and were replaced, as well as dead plant matter and animal feces that fell to the soil surface and were carried underground by worms and insects. Bacteria, archaea, and fungi grew and multiplied on this bounty, and they in turn were eaten by amoebas and their relatives, as well as worms, nematodes, and a host of other creatures living in the soil. Those creatures lived and died in a continuous cycle, and their bodies, both living and dead, were eaten by other creatures. The carbon-rich by-products of this underground community gradually accumulated and attached chemically to the microscopic, sheet-like surfaces of clay and silt particles in the soil. Thus carbon accumulated in the soil, much like money might fill a vault, with the size of the vault limited by the amount of clay and silt in the soil and the amount of surface area on the soil particles, as well as the productivity of the ecosystem.

Soil scientists previously believed that carbon accumulated in soil after it had been consumed many times over, finally left in a chemical makeup so hard to break down that microbes left it alone, very much like we eat the meat off a chicken drumstick and leave the bone at the side of our plate. This view changed in the last decade when scientists began looking closely at soil carbon with electron microscopes and realized that it was not made of bones or "humic substances," as they had called it for centuries. A lot of soil carbon was made of simple molecules produced by microbes, as well as the bodies of dead microbes themselves.

Scientists like Dr. Francesca Cotrufo started appreciating the role of microbes as the agents forming soil carbon, rather than the agents responsible for consuming and decomposing organic matter in the soil.[20, 21] The complex underground ecosystem doesn't just consume carbon put into the soil by plants, but it also transforms it, and in so doing, sets aside a portion of that carbon, bit by bit over time, in the soil carbon vault.

Francesca likens the way soil carbon cycles underground and supports the health of this underground world and the thriving of the plants above it to a savings account and a checking account.[22] As we need to put a deposit in our bank account every month to support our living expenses, plant roots and animal manure are necessary to support the health of the soil community. If inputs into the soil checking account are continuous, strong, and diverse, the microbial legions put aside the by-products that accumulate in the savings account vault. The beauty of natural systems is that they work as highly efficient production systems: Plants and the animals that graze on them continuously feed the belowground community, which in turn recycles the nutrients that plants need to grow, all the while setting aside some carbon in the vault. This process maintains the productivity of natural systems while storing carbon in the soil, until the vault fills up.

Several thousand years after that first plant colonized that sand dune on Neva's farm, the complex underground soil ecosystem had fully developed, and the clay and silt "vault" had filled up. No more carbon could be stuffed in. The vault held molecules from the first microbes that consumed the roots of the first plant that had germinated into the sand dune. It also held carbon from the microbes feeding on the most recent cohort of plants, and from every year in between. Some of that carbon likely was nibbled away and replaced every year, diminishing some in drought years and increasing a little in wet years, but at very small rates if the soil was not disturbed. After the vault filled, the total amount of carbon in the clay and silt vault remained in a relatively stable state of equilibrium.

When the clay and silt soil vault filled up, virtually every capital input of carbon and nitrogen the plants and their symbiotic microbe partners captured from the atmosphere cycled through the checking account, like a well-capitalized business. The soil and the plant and animal ecosystem it supported had become as productive as it could possibly be, while maintaining the ecosystem capital.

That vast store of carbon in the organic matter, along with the nutrients bound to it, was the incredible biological and biochemical richness that drew so many hopeful pioneers to the Great Plains. How much carbon did Neva's soil hold? Based on computer simulations developed from experiments in soil carbon around the world, my colleagues and I have built computer models of ecosystems like the soil on Neva's farm. We calculated that the top eight inches to one foot of Neva's sandy topsoil (twenty to thirty centimeters, where most of the carbon accumulates) likely held about twelve tons of carbon per acre (about 1 percent soil carbon) before farmers arrived.[23] That may seem like a lot, but it is actually a pretty small amount compared with most soils.

That is because sandy soils hold relatively little carbon. They have far less of the clay and silt with their sheet-like surfaces that

A view of the rich underground world in a field of the perennial grain Kernza® grown by Luke Peterson near Madison, Minnesota.
Amy Kumler

can bind soil organic matter, and they hold less of the water necessary to keep the soil ecosystem engine humming. And because they hold relatively little carbon, they tend to be far less fertile than soils with a greater balance of silt and clay. A different soil higher in clay near Neva's farm, in the same climate and growing the same plants, might contain twice as much carbon as Neva's sandy soil.

The same holds true for soils in different climates. For example, the soils in eastern Kansas receive twice as much rain and snow as at Neva's farm. The ecosystem there captures roughly two times more carbon through photosynthesis, and so as more biomass accumulates, correspondingly more carbon cycles in the soil. Prairie soils near Kansas City can typically hold far more carbon in the top foot or so than those in Neva's dry plains, or about thirty tons per acre (approximately 3 percent soil carbon in the topsoil). The poorly drained, silty loam soils in northwest Iowa hold more carbon still in their top layer, up to fifty tons per acre or more (approximately 5 percent soil carbon in the topsoil), because the microbes quickly use up the oxygen in waterlogged soils. Less oxygen means less decomposition, and carbon stocks build up more quickly.

Before the plow, the deep grassland soils of the Great Plains, the South American Pampas, and the Ukrainian Steppe held more soil carbon per acre than most other ecosystems, including tropical forests. The only ecosystems that hold more carbon are the deep peat soils such as those in the Everglades, tropical Indonesia, Arctic taiga forests and tundra permafrost, and mangrove wetlands.

To picture how much carbon these soils hold, consider a wheelbarrow filled with a mound of charcoal briquettes, equal to about a hundred pounds of carbon. It would take twenty such wheelbarrows to equal a single ton of carbon. For reference, the typical American automobile at the time this book was written burns enough fuel to emit between 1.25 and 1.5 tons of carbon into the atmosphere each year, or the equivalent of twenty-five to thirty wheelbarrows full of charcoal. Soils in northwestern Iowa before the age of the plow typically held the equivalent of one thousand wheelbarrows full of charcoal per acre. On the plains just west of Kansas City, the soil might hold 720 wheelbarrows worth. At Neva's farm, far drier conditions and sandy soil led to the equivalent of about 240 wheelbarrows scattered over each acre in 1912, the year her farm appears to have been homesteaded.

Homestead records indicate that is likely the year a farmer first hitched a plow to a team of horses or to an early tractor, pushed the plow blades into the soil, and overturned it to create a seed bed for a wheat crop. That is the point where everything changed.

Wheat began to pour from the land, and alongside it, the carbon the ecosystem had spent the preceding one hundred centuries building into the soil savings account. The perennial plant and microbial community's work would be undone in practically the blink of an eye.

> • <

In a way, Neva's land had likely been lost well before she was forced to sell it. Her farm lay square in the dusty cusp between two agriculture market poles—grains and livestock—along with millions of acres of other land on the dry western edge of the Great Plains. Growers acquiring land throughout the dry Great Plains faced a decision: What should they try to grow? They could plow the soil, though they probably shouldn't, but there was too much money to be made growing wheat, compared with raising cattle on the unplowed prairie. Little was there to prevent most people from breaking out the steel. So they plowed.

Why do farmers plow soil? Contemporary agriculture requires planting seeds for a new crop of different plants every year (known as "annual crops"). Monocultures of crops generally do not compete well against weeds, and tilling the soil is one of the most common ways to eliminate that competition. The perennial native plants on Neva's field would have to be killed before wheat could grow, and plowing the soil was the most effective method at the time to do that. Farmers also plow or till the soil to prepare the field to uniformly germinate a new crop. Other problems like compacted soil compel some farmers to plow.

Plowing the soil breaks open the soil carbon vault, releasing the organic matter that had accumulated over the years. Plowing shatters the soil aggregates and the organic matter. Plowing converted Neva's field from an ecosystem that included perhaps hundreds of perennial plant species, with deep and complex root systems, to a monoculture annual crop ecosystem with far smaller root systems. This shifted the carbon balance from one with most of the carbon belowground in roots to one with most of the carbon aboveground in straw and grain. Rain and snow, combined with the additional oxygen the disturbance introduced into the soil, ramped up the microbes' actions. It was like an around-the-clock, 365-day wrecking crew.

Unless farmers returned the organic matter fertility through compost, animal manure, cover crops, or some other source, they would burn through the soil organic matter capital. They would first liquidate the storehouse of tiny organic matter particles in the soil, and then move on to the organic matter fixed to the flat plates of clay and silt particles in the soil. During that process, microbes release tons of nutrients also bound within the organic matter, which effectively fertilizes the crops until the organic matter is all used up.[24] Additionally, converting an ecosystem from deep-rooted perennial plants like the Great Plains native grasslands to shallow-rooted monocultures eliminated carbon inputs into the deep soil below about a meter (three feet) in depth, releasing carbon and nitrogen stores that the deep-rooted native ecosystem had built and maintained for thousands of years.

That seemingly simple act set the soil and its ecosystem into a downward spiral that sent millions of acres into both ecological and economic bankruptcy. From the time the homesteaders began to plow, around 1912, to when Neva lost her farm in 1935, most of the topsoil and up to three-quarters of the ecosystem capital in soil carbon may have been almost completely lost. Soil organic matter and the carbon it contains are the natural source of soil fertility. Within limits, the more organic matter a soil holds, the higher the fertility, the greater the crop yields, and the better the soil's capacity to grow plants that can resist drought and disease. The actions of the plow, wind, Great Plains storms, and wheat led to such rapid soil carbon declines that within two or three

Plowing soil stimulates soil microbes to decompose organic matter, depletes soil ecosystems and fertility, releases greenhouse gases,
and exposes the soil to wind and water erosion. Mid-1900s, Gem
County, Idaho. *Heritage Image Partnership Ltd / Alamy*

decades after the plows first cut the sod, crops completely failed or were so poor that farmers needed to prop up the ecosystem with expensive chemical fertilizers or animal manure.

For a time, plowing the soil created free fertilizer. As the organic matter decomposed, nutrients essential to plant growth and chemically bound to the soil organic matter became free and available. As long as there was organic matter that would decompose, there were free nutrients available to grow crops. Farmers worked the soil before harvest to prepare seed beds and again after harvest to kill weeds, leaving the soil exposed for months out of every year. Great Plains winds and rainstorms eroded bare soil. Whereas spectacular wheat crops grew in the first years after the plow, the fertility rapidly declined, particularly in Neva's sandy soil, and the fragile topsoil blew away. Neva's soil probably was completely played out by the time the 1929 market crash signaled the beginning of the Great Depression.

A pervasive farming practice took hold in the region that hastened soil carbon decline. West of the hundredth meridian—a north-south longitudinal line that roughly divides in half the Dakotas, Nebraska, and Kansas—rain and snowfall decreases, and raising a grain crop without added irrigation becomes increasingly risky the farther west one gets. Farmers in eastern Colorado quickly learned that fields in the rain shadow of the Rockies yielded poorly compared with regions in wetter regions farther east. Farming extension bulletins from the time recommended farmers let the land lie fallow every other year. This meant tilling the soil to kill weeds and letting it gather moisture for two years for every single wheat crop. Farmers know this practice—growing grains every other year—as a "grain-fallow" system. Though grain-fallow fields exist on more than ten million acres in the Great Plains, they are not unique. Farmers grow crops in this system on every continent, and wherever it persists, soil carbon in the fields degrades to some of the lowest levels of any farming system anywhere.

Why does this happen? For every single crop, the soil experienced twice the tillage and only had a living root in it for about one-quarter of the time compared with the native prairie that had built the soil. Science has not documented any native ecosystems that behave in this way.[25] Ecosystems simply do not deliberately prevent plants from growing and keep the soil bare every other year if rainfall levels vary. They develop and evolve into different perennial plant ecosystems with diverse species that can thrive when rainfall and snowfall are unpredictable. In the end, the carbon in the roots and straw from the every-other-year wheat crop cannot replace the carbon leaving the soil when the organic matter, built up over millennia, decomposes. Chemical fertilizers became the only way to prop up the ecosystem and keep the wheat growing, which amplified the carbon loss and greenhouse gas emissions from the system.

Can we blame the farmers? As a cohort, they were essentially inventing, by trial and error, a dryland farming system in an ecosystem where agriculture had never been attempted at scale. Native American cultures living on these dry western grasslands had evolved a hunting-and-gathering culture, living off the meat of plains animals and edible prairie plants. Perhaps they farmed small plots in bottomlands to a small degree, or traded with or raided from the farming cultures to the east and south for agricultural foods.

Perhaps they settled on this way of life through their own trial and error with farming. At the time of the European invasion and the subsequent genocide of Indigenous peoples, notions of cultural superiority prevented most from examining the indigenous template for land use, learning from it, and adopting pieces we could use. Perhaps our conquering culture would have left the dry grasslands intact if we'd learned from their example or adopted native dryland farming systems such as those used by the Hopi to the southwest, the Kaw people to the east, or the Pawnee to the north, leveraging agricultural templates that had already been in place for centuries. Plowing the soils in ecosystems unsuited to farming annual grain monocultures became another tragedy layered upon the accumulated tragedies of the time.

There were tremendous market and government incentives to plow soil and grow wheat. All one had to do to "prove up" a homestead and gain title to 160 acres of land (called a land patent) was establish a residence and either grow a few acres of trees or attempt (but not necessarily succeed) to grow a commodity crop on a portion of the land over five years. The first few years after busting the sod must have felt like winning the lottery. Higher rainfall levels from about 1910 through about 1925 led to fantastic crop yields at a time of high commodity prices.

This new, essentially experimental, farming technique made the farmers tremendously vulnerable. Plowing the soil and leaving it bare for much of the year left them completely unprepared for the punishing droughts of 1931 and 1933, which were punctuated by violent, inconveniently timed storms in the intervening years. It is conceivable that Neva's wheat crops completely failed each year in the four years leading up to her selling the farm. Neva and her neighbors experienced an ecosystem backlash other farmers have experienced since agriculture's beginning. Neva lived from 1872 to 1955, which encompassed the seven decades it took to transform the plains from grasslands spectacularly rich with indigenous cultures and wildlife into the largest agricultural network in the world. In that process, Great Plains farming released into the atmosphere seven billion tons of carbon dioxide.[26] That is almost as much as the United States emits in a single year today, and equaled about a quarter of the fossil fuel emissions during that era. That pulse of carbon still overwarms us today.

> • <

The story of played-out soil is a very old one, recorded in the ice sheets of Greenland, the landscape of Europe, the bottomlands of the Maya civilization—basically almost everywhere archaeologists and biogeochemists have looked. Evidence appears nearly everywhere crops were grown. While helping with a plant survey in Germany, my colleagues and I dug a soil pit to characterize a plant collection from a fragrant wildflower meadow filled with wild oregano. Ancient stone walls marking former fields crisscrossed the meadow, and crumbling wreckages of medieval homes lay scattered here and there. The soil pit showed the topsoil was all nearly gone, eroded by centuries of land use. Near Piracicaba, Brazil, our team leader, Keith, and I walked along a road cut into a hill slope hosting a field of sugarcane. The topsoil remained only in a few low-lying ravines. Elsewhere the cane was rooted into decomposing sandstone. While vacationing in Italy, my wife, Leslie, and I walked paths and ancient roads through the fields and woodlands of an *agriturismo*—an agritourism farm. Wherever we went, the hard evidence of past land use lay evident. The topsoil was largely gone. Remnant pockets lay only in a few level bottomlands. The key ingredients propping up these farming systems today and making them even marginally possible were fossil fuel–derived synthetic fertilizers.

Our trip to Italy was during the fall, and one day we drove a winding highway to visit one of the dramatic hill towns in the region. On the route, we passed miles upon miles of fields that had been plowed directly up and down ragged, steep slopes. The soil would lay bare through the winter before the next crop of durum wheat was planted the following spring. It had rained in the days before we arrived and so, in places, rivulets had cut miniature canyons into the bare soil. I imagined that if carbon dioxide had a color, say purple, the entire landscape would lay bathed in a lavender haze as the microbial legions did their work decomposing the soil organic matter exposed by the plows' cut. Streams and rivers downstream choked in silt. I became increasingly frustrated as the scene played out in unending monotony. Finally, I couldn't hold back.

"Don't plow!" I cried out in my best faux-Italian accent. Leslie jumped in the passenger seat and stared at me.

"What?"

"Don't plow!" I pointed to the bare fields rolling past the windshield. I rolled down my window and leaned into the breeze. "Don't plow!" I shouted.

"Don't plow!" Leslie shouted back. She rolled down her window and leaned out. "Don't plow!" We cried out again and again, in unison with arms stretched out the windows in the classic Italian five-fingered, back-handed wave.

We flung the words out to nobody in particular, giggling like crazy people. I wonder, though, what was more absurd in that moment. Was it the hundreds of square miles of soil ripped open across the countryside? Or the two of us with our arms out the windows, shouting pointlessly?

> • <

Even with time and distance between me and that moment, I still can't get past the irony that in one of the great seats of food culture, we can find the clearest evidence of carbon and soil loss. In Rome, a city synonymous with flavor, eroded soil washed from farmland upstream into the Tiber River has filled in miles of what was once the river's estuary, surrounding the former port of Ostia with soil. Plowing devastated the soil and the agricultural landscape depending upon it. It was this process of farming and playing out the soil that helped drive Rome's insatiable need to conquer new lands. The same process of clearing land, growing cotton and tobacco, degrading the soil, and moving on drove American colonial expansion westward out of the original thirteen colonies.

What seems even more ironic is that agriculture's invention appears to have coincided with a unique period in the Earth's astronomical history to make human civilization possible. Evidence gathered from ice cores and peat bogs supports the idea that if agriculture had not been invented, the Earth's climate today would likely be well on its way into another glacial maximum. The Earth cycles in and out of cool and warm periods, depending on where our home planet is in the varying astronomical cycles that define its orbital distance from the sun, the amount the planet wobbles around its axis, and the extent of its axial tilt. Based on our understanding of where we are in those cycles today, rather than melting, ice sheets likely would be stable and expanding to some degree. The same would be true for ice covering the polar oceans.[27, 28, 29]

Dr. William Ruddiman from the University of Virginia examined the climate anomalies and compared them against plant pollen records reconstructed from peat bog cores aligned with other geologic evidence that indicated a consistently warm climate since the invention of agriculture some eight thousand years ago. During the development and advance of civilization and the age of technology, the climate had remained remarkably stable and warm. Ruddiman concluded that throughout this evolution in human society and the advent of civilization, the climate gradually warmed through the period, almost imperceptibly. Or put more accurately, the climate did not cool. Agriculture appears to have kept the climate warm.

Though my great-grandmother Neva's experience was uniquely American, she appears to have repeated the story of countless farmers in every habitable place where agriculture existed. People moved into new ecosystems, cleared land, and attempted to grow food. They brought with them their experiences with agriculture in other places and imposed those systems in the new land.

A mound of windblown soil on Neva Heilman's farm captured by a windbreak of tumbleweeds against a fence. Eroded soil is piled several feet above the field on the downwind side of the fence. Yuma County, Colorado. *Mark Easter*

Some succeeded, others failed, and over time, new agricultural systems arose. In nearly every case, ecosystems bled carbon into the sky.[30, 31, 32, 33]

Ruddiman published his hypothesis in a paper in 2003 titled "The Anthropogenic Greenhouse Era Began Thousands of Years Ago,"[34] and followed that paper with a popular science book in 2005 titled *Plows, Plagues, and Petroleum: How Humans Took Control of Climate.*[35, 36] Scientists have debated his hypothesis in the two decades since Ruddiman first formed it, and a consensus has gradually formed that he is correct. Still, it was difficult for me and my peers to wrap our heads around the notion that the world's farmers, acting independently throughout history, could warm the climate through the seemingly benign act of simply growing food. How could a morning piece of toast or a plate of dinner pasta be such a world-altering culprit?

On a brilliant autumn morning, I set out to visit Neva's farm to try to picture it more clearly.

> • <

Helpful workers at the Yuma County clerk and recorder's office located Neva's farm using land-transaction records combined with township and range maps. I had entered the location into mapping software and examined the landscape on my computer screen using satellite imagery. I had a vague sense of the place, but still wondered throughout the drive what I would find there.

I'd located the owners and called ahead for permission, and though they had declined to be interviewed, they'd agreed to let me walk on the fields near the roads. When I arrived, I found much of what I expected—a square field a half mile on a side, bounded by gravel roads on the west and south. The field had been divided in half into two eighty-acre parcels, which was typical in the region. One parcel would lie fallow, the other would grow wheat in any particular year. Unplowed pastures filled with native grasses lay across the gravel roads on two sides. A barbed wire fence plastered with tumbleweeds bounded the east side, forming an ad hoc windbreak that had captured a mound of windblown soil several feet above the level of the field. The field to the east had been restored to native grasses and forbs, and a sign showed that it was part of the Federal Conservation Reserve Program, set aside to preserve topsoil. The topsoil definitely needed preserving, as the surface of the crop field lay at least two feet below the surface of the unplowed grasslands to the west and south.

Gathering a spade and a bag from the car, I stepped into the field to collect a soil sample. I hopped onto the shovel's back and was a little dumbfounded at how easily it slid into the dry soil. The soil came up loose and pale brown, with almost no structure at all. It fell from the blade and settled onto the ground in a sandy, amorphous pile. I saw no sign of insects, worms, or other organisms anywhere. I pushed the soil back into the hole, leveled the divot, and walked a short distance farther and took another shovelful. The same thing happened. Then again two more times. The field was like a sandbox.

But something else struck me as surprising, and hopeful. Whoever was farming the land had planted a cover crop mix this year and harvested the crop as forage, but left the field untilled for the winter. A few bales of harvested forage still lay scattered about. Curious, I returned to my car, connected my touchpad to my phone's internet hotspot, and downloaded the past history satellite imagery I'd intended to use to examine the most recent crop history.

What I found there stunned me.

I began with the earliest available satellite records that interpreted and classified the crops that had grown on the parcel. The field had alternated between fallow and wheat years. But something interesting appeared in the land use history starting four years before my visit. The fallow periods ended and other crops appeared in the cropping sequence. Before my eyes was a diverse cover crop blend. The new farmers were ending the long, disastrous cycle that had depleted this part of the Great Plains for more than a hundred years. They were starting the soil on its long, slow journey back to health.

I stepped out of the car, leaned against the fender, and took a longer look around. The landscape, the breeze, the yucca-strewn sandhills carpeted with buffalo grass and blue grama and little bluestem were all familiar to me. Though I'd never been here before, the place suddenly felt like it was part of my family DNA. I pondered the stardust that in ancient times had become plants, and then soil, and was then liberated back to the atmosphere in a rush of capitalist ambition. I realized in that moment how ravenously hungry I was for good news about the climate. In the run-up to my visit to Neva's farm, I'd prepared myself, resigned myself, to find bad news—depleted and eroded soil, a farm completely played out. Suddenly, here I was, and I'd discovered what was probably one of the best possible ecological outcomes I could expect on privately owned cropland on this dry portion of Great Plains.

For a time, standing there next to what was once Neva's field, my cup runneth over. I reached into the car and pulled out the lunch I'd brought with me and spread it out on the car's hood. I imagined that some miracle had raised Neva from her grave and brought her to stand there with me in the October sunshine. In that daydream, I shared my sandwich with her. I filled a cup for her from my thermos of tea. And after a time, I asked her to tell me about her life here on this land.

> • ‹

"In the forty years I've been farming, I've never been more in touch with my farm and my soil as now." Curtis Sayles and I were crouched around a shovelful of soil pulled from a research plot near his home. Curtis's son-in-law and farming partner, Pat Einspahr, had run into town to replace a hydraulic hose needed to unload a thirty-ton load of millet. "We're dead in the water until Pat gets back. Let's have a look around," Curtis said.

The plot where we had taken the sample was part of an experiment Dr. Meagan Schipanski from Colorado State University had developed with Curtis and other farmers in the region. The soil in this plot, a deep-brown clayey loam named Richfield, had the same qualities I'd seen in other growers' regeneratively managed soil. It held tilth. Plant roots and mycorrhizal fungi ran through the cluster. Insect and worm tracks cut across the shovel profile. Nymphs and grubs fell from the soil clumps as we broke apart the shovelful. It was consistently damp throughout and had a lightness to it that I coveted for my own garden.

A short time earlier I had pulled into Curtis's farmyard near Seibert, Colorado. At the farmyard entrance stood a painted steel sign held between two elegant steel posts, with the perforated letters "Curt and Kelly Sayles" and cutouts of a tractor and combine. Next to it stood a square white sign with "AMERICA" standing out in neat blue capital letters near the top, and in a row underneath read the words "one nation under God." Covering the bottom half was a single painted square of a vibrant, red-and-blue bear claw quilt pattern surrounding a painted cross. At the end of their driveway stood a stucco-covered passive-solar home with a sloped earthen berm on the north side. A dormant prairie garden covered the berm. Wind turbine blades spun steadily above a large steel-sided equipment shed and grain bins behind the home, all of this wrapped inside a dense windbreak of eastern red cedar.

Curtis, a fit and young-looking man in his early sixties, was stepping out of his pickup truck as I pulled into the driveway. As he reached out a hand to greet me, he asked, "Have you had lunch yet?" Moments later we were in his semi-truck pulling a load of millet he and Pat had harvested that morning and driving to share a lunch prepared by Curtis's daughter and Pat's wife, Megan, at their home nearby. Over lunch we'd started a conversation about regenerative agriculture, and I'd tagged along while Pat and Curtis troubleshot their equipment problems and decided Pat needed to make the supply run. Which had led to us crouching over the shovelful of soil from his field.

We stood up, wiping our hands on our jeans.

"What is the cover crop you grew here?"

"This is what we call the Schipanski mix. It's a diverse blend of cover crops Dr. Schipanski proposed for these plots. We couldn't believe the weight gains our cattle achieved eating this mix. They gained three pounds per day!"

Meagan Schipanski is a soil scientist with expertise in cover crops, and Curtis and a group of colleagues had recruited her to help them develop new, regenerative farming techniques for their part of the dry Great Plains. The amount of weight gain Curtis described is typically achieved only by cattle crowded into concentrated animal feeding operations, or CAFOs, where they eat diets rich in grain concentrates and additives.

We stepped into another plot where a corn crop stood waiting to be harvested. It was part of an experimental treatment of the soil that had not been tilled but had no cover crop. We dug another shovelful. It held a lot of the same properties as in the cover crop, but without the network of roots and fungal threads.

"I haven't tilled this field since 1997. How long has that been?" Curtis looked at the sky for a moment. "More than twenty years."

"What is your soil organic matter doing here?"

"It was 1 percent when we got started. Now it is between 2.5 and 3 percent. I think it can go higher."

Before his innovations, Curtis's soils likely held about ten tons of carbon in the top one foot of each acre of soil. Twenty years later it held between twenty-five and thirty tons of carbon.

"You know what the best part is? The biology and the plants are providing all the fertility the crops need. I have completely stopped applying chemical nitrogen fertilizers," he said.

Cattle graze a dryland cover crop blend, developed by Dr. Meagan Schipanski, in between grain crops at the Sayles farm. Seibert, Colorado. *Curtis Sayles*

That was an extraordinary step for any farmer to take. Chemical fertilizers may be the most ubiquitous farm chemical applied to farm and pasture soils throughout North America. But implementing two simple actions—rotating in grazing livestock and planting nitrogen-fixing crops every other year—was a powerful step toward climate change mitigation. I'd noticed evidence of this during my drive to their home. Curtis, Kelly, Pat, and Megan farm 5,500 acres in this hilly piece of Colorado near the Kansas border. When I got within a few miles of their home, I noticed a change in the crops grown in the fields I could see from the road. Fields of sunflower and safflower appeared. Stubble and crop residues I didn't recognize showed on other ground. This was all different from the wheat and dryland corn alternating with tilled fallow fields seen almost everywhere else along the drive south.

Curtis was leveraging two key strategies to stabilize and increase organic matter in his soil.[37] The first was to eliminate practices such as tillage that broke open the soil carbon vault and made the carbon there available to microbes.[38] The second was to increase the carbon inputs into the soil, which in his case was to end the fallow cycle and plant cover crops, ensuring there was a living root in the soil every month of the year.[39]

In league with other like-minded growers, Curtis eliminated tillage and bare fallow periods from his fields. He alternates crops of wheat and other grains with legumes like pinto beans and garbanzos, which add nitrogen to the soil. They periodically plant rich mixes of cover crops into their rotations that they grow for their cattle to graze on. Their crop rotations are extremely diverse—including buckwheat and safflower—and they graze their cattle through their harvested fields to glean grain the combines missed and to leave manure on the soil to feed the microbes. Curtis began a refrain at lunch that he continued throughout the day, which boosted me every time I heard it: "It's all about the soil biology."

A short time before he took me out to visit his field, he had shown me some equipment he and Pat developed. A system of tanks, screens, and hoses allowed them to create compost tea—a mixture of compost and water they let ferment for a few weeks—which they then filtered to make a tea-colored compost extract. They briefly soaked their seeds in the mix before they planted them. "We saw a 15 percent increase in the sunflower yield with the seeds we'd soaked in this mix," he'd explained. "We are trying to stimulate the soil biology by doing this." Whatever the mechanism involved that improved that yield, their focus on soil biology was as unique as it was a very old story. Farmers and scientists the world over are now rediscovering that soil health is critically important to growing healthy food in a warming world.

At lunch earlier that day he'd also said, "We learned that if you have carbon in your soil, you will do better. It was as simple as that. I've never looked back."

> • <

Curtis Sayles is part of a new vanguard of growers who are collaborating with their ecosystems to restore the carbon that six generations of wheat-fallow farming mined from their soils. Dr. Schipanski calls them courageous. I agree. It is not easy for anybody to buck an established system in a business as risky as farming, especially in an ecosystem like the Great Plains where the margins can be so low. Developing the vision to turn their systems around came out of collaboration with neighbors, experimentation, and the frank awareness that, as Curtis told me, "Some of my soils had hit rock bottom. I needed to do something different. There was no place to go but up."

How far up does the soil carbon need to go to dull the sharp edge of the climate crisis? In 2017, Dr. Jonathan Sanderman and a team of scientists at Woodwell Climate Research Center (formerly known as the Woods Hole Research Center) asked the question: "How much carbon has been lost to the atmosphere from the soil due to agriculture?"[40] They used computer simulations tied to the most comprehensive worldwide soils and climate information available and combined it with current and historic satellite imagery used to predict forest losses. They concluded that 133 billion metric tons (also known as just "tonnes") of carbon have been lost from the top two meters (a little over six feet) of soil since humans invented agriculture and began clearing land to grow crops and graze livestock more than ten thousand years ago. About one-third of that carbon is believed to have been lost from croplands, and two-thirds lost from grazing lands. That is about 44 percent of the 259 billion metric tons of extra fossil carbon humans have directly put into the atmosphere since the industrial revolution began. Sanderman and his colleagues called this figure the "soil carbon debt."

Bison roam on the Great Plains grasslands, helping to repair a broken ecosystem and food system on over three hundred thousand acres of grasslands in the Dakotas, Nebraska, and Montana. *Jill O'Brien*

Does this mean that 44 percent of the extra carbon in the atmosphere came from the soil? Not exactly. Though much of the carbon lost from the soil has gone into the atmosphere, some found its way into other Earth system carbon pools.

Some eroded carbon piled up in lowlands downhill or downwind from the eroded fields, or migrated into waterways. Some eroded carbon likely found its way into marine sediments, where it may remain for the foreseeable future.

Of the carbon decomposed into the atmosphere, the oceans have absorbed much of it through the chemical processes leading to ocean acidification, where, for all intents and purposes, it will stay permanently. Undisturbed forests and grasslands accumulate some of the extra carbon back into trees, prairie plants, and soil.[41]

But even with all of that, some of those emissions remain present in the atmosphere, influencing the climate today, and persist as humans continue to clear land for agriculture at historically high rates.[42,43]

What this figure means in a more practical sense is that the soils of the world likely have enormous capacity to gulp up carbon to restore soil fertility and, in the process, reduce the severity of climate change by reducing atmospheric carbon dioxide levels. In virtually every analysis of cost-effective ways to take extra carbon out of the atmosphere (which the scientific community calls "carbon dioxide removal"), science consistently finds storing carbon in soils through improved farming practices, and in trees by restoring forests, to be the most cost-effective.

Can we remove all the extra carbon from the atmosphere just by changing the way we grow food and by planting forests?

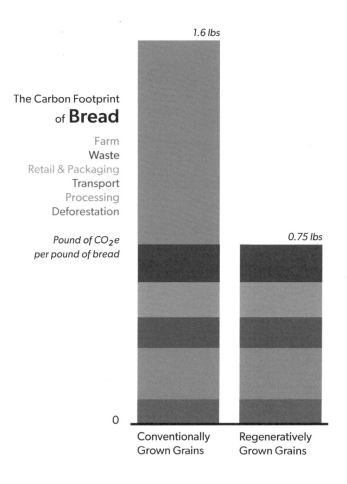

The Carbon Footprint
of **Bread**

Farm
Waste
Retail & Packaging
Transport
Processing
Deforestation

*Pound of CO_2e
per pound of bread*

1.6 lbs

0.75 lbs

0

Conventionally
Grown Grains

Regeneratively
Grown Grains

Growing grain regeneratively stores CO_2 from the atmosphere in the soil, reducing the need for fertilizers and offsetting emissions from fertilizers and fuel used to grow crops. "Farm" is the emissions from soil, fertilizer, burning fuel in equipment, and emissions from manufacturing equipment and buildings on the farm. "Waste" assumes 40 percent of products are eventually landfilled and become landfill methane CO_2e. "Retail and Packaging" includes manufacturing materials to contain products on retail shelves, and equipment, fuel, and energy use for retail establishments. "Transport" includes shipping grain to millers, flour to bakeries, and baked goods to retailers. "Processing" is grinding grain into flour and baking it into food products. "Deforestation" is clearing forests and plowing grasslands to create cropland to grow the grain.

No.

Will pulling carbon into soils and forests reduce the impacts of climate change?

Yes.

In fact, it is pretty much mandatory. The best information we have today indicates that we simply must begin repaying the soil carbon debt, even if nations end up collaborating on an aggressive technological pathway to a carbon-free energy, manufacturing, and transportation system.[44] Farmers like Curtis Sayles are beginning to change the way they grow food, reversing soil carbon loss and returning carbon from the atmosphere into the soil on millions of acres in the United States and abroad.[45,46]

Closing the soil carbon debt gap is starting to be recognized as one of the defining challenges in agriculture today. Nearly every study addressing how to engage agriculture to fight the climate crisis prominently cites eliminating bare fallow, which is still practiced on more than thirty million acres in the United States, almost 15 percent of US cropland.[47,48,49]

At the time this book was written, less than 10 percent of cropland sees a cover crop in the shoulder seasons or has eliminated a fallow period by planting a cover crop.[50] Farmers still intensively till more than 60 percent of US cropland every year.[51] There are myriad reasons for this—dealing with weeds, preparing seed beds, lacking finance for equipment upgrades, or the farmer simply lacks practical experience or access to technical resources to make a plan to do otherwise. Things are starting to change, however.

Two decades ago, only a fringe minority of innovators in North American conventional agriculture used cover crops in the shoulder seasons and eschewed tillage. Today, thousands of farmers across the United States are collaborating with land-grant universities, the Natural Resources Conservation Service (NRCS), state agriculture agencies, and private entities like the Soil Health Institute, the Rodale Institute, and Mad Agriculture, to chip away at the issues that lead farmers to till the soil or leave it fallow. Every year, conferences bring to light innovative tillage-free farming systems. New planting equipment helps farmers to plant crops without tillage.

Whereas reducing tillage does not necessarily increase soil carbon stocks everywhere it is practiced, growing cover crops and eliminating bare fallow periods are emerging as a positive leap forward to draw carbon from the atmosphere into the soil and reduce the need for farm chemicals and the emissions from manufacturing them. Combining the two with grazing animals— to eliminate tillage while using cover crops, and to let the animals help cycle organic matter and nutrients back into the soil— integrated as a system, is emerging as a carbon-farming system that reduces reliance on manufactured fertilizers while restoring and maintaining soils utilizing a more holistic approach to raising livestock.

> • <

On a Sunday morning not long after I visited Curtis Sayles, my wife and I bicycled from our home to the Moxie Bread Company in Louisville, Colorado. We'd tried to get there before the rush, but from two blocks away we could already see the line out the bakery's door. We locked our bikes together at the entrance and joined the queue. I pondered the delectable choices, then gave Leslie my order and went inside to snag seats.

I paused at the coffee station. Just beyond in the kitchen, an athletic-looking baker wearing a handkerchief around her neck and a backward trucker hat snatched a long-handled wooden peel, opened the oven door, and peered inside. She swung the peel like a bullfighter might artfully wield a sword, slid the wide wooden blade deep into the oven, extracted some loaves, examined them minutely, then slid them back in place and closed the oven door. They were not quite ready.

Past the kitchen chalkboard, the dining room crowd was in full weekend swing. There were families gathered, couples like Leslie and me out for a Sunday morning date, duos and trios of friends clustered laughing around a plate of pastries, and one or two earbud-clad singles intent on their computer screens. A boy about the age of four walked earnestly through the room, holding with both hands before him a well-made chocolate croissant centered on a napkin, like a priest might carry a holy relic.

In 1935, the town of Yuma, Colorado, had a bakery, run by a proprietor named Potts. I can imagine Neva stopping into the bakery for a pastry on a Saturday morning, after money began to circulate in the local economy again, and hints of optimism began to appear. Perhaps my grandparents and their daughter, my mother, joined her during a visit. As they sat there sipping urn-brewed coffee from porcelain cups and catching up on each other's lives, the bakery crew would have sweated out their shift in the back of the kitchen, checking loaves, shaping pastries, dusting cookies straight out of the oven with a little powdered sugar.

Like at Moxie, the aroma of baking wheat, toasted butter, and caramelized sugar would define the mood. The bakery mood. Happy. Anticipating. Satisfied. A hopeful place.

Leslie arrived with a wooden platter set with our breakfast and took a seat while I collected our coffees. I sat across the tiny table from her. As I picked up my breakfast pastry and inhaled, she leaned in and did the same.

"Yeah, baby!"

It was more of a declaration from Leslie than an observation. I took a bite and pastry pieces shattered off the crispy edges and littered the front of my shirt. The melded flavors completely took me over. Leslie tucked into her own pastry, and we talked about Neva as we shared bites and sips of coffee with each other. Bread had drawn a line that connected us across the decades. Bread—and carbon.

I'm reminded of her now whenever I pass one of the many wheat fields near my home.

The Unnatural Green of Desert Vegetables

I was floating downstream through Cataract Canyon on the Colorado River, not in some gray rubber raft or sleek wooden dory, but in the river itself. I was my own vessel, suspended by a life jacket, with only my head, floppy hat, and sandal-clad toes poking above the surface. It was 105 degrees in the shade, but the water felt like a late-summer swimming pool the color of a red chili and chocolate sauce. I no longer tasted the perspiration dripping onto my lips. The air smelled simply of river. The calls of canyon wrens and spotted towhees stippled the air, and the water burbled in a way that made me feel as if the river was completely satisfied with itself. I have no memory of the womb, but I wondered whether this was what it was like.

Previous spread: A fresh salad with savory seeds. *Amy Kumler*

Opposite: Fields of vegetables, pistachios, citrus, and alfalfa in the lower Colorado Desert, irrigated with water from reservoirs on the Colorado River. These reservoirs generate millions of tons of climate-heating pollution each year. *Pete McBride*

My companions and I had slipped from our comfortable rafts into the water while the rowers did some maintenance. Within moments of having settled in, I lost track of where they and the rafts were, and for a while, where I was. If ever there was a time in my life for emptying the mind and immersing myself in the moment, this was it. And yet, my mind began to wander a frustratingly distracted route through a series of topics that seemed like absurd scientific koans. I could not let them go. Eventually it settled on the topic of lettuce.

But not just lettuce. I thought about the dams, the gigantic concrete plugs on this river and its tributaries, and the deeply pooled water that lay behind them. Algal blooms surged above the dams, almost unheard of on free-flowing, high-elevation Rocky Mountain rivers. Millions of acres of dried-up, dying wetlands along the river's path and at its mouth no longer received the life-giving spring floods that had sustained them through millennia, and so were decaying a king's ransom of accumulated carbon and nitrogen and warming the planet. Lettuce was one of the culprits—lettuce, and a cornucopia of brightly colored vegetables and fruits grown to nourish people and lighten the weight of winter elsewhere on the continent.

More than 90 percent of the fresh vegetables eaten during the winter in the United States are grown in the region downstream of where I floated, irrigated with waters diverted from the Colorado River. A full four-fifths of the water that enveloped me would be applied as irrigation water to grow lettuce, broccoli, cauliflower, and other vegetables. That wintertime taste of summer would come at a cost that was unnaturally fraying

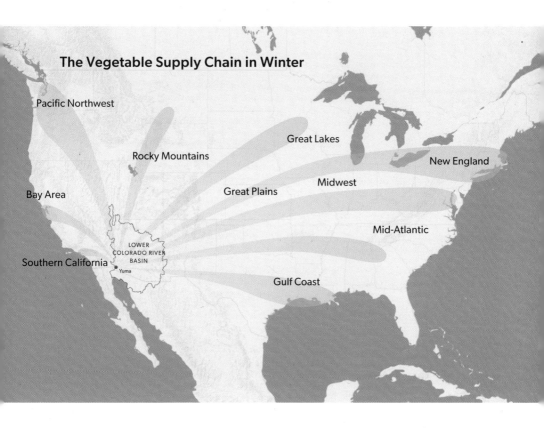

The Vegetable Supply Chain in Winter

Pacific Northwest

Great Lakes

Rocky Mountains

New England

Bay Area

Midwest

Great Plains

LOWER
COLORADO RIVER
BASIN

Mid-Atlantic

Southern California

Yuma

Gulf Coast

More than 90 percent of the lettuce and half of the other vegetables eaten during the winter in North America are grown in the deserts of the Lower Colorado River Basin using irrigation water from the Colorado River.

Sources: Sanchez, C.A., R.I. Krieger, N. Khandaker, R.C. Moore, K.C. Holts, and L.L. Neidel. 2005. "Accumulation and Perchlorate Exposure Potential of Lettuce Produced in the Lower Colorado River Region." Journal of Agricultural and Food Chemistry 53: 5479-5486. *10.1021/jf050380d; Heggie, J. 2020. "Can the Colorado River keep on running?"* National Geographic. *https://www.nationalgeographic.com/science/article/partner-content-colorado-river-preserving-stressed-water-resources*

89

Before the Colorado River was diverted for irrigation, its vast estuary held carbon in its soils and forests that likely totaled more than a billion tons of CO_2e. The Colorado River flowed to the sea for six million years, but little has reached the ocean since 1998. This abandoned boat now sits thirty miles inland, left over from a time when there were subsistence fisheries. *Pete McBride*

the edges of winter at both its beginning and its end, and diluting winter's heart. And also, ironically, contributing to the river's reduced flow, now forecast to ultimately cost us the future ability to grow these vegetables along the banks of the Lower Colorado River.

We may know more about the amount of water in the Colorado River than just about any other river in the world. On average, it collects and moves more than 5.3 trillion gallons of water a year.[52] Unimaginable, yet we have managed, in a single generation, to use it all up. When my grandparents were born in the early 1900s, a small portion of the Colorado River was being used by humans. By the time the last of them had passed on, all of the river was being used by humans. The Colorado stopped flowing regularly into the Sea of Cortez by 1981, when Lake Powell reservoir finished filling behind Glen Canyon Dam.[53,54] The river joined a famously auspicious group—the Yellow, the Amu Darya, the Euphrates, the Tigris, and the Rio Grande. Their geologically absurd fate is that they now merely trickle into their sandy beds some miles upstream of their formerly lush deltas. In the year my grandmother Margie was born, they met the ocean surf with a roar.

How could such a thing happen? Evidence shows that our desire for winter vegetables, and agriculture's capacity to deliver them, drove the Colorado River's extinction more than anything else. Evidence also shows that the dams and reservoirs, considered to be miracles of human engineering, disrupt ecosystems like no other. Their use sets off a chain of events that bleed carbon and nitrogen into the sky at rates exceeding most other land uses. And because of this, they add a heavy carbon burden to the fruits and vegetables coming out of the Lower Colorado River Basin—one that may be heavier than any other of its kind.

How could that possibly be? How could the straightforward act of damming a river, diverting its waters, and irrigating crops with the water create large greenhouse gas emissions? I set out for the lettuce fields to see for myself.

› • ‹

Early one morning in the first week of March, I drove Arizona's Interstate 8 from Phoenix to Yuma. The highway cuts a path through saguaro and creosote bush along the Gila River, among playas and intermittent hyper-green patches of irrigated alfalfa so bright against the desert pale that they startle the eye. The Gila, born in the snows of southwestern New Mexico, is so greatly diminished by the time it joins the Colorado River at Yuma that it appears to be more of a seep than the river that steam ships navigated in times past. I had meetings scheduled with farmers throughout the day, but arrived early enough to stop at a high bluff overlooking the desert agricultural landscape. The soil below was divided into smart, clean patches of crops cut into laser-straight rows of lettuce, broccoli, leafy greens, and other vegetables and fruits. Uniform, wooly fields of durum wheat lay like giant squares of dense, sea-green foam. In a month their seeds would ripen and be harvested, ground into semolina, and mixed with water to be molded into pasta in factories around the world. The greens were destined for plastic clamshells; the romaine heads to be loaded into three-packs, the broccoli heads and everything else to be shipped some hundreds to thousands of miles before they sat on grocers' misty produce shelves.

There seemed to be movement in every field. Water trickled from a gated pipe down thousands of narrow lines to laser-leveled beds of butterhead lettuce. A team of harvesters worked around and on a sanitized, stainless steel harvesting platform that crept slowly across a field of iceberg lettuce the size of bowling balls. Men and women loaded trucks with boxes of romaine and spinach whose roots had been in the soil just minutes earlier. The greens would arrive within the hour at a gigantic, refrigerated warehouse where they would chill for a day and a half to thirty-four degrees Fahrenheit before being loaded onto trucks and airplanes headed across the continent. Everybody within sight seemed to be moving with a sense of urgency as they either tended or harvested the bounty below, working at a pace that could make one think a hurricane was approaching and threatening the crop. The engineer in me marveled at the superb organization of it all, as well as the stunning amount of water required. A typical one-pound head of lettuce produced in the area required about thirty-one gallons of irrigation water applied to the crop, not to mention the additional 10 percent (about three gallons) of water evaporated from the reservoirs upstream.[55]

In conversations with farmers and extension specialists throughout that week, I learned that the winter vegetable business is a minutely planned enterprise running 365 days per year. Winter vegetables grown and harvested in October through March alternate with hot-season crops like alfalfa, melons, and peppers grown through the warmer months. To break disease cycles, durum wheat periodically replaces a winter vegetable crop. The soil might be tilled more than a dozen times each year to prepare seed beds, kill weeds, and construct furrows for irrigation. The harsh intensity of these practices has caused the soils to bleed organic matter until they have some of the lowest concentrations of carbon (and some of the highest concentrations of salts) of any agricultural soil in the United States and Mexico.

An error leading to a few days' delay in March could hold back the harvest of an October melon crop, which could in turn delay the entry of next year's romaine heads into the winter market long enough to slice tens of thousands of dollars of revenue from a single field. Meanwhile, the orderly irrigation canals are filled with most of the remaining water in the Colorado River before it crosses into Mexico. From Yuma's bluffs I could see the concrete line of the Imperial Dam several miles upstream. After its final pitch on US soil, what is left of the river creeps downstream through Mexico's own agricultural mirror image of the farm landscape in Arizona. Downstream of that is a small fraction of the Colorado River's formerly lush wetlands that the conservationist Aldo Leopold wrote about in "The Green Lagoons," chronicling a monthlong canoe journey through the expansive wetlands of the Colorado River Delta that existed at the time. Inspired by the explorer Hernando de Alarcón's visit to the gulf in 1540, Leopold wrote this of his experience in the wetlands:

> When the sun peeped over the Sierra Madre, it slanted
> across a hundred miles of lovely desolation, a vast flat
> bowl of wilderness rimmed by jagged peaks. On the

Migrant workers harvest lettuce irrigated with Colorado River water. The Colorado River irrigates cropland producing more than 90 percent of the vegetables eaten in the winter in the United States and Canada. Yuma, Arizona. *Pete McBride*

*map the Delta was bisected by the river, but in fact
the river was nowhere and everywhere, for he could
not decide which of a hundred green lagoons offered
the most pleasant and least speedy path to the Gulf.*

Today, this once-vast wilderness consists mostly of dried-out mud flats and sand dunes.

Irrigating crops in the desert of the Lower Colorado River regularly requires up to six standing feet of water per year. Four feet or more per year is commonly applied to grow the crops,[56,57] and up to two additional feet is applied to leach into the groundwater the salts from the saline surface of these desert soils.[58,59] In the below-sea-level Coachella Valley over in California, up to three additional feet of water is splashed onto vineyards in November and December every year simply to cool the vines, through evaporation, to mimic cool winter temperatures, thereby increasing spring flower densities and therefore higher yields the following summer.[60] Applying feet of water to permeable desert soils washes into the groundwater soluble nutrients remaining in the soil from the previous crop.[61,62] The groundwater and the landlocked Salton Sea accumulate the salts and nutrients. Fertilizer must be reapplied to soils after these events, at rates far higher than what is needed to achieve comparable yields in other parts of the country.

Whenever I am in a grocery store and see the plastic clamshells of leafy greens, rubber-banded bunches of broccoli, and bagged heads of romaine hearts, I am transported back to the hyper-green, quilted patchwork laid out on the floodplain. That dish of vegetables comes with a hefty side of global warming.

> • <

In the late 1980s, scientists began asking the question: "Are dams and reservoirs helping to warm the planet?" In the four decades since that basic inquiry began, researchers have examined the details of the life cycle of dams and reservoirs. They have found emissions wherever they looked and uncovered new classes of emissions that have yet to be fully quantified. A proportion of reservoirs are thought to store more carbon than they release.[63] But that appears to be relatively rare, especially when examined in the context of the reservoir's complete impact on its water-sheds downstream; carbon lost from soils, grasslands, and forests when reservoirs first fill up behind dams; and emissions from the full cradle-to-grave life cycle of the reservoir. The larger context of findings has coalesced over time into a relatively clear under-standing that most reservoir systems have a large carbon foot-print, albeit invisible to the naked eye unless one knows where to look.

The emissions are there regardless of whether or not hydro-power turbines spin within the dams. The emissions are often difficult to detect without advanced equipment and the unique perspective of life-cycle analysis. Measurements and model pre-dictions from reservoir and hydropower systems internationally show emissions so large they rank among the greatest sources of methane in the world. The electricity produced from many hydro-electric dams has a carbon footprint comparable to or greater than any other fossil fuel source of energy.[64,65,66] There is still much to learn; however, the upshot is that reservoirs are giant methane factories.[67,68] The methane from reservoirs is a potent source of climate-baking emissions (other sources include leaky natural gas wells, melting arctic permafrost, and cow rumen).

Emissions were first measured in the 1990s, when field equipment and methods were developed that could collect and quantify trace gases like methane and nitrous oxide coming off the surfaces of water bodies. As data accumulated, it became clear that greenhouse gas emissions were being emitted from multiple parts of the system.[69] To get a clearer picture of how the science has developed in the two decades since its inception, I reached out to Dr. Philip Fearnside at the National Institute for Research in Amazonia, in Manaus, Brazil. His research into the impacts of tropical reservoirs includes greenhouse gas emissions as well as changes to the ecosystems around the reservoirs and water quality impacts downstream.

"As far as I know, the first publication on this was Rudd in 1993," he wrote, referring to a synopsis written by Dr. Paul Rudd and colleagues that described how methane accumulated in enormous, landscape-changing hydropower reservoirs constructed in Quebec. Those first emissions measurements set off alarm bells. Researchers responded by taking measurements in tropical and subtropical regions as well as northern climes. In 1995, Fearnside published a paper on the emissions from the Balbina Reservoir in the Amazon, showing that emissions for the electricity there were worse than if one burned fossil fuels for power.[70] The research set off an ongoing flurry of further studies.

Science has since documented that the emissions from dams and reservoirs span decades, with heavy emission spikes at the beginning of a dam's life, and with a long, steady stream through the life of the dam and extending until the dam is removed. A final spike in emissions is believed to occur when dams are taken out of service. The waters standing stagnant behind concrete dams and the mud they deposit there tell the story.

> • <

At its core, ecology is the science of relationships between the Earth's organisms. Those relationships are defined by the physical environment and the organisms' life within that environment. River water temperature, chemistry, amount of sediment, and annual variations in the river's flow all deeply influence the plant and animal communities within rivers and along their banks. Decisions made and concrete poured more than a thousand river miles away can affect river conditions far downstream, creating physical conditions that may have never existed during the river's evolutionary development. Changes in organic matter, nutrients, waterborne silt, water temperatures, and the presence of new species or absence of historically present species drive relationships between the organisms and the ecosystems themselves into the margins of their evolutionary plasticity.

Through these relationships, carbon and nitrogen are fixed and deposited into the ecosystem, and then consumed again and again, growing into microorganisms that are in turn consumed by larger organisms or decompose upon the organisms' death, cycling further as food and nutrients for the ecosystem downstream. It is a steady pipeline of carbon and nitrogen into and through the ecosystem—but the pipeline leaks. Some of that carbon and nitrogen continuously leaks out as greenhouse gases. The extent of the leaks that flow through the pipeline are all determined by

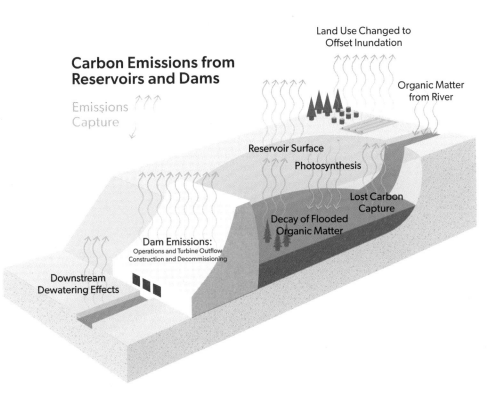

Carbon Emissions from Reservoirs and Dams

Emissions
Capture

Land Use Changed to
Offset Inundation

Organic Matter
from River

Reservoir Surface
Photosynthesis

Lost Carbon
Capture

Decay of Flooded
Organic Matter

Dam Emissions:
Operations and Turbine Outflow
Construction and Decommissioning

Downstream
Dewatering Effects

Carbon dioxide is emitted from fossil fuels burned in the construction, mining, and cement manufacturing during dam construction. Additional CO_2 is emitted from the energy required to operate and maintain the dam and reservoir. Decomposition of downstream wetlands and riparian forests due to dewatering effects emits CO_2 and nitrous oxide. Methane is emitted from hydroelectric turbines that draw water from the reservoirs' methane-rich deep-water layers. Decay of flooded in situ organic matter, organic matter brought in from upstream, and organic matter from photosynthesis by algae and aquatic plants results in CO_2 and methane emitted from the reservoir surface. Land use changes when people living in the reservoir footprint must relocate leads to CO_2 and nitrous oxide emissions. Lost carbon capture is carbon capture by forests, grasslands, and soils that no longer happens when the reservoir is flooded. Dam decommissioning leads to methane emissions from sediments captured behind the dam and exposed during the drawdown process.

the relationships between the organisms and the conditions in the water, which are increasingly driven by the actions of concrete spillways far upstream. Every small change in that carbon and nitrogen balance has consequences for the atmosphere, and the climate.

The water could produce hydroelectricity and become golf courses, swimming pools, or pitchers of water on dinner tables throughout the desert southwest of North America. Some of the water becomes lettuce, alfalfa, and cantaloupes. A lot of it will simply evaporate from reservoir surfaces into the desert sky. All of it will be dammed, diverted, processed, boiled, evaporated, drunk, or used for some other human purpose, many times over. Because of this, the carbon and nitrogen molecules laden in the river's flows are destined to fates far different from just a century earlier when rivers largely ran free.

Millions upon millions of tons of carbon and nitrogen that once ponded into delta soils, or the immense carbon stocks stored in the coastal wetlands, or in the wood of lush riverside forests, or that were never flushed from soils into the river in the first place, are now destined for the atmosphere to add to Earth's insulating blanket. The fifteen dams along the Colorado River's main stem and the hundreds on its tributaries have accumulated a legacy of disruption. The most famous of these dams has become infamous for reasons that may outlast its legacy.

Hoover Dam, once called the eighth wonder of the world, stores enough water to irrigate two million acres in California and Arizona.[71] It was built by federal and state governments to stimulate the US economy during the depth of the Great Depression and put people to work. Between 1931 and 1936, the federal government employed over twenty-one thousand people to build the dam.[72] Stories of the gigantic dam's rise captured the public imagination at a time when little was being built elsewhere. Newsreels shown in movie theaters around the country featured "high scalers"—men suspended by ropes and operating jackhammers, sledgehammers, and pry bars on cliff faces hundreds of feet above the canyon floor. Four and a half million cubic yards of concrete were poured into the concrete buttresses wedged into the canyon walls it spans. More than two million cubic yards of rock and gravel were moved to secure the seam between the concrete dam and the bedrock and to construct barriers to protect the workers at the dam site. The carbon dioxide emitted from the project matched emissions from the entire city of San Francisco at the time and equated to the yearly emissions from about 636,000 modern American automobiles. Portland cement, the binding agent in concrete, was at the root of the issue.

Manufacturing cement is one of the largest single sources of greenhouse gas emissions in the world, totaling more than 10 percent of the annual greenhouse gas emissions worldwide.[73] The process requires burning copious amounts of coal and natural gas to bake limestone and other ingredients into Portland cement. The emissions from burning fossil fuels to manufacture the cement, combined with blasting and moving rock in the way of the dam, created a carbon dioxide burden totaling about three million tons. This was just the first pulse of climate-warming emissions in the life of Hoover Dam and Lake Mead reservoir behind it.

Greenhouse gases began to stream from Lake Mead's surface as soon as the river pooled behind the dam. When the turbines began to spin, methane streamed through the turbine outflows downstream. Among all their other intended and unintended uses, reservoirs convert into climate-warming gases the copious organic matter found in the reservoir. Algae from the surface, organic matter washed in from the upstream watershed, and organic matter in the carbon and nitrogen in the soils and riverside forests inundated by the reservoir all become food for microbes present throughout the ecosystem.

Microbes feeding on organic matter in the reservoir use up the oxygen in its deepest layers, at which point they shift from producing carbon dioxide as a waste product of their metabolism to producing methane. That methane diffuses or bubbles toward the surface. Some is consumed by microbes in the oxygen-rich layers near the surface. Hydroelectric turbines like those at Lake Mead draw water from the methane-rich depths, shunting the methane straight into the atmosphere. Without the turbines, much (but not all) of that methane would become food for microbes in the oxygen-rich layers near the surface and would be converted to carbon dioxide. The methane emissions coming off the reservoir surface or through the turbines continue as long as the turbines spin and the water lies stagnant behind the dam.

As night fell on my last evening on the Colorado River trip that opened this chapter, I walked down to the water's edge on a long sandbar. The river had washed us into the upper reaches of Lake Powell, which pools behind Glen Canyon Dam about 375 river miles upriver of Lake Mead reservoir. That afternoon we had journeyed through the high canyon walls and across the lake's still surface. Had Glen Canyon Dam never been built, I would have been resting dozens of feet lower, along a running river lined with cottonwoods and wetlands holding carbon and nitrogen stores in their trunks and soil. The reservoir had blocked the riverside ecosystem's ability to sequester carbon. It created a tremendous carbon mitigation opportunity cost.

I sat at the water's edge and sipped a beer. Barry Lopez's essay "The Grace Note of the Canyon Wren" came to mind as the unmistakable descending call of that lovely bird echoed off the sandstone walls. Crickets began making a racket so loud I worried I might not be able to sleep. Bats flew erratic lines overhead as they cached insect calories for themselves and their babies in their cliffside rookeries.

As I sat there, I recalled a documentary film describing humanity's role in the climate crisis. The film depicted greenhouse gas emissions in vivid colors. Bright-purple carbon dioxide streamed from automobile exhaust pipes and electricity plant smokestacks. Had I made the film, I might have added images of yellow methane pulsing from the mouths of cattle chewing their cuds, and from lagoons of liquid dairy manure and rice paddies. Red nitrous oxide would stream from farm fields after fertilizer was spread on the soil. That evening I wondered how the scene on the reservoir surface stretched out before me would be different if we could see the emissions coming from it. Brief, intense yellow and red ribbons of methane and nitrous oxide would pop up here and there through the purple carbon dioxide fog shrouding the water's surface.

After twilight fell, I knelt beside a mudflat at the water's edge. Steady blurbs of gas had been popping from the mud's surface. I held a butane lighter above a spot where I'd seen the bubbles pop frequently and waited. Before long the mud surface bulged faintly. I flicked the lighter and lowered it to the surface. A moment later the bubble popped. A brief, blue flame with a yellow fringe flashed for a moment. Methane. As the reservoir surface rises and falls and its banks alternately wet and dry, it stimulates microbes to decompose the carbon and nitrogen in its banks into flammable methane and inflammable nitrous oxide at rates that at times match the emissions streaming from the reservoir surface. Integrate these over the miles upon miles of shoreline as a reservoir rises and falls (particularly one as variable as Lake Powell), and the numbers really add up.[74,75]

What happens at the end of a reservoir's life? Engineers have conceded that removing the mud that piles up behind a dam is an impossibly huge task. Simply leaving the dams and mud in place creates a safety hazard downstream. The Colorado River carries a greater silt burden than most rivers.[76] The consensus among engineers at the time the dams were built, and still today, is that when the reservoirs fill with sediment, they stop operating and must be decommissioned to allow the rivers' flows to safely continue. As they do, over time they will erode the billions of tons of sediment piled up behind the dams and carry it downstream. As the banks erode, much of the undecomposed carbon and nitrogen within the sediment gets exposed anew to microbes. There comes at that time a final pulse of greenhouse gas emissions.[77,78]

A dam was removed, or "decommissioned," in my own community in 2013. River conservation organizations worked with the City of Fort Collins to decommission abandoned irrigation diversion dams on the Cache la Poudre River to improve aquatic habitat and water quality, and allow for native fish and other aquatic animals to freely move up and down the river.[79]

On a bluebird winter afternoon, I met my friend and colleague Dr. John Bartholow where the Josh Ames Dam was being deconstructed. John had originally proposed that the dam be removed, and he shepherded the decommissioning process through the long, sometimes maddeningly slow process of public review, decision-making, and consensus-building that defines many city governments. He had been photographing the dam's deconstruction over the weeks of its demise. The dam, originally about eight feet high and spanning about a hundred feet, had been removed two weeks earlier. Workers operated a backhoe to reconnect the river with wetlands nearby.

I surprised John with a bottle of bubbly to celebrate his years of work. We drank with delighted smiles before scrambling to the river's edge to where years of accumulated mud had once rested at least two yards thick. I squished a carbon-rich, black handful through my fingers. Snail shells and leftover insect carapaces oozed between my fingers. I was squeezing many decades' worth of accumulated and decomposing bug poop and dead microbe bodies. We talked about the Colorado River and the hundreds of billions of tons of mud that lay in Lake Mead reservoir. Much will inevitably erode away after the dam can no longer operate. At the present time, no reliable predictions exist about how large the

Lake Mead reservoir beyond the Hoover Dam. The Colorado River is overallocated and the projected reservoir capacity looks grim despite the current wet winters. *Pete McBride*

emissions from that process will be. All we do know is that they are likely to be real.[80, 81]

Were the river and the rocks still in their native state, most of this carbon and nitrogen destined to flux into the atmosphere from Lake Mead's sediments likely would have remained in the soil and trees blanketing the river's banks and in the spectacularly productive delta that once lay at the river's mouth. Little of the roughly 1.9 million acres of the Colorado River delta wetlands remain. The river's terminal fate lies in the farm fields well upstream of the Gulf of Mexico. What was once one of the greatest subtropical estuaries in the world is now fed by a trickle of saline leftovers from cities and agricultural fields upstream. Tens of millions of tons of carbon and nitrogen stored in the wetlands, and forests there are now gone. Nearly all of it has likely been added to the atmosphere's dangerous, climate-heating blanket.

> • <

The legacy of these emissions eats at me. Over the course of nearly two decades of conservation work and two decades of local eating and greenhouse gas research, I have to concede a complex personal relationship with dams.

It is because I am in love with all kinds of natural spaces—prairies, peaks and valleys, glaciers, the vast expanse of oceans, the chilly blue of lakes—that rivers especially draw me in. Research shows that many people in the world feel the same way.[82, 83, 84, 85] Rivers are grand ecosystem integrators. Rivers coalesce resources in every ecosystem they traverse. They are hotspots of biodiversity, of photosynthesis, and of the sheer beauty of functioning ecosystems.

I spent much of my youth walking the river bottoms in central and southwest Nebraska. We gathered morel mushrooms and fished for white bass in the spring, set trotlines for catfish in the summer, and hunted in the fall. Thirty-five years of water have flowed under the bridges of my life since my family's farms were sold, and yet my brother and I can still close our eyes and describe in detail nearly every foot of Medicine Creek where it flowed through my mother's parents' farm.

Whenever I am on the road and cross a bridge over a waterway, I slow the car to see the river's flow and scan the forest on its banks. I locate the green-and-white road sign identifying the waterway's name and speak the river's name aloud. These rivers, fords, sloughs, wetlands, and reaches all have uncountable names, transcending thousands of years of time through the experiences of people living here long before the European invasion of North America. As humans we name places that are culturally significant, and our love of them is defined by their names—and though humans might not name every hill and dale they come across, we can be damned sure that they name every river.

Feelings of clarity and openness wash over me on undammed rivers. I once camped along the Blackstone River in northern Yukon Territory, a day's hike from the nearest road. I was on a black sand beach at the water's edge with my wife at the time, the first night of a long backpack trip through the region's remote Tombstone Mountains. The river ran fine and clear. Downed trees captured silt in its corner flows. Eddies and sweeping back currents carved out the banks where the river swung in its serpentine path. Caribou crossed the river upstream of camp, shaking the water off their coats beneath a snag on which perched a hawk owl. There were no reservoirs upstream, no diversions, no houses leaking their septic tank contents into the river. It was simply eco-system processes run amok. The river remade its own beauty each day, season, and year. I sat awake far into the Arctic twilight. I felt like I was sitting at the feet of a master painter casting her brush upon canvas, but the brush was a hundred caribou, a thousand birds, uncountable grains of sand, microbes, blueberry rootlets.

In contrast, dams feel like a vandal's slash through a finely woven fabric. They raise the hair on the back of my neck the opposite way the beauty of the Blackstone did that summer evening. However we attempt to stitch the ecosystems back together after dams are built, the seam bulges like a scar and the work will never be the same until the dam is gone and the river reweaves the tapestry.[86]

The emotional conflict I and so many others face is that our lives are intertwined with the existence of dams. Just like fossil fuels are seemingly unavoidable in our daily existence, the same can be true for dams and reservoirs. More than half a million reservoirs larger than 2.5 hectares (5.5 acres) exist in the world today. Approximately sixty-two thousand are classified as large dams—more than fifteen meters high and holding more than three million cubic meters of water.[87,88,89] Only about one-third of rivers longer than one thousand kilometers km (620 miles) remain free-flowing, and only a quarter of them flow uninterrupted to their saltwater estuaries.[90] Only one major river in the lower forty-eight states of the United States—the Yellowstone—remains undammed on its main stem. Most of the food grown in my watershed required some irrigation water diverted from my home river and from a half a dozen other rivers in completely different watersheds, dammed and diverted through ditches and tunnels across and under mountain ranges spanning the skyline to the west of my home. I flush my toilets, brush my teeth, grow my own fruits and vegetables, bathe, and cook with water from these rivers funneled through reservoirs. Their connections to our lives seem impossible to escape.

Does that mean alternatives are not possible?

Michelangelo's *David* was once a block of stone buried within a mountain of Italian marble. Da Vinci's *Annunciation* was once merely pigment, canvas, and brush. Before the invention of the transistor and other solid-state devices, creating electricity from the sun wasn't possible. The first digital computers were enormous physical devices that filled entire buildings. Wind turbines that could generate gigawatt-hours per year were simply not possible until the last decade.

Just as the transition from the fossil fuel era to the renewable energy era defines our lives today, reimagining our water needs and the systems that meet them, while rewilding rivers, could define the next era. Crises in water delivery systems and a projected global shortage of fresh water[91] is driving innovation. Rising temperatures are leading to high evaporation rates from reservoirs.[92] To quote the author of one study, "The total reservoir evaporation can be larger than the combined use of domestic and industrial water."[93] Said differently, more water can be lost by evaporation from reservoirs than they actually deliver. Storing water belowground in aquifers is expanding in practice and scope throughout the world.[94] We are on the verge of dramatic, critically needed innovations in meeting our water needs.

The CAP (Central Arizona Project) canal near Phoenix, Arizona. The canal diverts water from Lake Havasu reservoir on the Colorado River near Parker, Arizona, and carries it 336 miles (541 km) to Phoenix and Tucson, Arizona. *Pete McBride*

Dams are being decommissioned and rivers restored throughout the United States. What about the dam holding back Lake Mead reservoir that was once called the eighth wonder of the world, and its sister project 375 miles upstream, holding back Lake Powell reservoir? Give us back the wetlands, porpoises,[95] fish, birds, cottonwoods, and everything else the Colorado River ecosystem supported. And the climate-baking carbon the dams released.

Would I also trade those flows for the almost ridiculously easy-to-buy selection of winter vegetables from my grocer's produce aisles? Fortunately, it isn't clear that is even necessary.

> • ‹

Earlier in this book I introduced Sunspot Urban Farm, a small, community-supported-agriculture and market farm operating near Fort Collins, Colorado. The farm grew enough produce to supply eighty families all the vegetables and eggs they could consume for about five to six months out of the year through Community Supported Agriculture (CSA) shares, while supplying local grocers and restaurants with produce for their shelves and menus. Originally conceived by the horticulturalist Dr. Booker Whatley at Tuskegee University, the CSA model is designed to connect local consumers with local farmers.[96] CSA shareholders take on some of the risk of agriculture by purchasing a share in the farm before the season begins. They receive produce from the farm throughout the growing season. The couple running Sunspot, Amy Yackel and Rod Adams, began the venture in 2011. They grow nutritious vegetables and fruits with a minimum of fossil fuels, without the aid of synthetic agricultural chemicals like fertilizers or pest control sprays.

The two of them had recently expanded to a small farm on the town's border, and my colleague Amy Swan and I met them there one chilly October afternoon with snow in the forecast.

Like many farmers I know, the two of them have day jobs. Amy Yackel (whom I'll refer to as farmer Amy, to avoid confusion with my colleague Amy) holds a PhD in wildlife biology, and works for the US Geological Survey, researching snake biology and ways to control invasive Burmese pythons in the southeastern United States and invasive brown tree snakes in US Pacific Island territories. Rod teaches during the winter at the local community college. The two of them appeared from behind a building to greet us, dressed in overalls, sleeves rolled up despite the chill, revealing the tanned, strong hands and forearms of people who work outdoors.

Our conversation immediately turned to the weather as the two of them began an animated tour of the fields. In one of their "high tunnels" (long, tall hoop houses covered with polyethylene that extend the growing season without requiring heaters) we found spectacular-looking poblano peppers dripping from deep-green pepper plants. Slim, aromatic cucumbers and globes of tomatoes hung from plants lining the opposite pathway. The bumpy, deep-green leaves of dinosaur kale lined the path.

"This field was barren clay when we bought it—a pasture that had been grazed down to nothing," said farmer Amy as she lifted boards from what I thought was a covered walkway, revealing a deep pit filled with decomposing leaves. "This is our worm pit."

Rod knelt down and dipped a hand into the pile, lifting out a dark-brown mass of moist, crinkly material, wriggling with red-orange worms that dropped back to the pile and burrowed back down out of the sunlight. He tipped an ear to the pit and pointed. "Listen!" he said.

A faint rustling came to my ears, generated by the worm-pit community doing its work on the season's detritus. My colleague Amy and I put our own hands into the pile. The earthy handful, about halfway in the process between dead leaves and fully digested compost, felt moist and clean with a faint warmth emanating from its depth. For lack of any other term to identify it, the mass smelled "wormy." The luscious vegetables growing all around us, growing in the previous year's worm compost, demonstrated the connection to the worm's work.

"The pit goes down three feet deep," said Rod. "We fill it with leaves and farm waste. In the spring it becomes a home for chorus frogs and Woodhouse's toads."

"There is some really good stuff happening here," said farmer Amy.

The story behind Sunspot Farm's beginning eight years earlier mirrored many other modern farm origin stories. Rod described it this way: "Farming and working for ourselves fulfilled what we were trying to achieve in our shared search for a good life. And growing food for people feels like an uncontroversial good."

"It's very satisfying," added farmer Amy.

Not only did they want to grow food, but they also wanted to do it in a way that engaged the local community. And they wanted something that would include Lois, farmer Amy's mother. She was eighty years old at the time, living in Florida, with failing health and declining spirit. They wanted to bring her home to include her in their lives. The farm seemed a natural fit.

"In some ways, bringing her here is the larger reason for starting this farm. It literally saved her life," said farmer Amy.

I thought back to her mother's thoughtful face as she sat chatting with customers and processing vegetables for CSA shares earlier in the year. Then farmer Amy told us about a spontaneous visitor they'd had their first year of operation. They were working in the vegetable beds of their front yard when a school bus pulled up and stopped. The driver opened the front door and leaned out.

"You have GOT to tell me what is going on here! Whenever I drive by, the kids are all just glued to the windows!"

That led to a field trip of excited middle schoolers who circulated through the farm, learning about carrots, spinach, chickens, and worms.

"Not to one-up Amy's story, but I've got another," said Rod. "That same summer a hailstorm poured icy hell on the farm. Our neighbors ran out with their umbrellas, shielding the vegetables!"

What is the source of the nutrients for the farm's crops? Leaves from the neighborhood's fall cleanup. Rod put out the word to neighbors and CSA share members that they would take any material from the annual fall yard cleanup, which they would use to cover the vegetable beds through the winter and make compost.

"That first year we were literally buried in leaves!" farmer Amy said. "We knew by then that we were on to something."

Organic vegetable farmers throughout the country are taking a similar approach to feeding their soil. Ray Tyler from Rose Creek Farms in Selmer, Tennessee, which supplies vegetables year-round to multiple farmers markets and ten local grocery stores, accumulates their neighbors' leaves every fall to compost into the nutrients their crops need. Customers I interviewed describe their produce as "spectacular." Duncan Family Farms, an organic producer in Goodyear, Arizona, took it a step further. They contracted with the city of Goodyear to divert as much of the city's organic waste from the landfill as possible, directing it instead into their composting facility. It became a second income stream for the farm, saving the city money and providing the nutrients to feed the soil under their crops on thousands of acres.

Sunspot Urban Farm's system revolves around two simple principles—building organic matter in the soil and keeping the soil covered year-round. At the end of the growing season the fields are covered with a deep layer of leaves. In the spring the fields are layered with the contents of the worm pit and secondary piles of compost. Winter-hardy greens like spinach grow as cover crops, keeping cash coming in while ensuring there is a living root in the soil at all times.

"After we started layering leaves on the field over winter, we realized it was a no-brainer. Before then, in the spring this heavy clay soil was so hard and dry it sometimes required a pick to break it up for planting. After the first winter with leaves on the field, the soil in the spring was moist, springy, dark, and full of tilth," Rod explained.

And here is where their story intersects with reservoirs. A by-product of their soil fertility program has been a dramatic drop in their irrigation water needs.

"We can delay starting our irrigation program by several weeks in the spring, compared to other growers. The soil has plenty of water for the germinating plants," said Rod.

Hearing this, my colleague Amy bent to examine the drip tape laid out in the rows through their fields. From a distance, the long, black plastic lines looked as if somebody had stretched precise strips of electrician's tape down the rows. Instead, it is a thin plastic tube, pressed flat, with water emitters every several inches along its length. The tube expands when filled with water, and drips it out directly onto the soil surface, cutting evaporation losses and delivering moisture directly to the plant roots. The tape lasts a decade or more, and like the materials for their greenhouses, it can be recycled at the end of its life. Manufacturing the metal and plastic for the high tunnels and drip tape added about a quarter of a metric ton of CO_2e per acre of land. Amy and Rod monitor the water in the soil and deliver the amount of water needed for each crop. Their system and equipment don't allow it yet, but other farmers use drip tape to deliver soluble nutrients, compost tea, and other soil amendments to the crops.

My colleague Amy moved on to inspect the soil as the forecasted snow began to fall. There was so much more to talk about, and none of us wanted to leave the field. The soil surface was the color of deep milk chocolate, flecked with darker remainders of compost as if tiny dark chocolate drops enriched the mix. "How much organic matter do you have in the soil?" she asked.

"We started out at about 2 percent. We are up to 5 percent now," answered Rod.

By diverting the leaves from the landfill into compost, Sunspot Urban Farm avoided significant methane emissions. Recycling the nutrients in the leaves into compost to grow vegetables avoided additional emissions from manufacturing synthetic fertilizers (described in a later chapter titled "The Corn Eaters"). It supported more efficient use of rainfall and irrigation water. However, moving the carbon from one location to another to maintain high organic matter levels in the farm's soil doesn't sequester additional carbon from the atmosphere.

The snow shifted to a light scattering of rain, and we began walking back to the car. I looked around at the farm as we walked, marveling at how much more efficiently the soil holds the irrigation water precisely delivered through the drip tape to the plants.

We said our goodbyes and drove slowly down the driveway. My colleague Amy watched the field as we drove past, then looked at me and said, "You know, Mark, I don't know exactly which of all these things they are doing leads to it, but Amy's and Rod's vegetables are absolutely delicious."

> • <

How do the emissions from growing vegetables in the Lower Colorado River compare with the produce from operations like Sunspot Urban Farm? A conservative estimate of the carbon footprint from the reservoir surfaces in the entire Colorado River system indicates emissions likely exceed 1.3 million metric tons of CO_2e per year. The US Environmental Protection Agency's carbon calculator predicts that is equivalent to driving about 15.6 billion miles in a typical American passenger vehicle. Those surface emissions add up to about six-tenths of a metric ton of CO_2e per acre of irrigated cropland. Add in the methane emissions through hydropower turbines, carbon lost when the reservoir was filled, and those from lake sediments, and the number likely triples to nearly two metric tons of CO_2e per acre.

What does this mean for your own plate?

A typical, one-pound bag or clamshell of spinach grown in Southern California or Arizona carries a greenhouse gas emissions burden of about three pounds of CO_2e delivered to your home.[97] That emissions load comes from four main sources: about a pound comes from manufacturing and applying fertilizers, as well as the fuel burned to farm the product and process it into bags. Another pound comes from shipping it to the grocer and keeping it fresh until you buy it. Approximately another pound comes from the irrigation system. An additional burden occurs from any portion thrown into landfills.

The carbon footprint of Sunspot Urban Farm's veggies is roughly a quarter of that produced by veggies farmed in the Lower Colorado River region. No manufactured fertilizers are used on the farm.[98] The compost made on the farm and applied to the soil fertilizes the crops, and emissions from making the compost are about one-third those of manufacturing an equivalent amount of fertilizer. The produce is shipped less than five miles, compared with the average of 1,200 miles for that coming from Yuma. (Shipping emissions per pound of produce vary between growers, and inefficient shipping can increase emissions, but shortening the supply lines is one of the clearest paths to reducing shipping emissions overall.) The emissions to manufacture the drip tape and high tunnels are a small component of the farm's carbon footprint since the materials are recycled when they can no longer be used. On a pound-for-pound of produce basis, the crops

Rod Adams adds organic matter to a very biologically active community compost pile (temperatures range from 120–150° F) at the Sunspot Urban Farm. Fort Collins, Colorado. *Amy Yackel Adams*

require one-half or less of the amount of irrigation water required in Yuma. The extra organic matter stored in the soil through their farming practices offsets other emissions. Sunspot Urban Farm's vegetables, and those of other farmers using similar practices around the country, are about as close to a carbon-neutral source of produce as one could find. But can one find fresh vegetables during February? It turns out the answer is yes.

> • ‹

Twice per month, the Fort Collins Winter Farmers Market takes over the vaulted space of a building in the city's Old Town. Our noses were flushed with the cinnamon spice of hot cider as Leslie and I stomped snow from our boots at the entrance. We paused for a moment and Leslie laughed out loud.

"Did we bring enough shopping bags?" she asked. More than forty vendors and hundreds of shoppers were crammed into the packed space.

Since 1992, when Eliot Coleman first published *Four-Season Harvest*, his treatise on farming winter vegetables without heated greenhouses, the possibilities for nourishing people with produce grown in winter expanded dramatically. Coleman and other winter-farming pioneers researched cold-weather farming techniques used for centuries throughout Europe, brought them home, and adapted them to the United States. For Coleman, that was Maine. With his wife, Barbara Damrosch, and a phalanx of winter-farming optimists, Coleman developed ways to make the techniques work while making a living doing it. Every commercial vegetable farmer I know owns Coleman's trilogy of works describing how to grow and harvest fresh vegetables every week of the year. Leslie and I reaped the benefits on that February morning.

Let me tell you what we did not find: butter lettuce, lipstick-red sweet peppers, lemon cucumbers, or watermelon.

But here is what we had when we left the market a half hour later (after I'd run back to the car for more shopping bags): spinach, kale, escarole, carrots, yellow Finn potatoes, celery root, yellow onions, three types of winter squash, dried beans, farm-fresh eggs, freshly ground wheat flour, a fresh chicken butchered the night before, mushrooms, peach jam, pear jam, a jar of honey, freshly made pasta (made from locally grown wheat and eggs), and an aromatic bottle of cider fermented by my friend and colleague Tim. That night we made a feast.

It feels ironic to carry fresh tomatoes and tender heads of butter lettuce from the supermarket across the threshold of my home while the snow falls outside. Not so for the produce we brought home from that market. All of it had been grown locally, a lot of it harvested the day before, the remainder harvested the previous autumn and stored for sale that day.

Is growing this sort of produce practical in our region? "It's possible, really a matter of scale, and of developing the markets," answered Adrian Card, my extension colleague at Colorado State University who specializes in working with local vegetable growers. "We have the soil and the climate that can support it. The growers are developing the know-how. But it isn't a simple problem to solve."

I asked him for clarification. "Labor is probably the biggest problem. Growing vegetables and fruits is a lot of work. We don't have the agricultural labor force here on Colorado's Front Range,

Vegetable beds at Sunspot Urban Farm. Fort Collins, Colorado.
Rod Adams

or in many other parts of the country where food could be grown locally, using climate-friendly and river-friendly methods, without developing the labor network to help make it happen."

This refrain—lack of an agricultural labor pool, consumer expectations, lack of distribution systems—is repeated over and over again by growers and supply-chain managers interviewed throughout the country.

He went on, "We'd have to expand the local food processing and distribution system. People have responded to that need already and networks are improving. I don't think this will be a huge problem to solve, but the distribution network will have to be developed further."

"Restaurants overall would have to become more innovative, and less dependent on a homogenous menu. I think the signs are there, however, that locally produced foods that have a lower impact are what people want."

Can the soils and climate in and near Colorado's Front Range urban corridor sustainably feed the five million people who live there? What about the urban centers throughout the world that rely on food grown in far-flung places, using increasingly endangered water supplies and transported with increasingly dangerous fossil fuels? Fossil fuels enabled a concentrated population to settle the landscape without considering whether the local ecosystem could feed them. Restoring society's connection to local food landscapes and transitioning farming and shortening supply chains to what can be sustained locally in landscapes more suited to growing food can reduce the food burden on the Colorado River and other rivers like it throughout the world.

The Salmon Forests

The grizzly was magnificent, a deep chocolate brown with blonde highlights. His massive, round head was beset with luxurious fur, his muscles rippled every time he lunged for a fish through the crystalline waters of the Brooks River. Salmon had only started migrating a few weeks earlier, and would be passing through for several more, and yet fat already rolled off his long back and hips and swelled his prodigious belly. Let's call him Bear #1.

When he caught a fish, he sat down like a dog on the rock he had claimed midriver and held the fish in his front paws. After crushing the head in his jaws, he turned the fish around to eat the tail, then turned it back again to eat the head, munching like a dog eating kibble. Finally, he delicately skinned the fish and

Previous spread: A wild-caught sockeye salmon and grilled vegetables. *Eric Bissell*

Opposite: When salmon die after spawning, their bodies fertilize the surrounding ecosystem, supporting forests that shade the spawning grounds, filter rainwater, moderate storm flows, and stabilize riverbanks. Great Bear Rainforest, British Columbia. *Tavish Campbell*

devoured the skin, and then after cleanly eviscerating the fish, he slurped down any eggs he found. He released the carcass back into the current to where the birds, wolves, foxes, fish, other bears, and insects were waiting downstream. His catch rate approached 100 percent and he rarely sat for more than a few minutes before catching another salmon and repeating his ritual. The dozen or so other bears at the falls kept their distance from him, and each other, focusing on their own catch method and eating routine.

The day before had been my first at the falls, and I'd come away with the notion that the place was one big happy fish party. As I approached the platform on the trail early in the morning of my second day, there was no way I could have known what was crashing through the brush past me as it fled the falls.

I didn't learn this until later, but the trouble began when Bear #2 stepped into the water from the opposite bank. Bear #1 was in the best spot in the falls. Bear #2, equally magnificent, stepped into the water and began slowly moving toward Bear #1. With Bear #2's first step into the water, all the bears within sight stopped whatever they were doing and skedaddled. Some walked deliberately, some trotted, some ran. All watched over their shoulders as they went. The ranger on the observation deck cautioned the people there to remain quiet and radioed to the visitor center to hold approaching visitors for a while. Then he moved back down the long ramp to the gate to hurry other approaching visitors into the safety of the fenced-in platform. I had already left the Brooks Falls visitor center in Katmai National Park sometime earlier and was still on the trail on the way to the platform, with no clue of the drama about to unfold.

As Bear #2 moved closer, he and Bear #1 began popping their jaws at each other, looking askance, and deliberately swatting the water around them—all classic methods to signal aggression. Bear #2 paused a dozen feet away when his competition caught a fish. Bear #1 moved back to his rock, eyed Bear #2, crushed the fish's head, then set the fish down on the rock and placed a front paw on it. He seemed to be saying, "This fish, and this spot, is mine." After an interval, Bear #2 moved closer, setting up to fish within feet of Bear #1. Then he lunged after a migrating salmon swimming between the two of them, swiping Bear #1 with an outstretched ring of claws, and the fight began.

They slammed into each other like thousand-pound-plus sumo wrestlers, slashing with inches-long claws and terrifying, gaping maws. They shattered the water as they tumbled through the current and spun up onto the bank underneath the platform and out of sight of the viewers. Their roars were so replete with rage, dominance, and ferocious strength that my testicles shrank into my groin. Those roars froze me on the trail approaching the platform, perhaps fifty yards away.

More than a ton of fighting grizzly bear bodies slammed into a pylon and the platform above trembled. People cried out. And then, only seconds after it began, the fight was over. The roaring abruptly stopped, and a large body scrambled up the bank past me and away. A relative silence came, but for the steady rush of the falls. The people on the platform could see nothing. Salmon continued their upriver migration. The people whispered to each other, "Who won? Are they dead?" The silence continued. The ranger stepped forward, held everyone in place, and then moved

back to the gate. I waited on the trail, eyeing a climbable tree close by in case I needed it. Suddenly I really had to pee.

After a time, Bear #2 stepped out from under the platform, into the river, and occupied the spot formerly claimed by Bear #1. There he stood on all fours, casing the scene, sides heaving. Blood dripped from his face. Raw flesh showed through an eight-inch gap of missing skin on his rib cage. This is the scene I came upon after the ranger hustled me through the bear-proof gate onto the platform. The others present recounted the story in breathless whispers, showing me their recorded video, eyes still wide. After a time, Bear #2 lunged into the water and emerged with a salmon in his jaws. He moved onto the flat rock, sat down, and began to eat. The other bears began to warily creep back in from the margins.

Seventy river miles directly downriver, Indigenous Alaskans prepared to set their nets along the estuary banks. Commercial men and women fishers jockeyed their boats into position where the river met the sea, awaiting a radio call from the state of Alaska announcing that the sockeye salmon season was open. The yearly race, and in some cases the fight, to fill freezers and catch quotas was about to begin.

> • <

A Bering Sea fisherman once told me that he has never quite felt the way he did while returning to shore with an open skiff

Bears and other predators and scavengers cycle ocean-derived nutrients from salmon into the surrounding ecosystem through their feces and through their bodies after they die. Katmai National Park, Alaska. *Michael Melford* bursting full of salmon, the ocean water just inches from the gun-wales. "I feel wealthy in moments like that," he said. Perhaps the bears felt some bearlike version of that feeling, standing in a river with a steady flow of fish swimming within reach. I had a similar experience a few hours after the bear encounter, standing in my fishing waders in the middle of the Brooks River. The following day I would set out with my wife at the time, Jan, to paddle our folding kayak on a lake-and-river circuit, the Savonoski Loop, accessible from Brooks Falls. The trip would require dozens of miles of lake paddling, a two-mile portage, and a breathless run of the Savonoski River. We had planned plenty of time for the journey and a fine weather window was predicted to open the following day. Pursuing wild fish in wild rivers with a fly rod consumes me like nothing else. I couldn't wait to experience what it was like to catch a wild salmon.

The afternoon after the fight at the falls, I waded into the water with my fishing rod rigged with a fly some kind fishermen had given me the night before. The gentle pull of the current around my legs, the scent of soil and water and fish, the scattering of light off leaves and the river surface lit up familiar receptors in my brain and took me to a happy place I feel whenever I am working a wild river. After this quiet reverie, intermittent bumps against my legs and a vague sense of movement in the water distracted me. I looked down. My polarized sunglasses cut past the reflecting glare, and my heart leapt when I realized I was completely envel-oped in a school of migrating sockeye salmon. They were slowly finning as they held themselves in formation against the current, just inches apart from each other. Downstream another pod of fish waited below this one. I imagined salmon stacked up in the Naknek River all the way from the ocean to Naknek Lake immediately downstream of me, and then to the river where I stood. I cast my line into the water and began to work the fly toward the pod of fish below. A short time later, an urgent tug bent the rod, the water boiled, and the struggle to land the fish began.

The rush of that moment has stayed with me ever since.

Later I landed a powerful, silver-and-blue sockeye, bright from the ocean. After she tired and came into my net, her marvelous beauty came into full view. I suddenly felt a spasm of regret as I recalled her journey—seventy miles swimming upstream from the saltwater estuary. That impressive distance defined this particular fish's life cycle, but actually paled compared to the journey of other salmon. Endangered sockeyes swim nine hundred miles upstream through the Columbia, Snake, and Salmon Rivers of Oregon and Idaho (navigating many dams along the way) and climb more than sixty-five hundred feet (1,980 meters) in elevation to spawn in a high-elevation, pristine waterbody known as Redfish Lake. Chinook salmon traveling from the Bering Sea up the Yukon River swim more than two thousand miles and climb more than two thousand feet (610 meters) to their spawning grounds above the town of Whitehorse in the Yukon Territory, Canada.

I eased her into an eddy, gently tugged the barbless hook from her mouth, wet my hands, and grasped her tail to slowly move her back and forth and flood her gills with the cold, oxygenated water. From the side she was a brilliant silver, just days out of saltwater, a spectacular reflecting slab against the dark, clean gravel underneath. Some weeks later she would turn red, as her back and sides atrophied. The jaws of her male companions would arch into knobby hooks. The females would carve out circular beds, known as "redds," into the clean gravel of the lakes and streams in their spawning grounds. They would partner with a male, engage in a courtship dance, and in a gape-mouthed rush, the pair would simultaneously release their eggs and sperm into the redd. The female would cover the fertilized eggs lightly with gravel, and the two would protect the redd from predators for a time.

Then they would die.

That story was on my mind as I cradled the fish in the water while it breathed. After about ten seconds of this, the muscles in her back flexed a little, and I let her go. She eased herself upright and held herself in stasis next to my legs, transforming suddenly into a blue-black torpedo, almost invisible against the river bottom. Her gills moved steadily for about a minute as she regained her strength, and then with a tail flip she disappeared into the current. I reeled in my line, clipped the fly to the cork handle, and worked my way back up to the bank. It was enough.

All around me the leaves of the riverside trees and willow shrubs flickered in the afternoon summer breeze. The nutrients necessary to fertilize these trees had nearly all come from salmon like the one I'd just released. The salmon had collectively built and sustained that forest with their bodies.[99]

In an intricate feedback loop, the salmon carried nutrients from the ocean up to the forest in their bodies, laid their eggs, and then died and were eaten by the animals upstream. They fertilized the forest soils in the defecations from the animals that ate

The Salmon Forests

After spawning, the decomposing bodies of salmon fertilize the spawning grounds, creating healthy insect populations that their young feed on after emerging from their eggs. Bute Inlet, British Columbia. *Tavish Campbell*

them, and from the bodies of those animals when they died. The forests held the soil and constrained the rivers and lakes, filtering runoff, shading the water, maintaining the cold, clear, clean water salmon needed to breed and their young to survive. It was a feedback loop sustained up and down the northern temperate coastline of the Pacific Ocean, from California to Alaska, across the Bering Strait to Kamchatka, and down to Japan, Korea, and China. A somewhat less amplified version of this system spans the tundra ecosystems lining the Arctic Ocean. Forests bordering rivers along North Atlantic coastlines carry the same carbon legacy from Atlantic salmon, striped bass, and a host of other spawning fishes. These are the salmon forests. They hold and maintain billions of tons of carbon. They are some of the most impressive, and most critical, lungs of the planet.

> ● ‹

As one moves south into the warm ocean climate of the tropics, a similar story plays out. Equally delectable ocean foods are on the menu in these ecosystems, and with similar carbon stories. Like the towering forests lining the coastlines of the northern Pacific Ocean, mangrove forests occupy bands along the coastlines and estuaries of every tropical ocean on the planet. These forests have evolved to live on the border between land and ocean, in coastal salt water and brackish river estuaries. Described in one study as "nurseries for the world's seafood supply,"[100] mangroves provide critical habitat for some of the most economically important seafoods on the world's table, including shrimp and crab. In an ironic scientific twist, these seemingly diminutive wetland forests compete with skyscraper redwood forests in their ability to capture and store carbon.[101,102] Like with the salmon spawning habitat in the headwaters of the Pacific Ocean watersheds, and the ecosystem processes that lead to it, mangrove forest carbon is critical to maintaining wild fisheries the world over. The understanding that these bands of coastal forests are such enormous carbon sinks has come into focus only in the last two decades. In contrast to redwood forests, however, mangrove forests hold most of their carbon below the water's surface, and belowground.

Mangroves have inverted the notions about where the carbon resides in forests. The most carbon-dense redwood forest holds about ten times as much carbon aboveground in its trunks, branches, and leaves as the most carbon-dense mangrove forest. In contrast, mangroves maintain dense networks of roots and other unique woody organs under the water's surface and in the soil below. Evolutionarily unique structures lie below and at the surface to remove the salt from the water the trees live in and collect oxygen to drive the trees' metabolism from the atmosphere and the water.

These dense networks of woody structures create habitat for a myriad of organisms. The diverse ecosystems below the surface are fed by a stream of leaves falling from the trees above. In a single year, mangrove leaves along with exudates from the woody structures and roots below the surface provide more plant matter for critters living there, by weight, than exists in a ten-foot-high field of corn or sugarcane grown on the same amount of land. Also, in contrast to redwood forests, oxygen in the soil beneath mangroves is in short supply. Without oxygen the process

Mangrove wetland forests hold some of the largest known carbon stocks per acre of any of the planet's ecosystem, rivaling the carbon stocks in redwood forests. South Water Caye Marine Reserve, Belize. *Brian Skerry / Minden Pictures*

of decomposition slows and shifts. Detritus from all that feeding activity in the water accumulates as masses of under- and un-decomposed plant parts, the remains of the bodies of animals and microorganisms, and other organic material to form deep, dense mats of peat in the soil.

How much carbon do these forests hold, exactly? Redwood and mangrove forests can hold more than a thousand tons of carbon in an acre in their trunks, branches, and roots, along with hundreds of tons per acre in the soils.[103] That is the equivalent of about 25,000 wheelbarrows full of charcoal, or about 250 times more carbon than an Indiana cornfield holds when it is harvested. Temperate rain forests along the north Pacific Rim hold approximately 240 tons of carbon per acre, or about 5,000 wheelbarrows of charcoal or 40 times more than said cornfield. The forests and tundra lining the Bristol Bay watershed downstream of Brooks Falls hold between 100 and 300 tons of carbon per acre, or up to 6,000 wheelbarrows of charcoal and 50 corn fields worth of carbon. All these ecosystems, among the most productive in the world for their climates and their vast storehouses of carbon, owe their richness to salmon, shrimp, crabs, other fish, and the creatures that eat them.

Ironically, carbon-rich mangrove forests are being clear-cut throughout the tropics precisely to raise more shrimp and fish that they provide the nursery for.

> • <

Between eight hundred thousand and a million years ago, an exceptionally dry and cold glacial period created climate conditions that appear to have nearly wiped out the human population on Earth. Evidence suggests that a few thousand survivors subsisted on the coastline of South Africa for several millennia, living on a diet of shellfish, finfish, and sea mammals. Eventually the climate warmed enough to allow humans to multiply and disperse. The archaeological record shows that humans have sought life along coastlines ever since. Archaeologists theorize that Homo sapiens' big brains may have evolved out of our access to the rich omega-3 oils from a seafood diet.[104]

Food from the world's oceans, lakes, and rivers appears to have become a permanent part of the human diet ever since. In virtually any large supermarket or chain restaurant, you will find seafood on the shelves or menu. More than three out of four of the offerings will feature salmon, tuna, or shrimp. Until about 1972, this seafood triumvirate comprised nearly all of the wild food hunted in the open oceans and along the coastlines.

Except for a few Indigenous hunting-and-gathering cultures, the majority of the food we humans eat is domesticated or cultivated, except for fish. More than half of the fish humans eat today still comes from wild fisheries in the world's oceans. And many of these wild fisheries have surprisingly low carbon footprints. All have the potential to be even lower. Whether it is Pacific salmon or tropical shrimp or myriad others, wild fisheries are intricately linked to the enormous carbon stocks within the ecosystems that support them.[105,106] The forests and soils might not be there but for the salmon or the shrimp, and vice versa. Studies show that carbon stores in these ecosystems are directly linked to healthy, diverse ecosystems that maintain them.[107,108,109,110]

Unfortunately, demand for fish has increased beyond the ocean's capacity to deliver. As human populations have increased, and income and quality of life have increased for many, fish farming—aquaculture—has expanded dramatically on every coastline except Antarctica. Like with the wild fisheries, many farmed fish have surprisingly low carbon footprints, but with alarmingly high exceptions.[111] Their impacts go well beyond their carbon footprints. Fish farming, like confined feeding operations of dairy and beef cattle, pigs, and poultry, have pollution and disease problems of their own. Industrial fish farming is essentially a new form of agriculture, with novel, new, carbon-shredding and -shedding ecosystems.[112] And as we are learning, farmed fish too often carries with it a burden of depleted ecosystems, pollution, and disease.

And conflict. Demand for seafood has literally brought countries to war over fishing rights. Some fishers routinely cut each other's nets and battle for the most productive catch spots. Advocacy groups and regulatory agencies engage in pitched policy battles over the fate of fisheries, with one question at the center of the conflict: Can the oceans and rivers keep up with the demand?

The answer from scientists monitoring the world's fisheries had been largely yes until about 1970, when the answer suddenly became ambiguous. The previous year something unimaginable had happened: The North Atlantic cod fishery collapsed.

Until then, it had been the greatest fishery in the world, with known annual catches just shy of two billion pounds. The catch peaked in 1968, then fell off a cliff. Since the crash, the cod population has hovered at around just 1 percent of historic stocks, with little sign of recovering. The reason for cod's collapse—vast overfishing—is well understood. But its failure to recover after commercial fishing ended largely remains a mystery. Mark Kurlansky, author of the seminal book *Cod: A Biography of the Fish that Changed the World*, wrote the following:

> *Man wants to see nature and evolution as separate from human activities. There is a natural world, and there is man. But man also belongs to the natural world.*

The impacts on wild fisheries are piling up. Overharvesting continues. Burning fuel to power the boats emits carbon, and seafloor trawling releases the carbon stored in the organic matter in seafloor sediments in much the same way as plowing the prairie releases carbon from the organic matter stored in soils.[113] Ocean floor biodiversity also suffers from trawling, with ecosystem impacts rippling through the food chain and impacting other fish stocks.[114]

These chilling concepts remind us that there are limits to what ecosystems can provide. Annual worldwide fishery surveys indicate that the total ocean catch leveled off in the mid-1970s and has slowly declined since. As fish stock inventories have come into focus across national boundaries, the answer to the question "Can we sustain our wild-caught fisheries at current harvesting rates?" has become a firm, emphatic no. An exhaustive 2018 report to the United Nations Food and Agriculture Organization (FAO) on the state of the world's fisheries (updated yearly) soberly explained why:

The fraction of fish stocks that are within biologically sustainable levels has exhibited a decreasing trend, from 90.0 percent in 1974 to 66.9 percent in 2015. In contrast, the percentage of stocks fished at biologically unsustainable levels increased from 10 percent to 33.1 percent in 2015, with the largest increases in the late 1970s and 1980s.[115]

As demand for seafood outstripped the wild-caught supply, industrial-level aquaculture expanded to fill the void. Humans have been farming fish at low levels since at least 2000 BCE; however, the invention of dried feed pellets in the 1950s and the simultaneous invention of industrial refrigeration enabled white-fish farming to expand dramatically in Asia, and trout and catfish farming to be taken to scale in North America.[116] In the decades since the wild ocean catch peaked, farmed shrimp and Atlantic salmon have become highly lucrative seafood markets. Fish farmers raise their products in baskets, nets, pens, tanks, ponds, in rushing water or stagnant pools, whatever the fish's needs and local governance allows. They can be found in the open ocean, in bays and bayous, along shorelines cleared of their wetlands. Wherever they are raised are rough imitations of the fish's natural environment, but with fish populations concentrated far beyond what the wild could sustain. In many of those cases, the problems the fish farms introduce outstrip the income benefits they bring.[117]

> • ‹

"I feel like I have this analysis paralysis, trying to do the least-worst thing for the environment."

This announcement came at the end of a delicious dinner that a dear friend had made for her husband, my wife, Leslie, and me, lovingly prepared with conscientiously selected ingredients. This conundrum that so many people face is present with seafood more than perhaps any other food category. The backstory of so much seafood—overfishing, pollution, degraded ecosystems—can be simply overwhelming. For those who can afford to make environmental choices, how are conscientious shoppers and diners to choose? Especially in a landscape as diverse and complicated as seafood? And perhaps more fundamentally, should the method of shopping sustainably be placed on the individual consumer, rather than measures being taken by the government to ensure the seafood supply can be sustained in the first place?

Are there good seafood choices that can be sustained in the long term? This is the dilemma that the organization Seafood Watch,[118,119] based at the Monterey Bay Aquarium, has grappled with for more than two decades. Seafood Watch first released written reports, then published online tools to advise on seafood choices and help ease the analysis paralysis consumers face. In 2018, they added the online Seafood Carbon Emissions Tool[120] to focus attention on the carbon footprint of different seafoods, enriching an already important dialogue about ocean conservation.

In clear and easy-to-understand graphics, the tool shows the difference between wild and farmed fishes in different seafood groups. Emissions range from less than one pound of CO_2e per pound of seafood for some fishes, to fifty pounds or more of CO_2e for others. In some cases, farmed versions of the same fish had higher carbon footprints than the wild-caught fish. In others it was the reverse. How could that be?

I contacted Lisa Max at Seafood Watch, who at the time helped lead the team developing the Seafood Carbon Emissions Tool. She graciously arranged for me to meet with her and her colleague, Tyler Isaac, at their offices along a cool and misty Monterey Bay. I asked them about the wide range of emissions reported in the tool, and why there was such a disparity between farmed and wild fish.

"The carbon footprint from seafood comes down to fuel, feed and bait, and ecosystem carbon," Lisa explained at the beginning of a long and thoughtful conversation. Fuel. Feed and bait. Ecosystem carbon.

I asked them to explain. We first tackled fuel.

"Fish are either caught in the ocean, or they are farmed via aquaculture in salt water or fresh water. Catching fish in the ocean and refrigerating it before processing requires fuel."

Fish flesh may be one of the most perishable food items humans eat. Once harvested, it must be quickly chilled, processed, packaged, and then shipped in its chilled state to the consumer. Fresh fish is very often shipped by air; frozen fish can take a more leisurely route by ship and by truck. Refrigeration and operating packing equipment requires energy, which in a fish-processing facility might be electricity, or out on a ship might be from diesel fuel.

Next, we tackled feed and bait.

"Hook and line fisheries require bait," explained Tyler. "In order to bait a hook, you have to first catch the fish that is the bait."

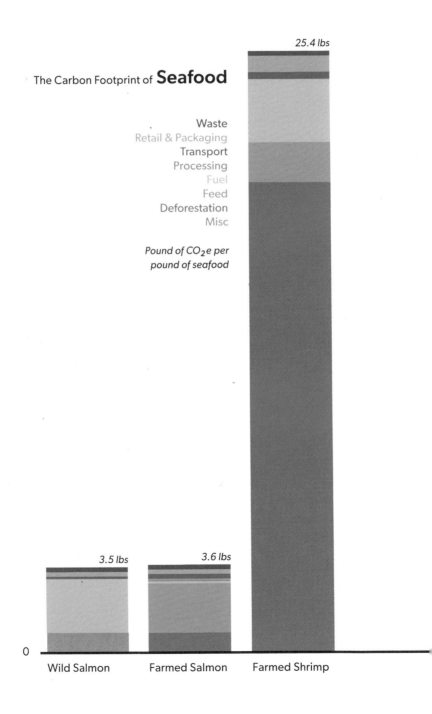

The Carbon Footprint of **Seafood**

Waste
Retail & Packaging
Transport
Processing
Fuel
Feed
Deforestation
Misc

Pound of CO$_2$e per pound of seafood

25.4 lbs

3.5 lbs   3.6 lbs

0

Wild Salmon   Farmed Salmon   Farmed Shrimp

I thought of the commercial hook-and-line anglers I'd seen in southeast Alaska, where on small and large boats with crews from one to twenty, buckets of herring on the deck provided the bait the fishermen twisted onto hooks that went into waters rich with coho and king salmon. Every fish caught required a herring on the hook. Similar line-caught fisheries the world over rely on the same methods, with different baits.

Farmed shrimps/prawns have the highest emissions due to deforestation to create fishponds. Farmed shellfish (oysters, mussels, clams, and scallops) have the least since they require no feed and they fix atmospheric CO_2 into their shells. "Waste" assumes 40 percent of products are eventually landfilled and become landfill methane CO_2e. "Retail and Packaging" includes making containers for products on retail shelves, equipment, fuel, and energy use required in retail establishments. "Transport" includes shipping fish to markets and delivering products to retailers. "Processing" is preparing fish for retail sale. "Fuel" is energy used on fishing boats and in initial processing facilities. "Feed" includes emissions to grow crops, catch wild fish for fish feed, and manufacture fish feed. "Deforestation" includes emissions from clearing mangroves and other forests, as well as disturbing intact grasslands to build ponds to raise farmed fish and grow food for those fish. "Misc" is nonenergy and nonfeed emissions before the fish are delivered to market.

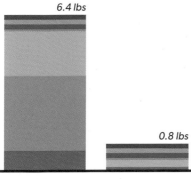

6.4 lbs

0.8 lbs

Farmed Trout Farmed Shellfish

"The footprint of the bait fishery is real, but it is relatively small. Aquaculture is different. In aquaculture, up to 90 percent of the carbon footprint is from producing the feed," added Lisa.

"Why is it so large?"

"Finfish and shrimp have to be fed. The carnivorous ones like salmon and sea bass are still typically fed a diet that includes at least some fish, supplemented with crops like soy and corn and oilseed crops like canola. Those feed fish, typically anchovies, sardines, menhaden, and herring, have to be caught out in the ocean and processed into feed. That all requires fuel, which generates emissions."

Tyler then pulled up a map of the world on his computer screen, and pointed out some of the famous "reduction fisheries" of the world, where feed fishes are caught and processed. Anchovies off the coast of Peru, sardines off the coast of California, herring off the coast of Alaska, menhaden in Chesapeake Bay and other parts of North America. These and other distant waters feed the demand for fish to feed to other fish in aquaculture.

"When caught, the feed fish must be refrigerated and processed quickly. Some get canned for human use. For most, however, the oils are extracted for fish oil capsules people eat, or processed into livestock feed," Tyler said. "The fish solids are dried and processed into a form that can be fed to fish in aquaculture."

Fish food for a Norwegian salmon farm or a Vietnamese shrimp farm requires processing ingredients and shipping them around the globe. I pictured the carbon emissions piling up.

"In contrast, vegetarian fish like tilapia can be fed a plant-based diet, but there is still a burden generated to grow that feed, typically corn and soybeans and plant-based oils, usually canola," Tyler continued.

As aquaculture expands, it is moving closer and closer to the CAFO feeding model adopted by beef, dairy, pork, and poultry producers around the world. Corn, soybeans, and vegetable oils like canola dominate the feed mixes of vegetarian and omnivorous fish, and even carnivorous fish like salmon. Farmed carnivorous fish diets still come in part from the worldwide reduction fishery, and increasingly, processing leftover by-products from other fisheries such as salmon and cod. Fuel for catching, processing, and refrigerating the fish dominates the fish-based diets, whereas emissions from growing crops dominate the vegetarian diets.[121,122]

Based on my research before the visit, I was afraid to ask the next question. "What about shrimp farming?" Like several billion other people across the planet, I adored almost any dish containing shrimp.

"Shrimp are largely grown in coastal waters along South America, China, and Southeast Asia," Tyler replied. "There can be huge carbon losses from coastal wetlands, especially mangroves, if they are cleared to make way for shrimp farms."

Wild-caught shrimp carry a carbon footprint of about eight to fifteen pounds of CO_2e per pound of shrimp, comparable to pork's carbon footprint. In cases where coastal wetlands are cleared to make room for them, especially mangroves, the carbon burden can be greater than fifty pounds of CO_2e per pound of shrimp. In those cases, farmed shrimp carry a carbon burden comparable to beef or lamb. Although clear-cutting mangrove forests for aquaculture has lessened significantly since 2000,[123] it continues in some areas.

The carbon burden of that forest loss is present in shrimp wherever forests were cleared to create the aquaculture ponds.

"What is the aquaculture industry doing to reduce the pollution and disease problems?"

"Recirculating tank systems are being developed to isolate farmed fish from the ecosystem and effectively reduce pollution, fish escapes, and disease. Unfortunately, some of the greatest greenhouse gas emissions in aquaculture are in recirculating systems," Tyler explained. "Besides emissions from feed and fuel, the energy required to aerate and filter ponds and tanks in which fish are raised cause even greater emissions if the energy is not sourced from low-carbon energy sources like wind and solar."

"But those systems have some of the least environmental impacts. They are enclosed, and fish escapes are rare," he emphasized.

Recirculating aquaculture systems (RAS) do resolve many of the problems present in aquaculture, but their potentially high carbon footprint can make them a mixed bag. They are now the focus of intense innovation within the industry. The best systems are those that clean and reuse water by removing the fish waste and converting it to a soil amendment and fertilizer, or anaerobically digesting it to convert into fuel like what is done at state-of-the-art dairy farms. Using low-carbon energy from wind, solar, and geothermal sources reduces the fish farms' energy carbon

A sustainable farmed-seafood future might look like this: Atlantic salmon raised in fully enclosed recirculating tanks to protect wild fish from fish escapes and to eliminate pollution releases into local watersheds, nourished by a sustainable feed based on soldier flies, powered by renewable energy, and near population centers. Centre Burlington, Nova Scotia. *Courtesy of Sustain Blue* footprint. Isolating them from natural watersheds can eliminate impacts from escaped fish and diseases. RAS can grow a variety of foods like salmon, trout, and shrimp. One of their greatest advantages is they can be built near or even within the urban centers where the meat is sold.[124,125]

This dramatically shortens the shipping distances required to fly fresh Atlantic salmon from places like Norway, Scotland, Chile, and the Canadian Maritime provinces to markets around the world. A good example of this is the Atlantic salmon farming facility integrated into the circular economic system known as the "Halifax Model," which has the potential to address the environmental problems inherent in sea-based aquaculture.[126] Food waste from nearby urban centers feeds insects raised to feed salmon. Algae are grown in contained biomass fermenters as fish feed. Low-carbon solar and wind energy powers the facilities. Waste from the insect farms becomes bait for lobster traps or high-quality soil fertilizer, and waste from the RAS system is used to produce energy and a compost-like soil amendment for nearby farms and ranches. Water is cleaned and recycled back into the system, hence little water is consumed.

I finally posed the question that is central to this book. "What are the best low-carbon choices for seafood?"

Lisa chimed in. "Farmed mussels are probably the best choice. Farmed oysters, clams, and scallops are a close second."

I recalled a succulent meal of mussels cooked in olive oil, white wine, and parsley, hosted by Italian friends in a beachside restaurant along the Adriatic Sea. Between sips of wine harvested from grapes on the slopes above, we lifted the mussels from a steaming kettle and stripped the meat from their shells and swallowed them whole. When the mussels were gone, we dipped chunks of crusty bread into the juice and chewed the glorious, saucy mix. I had no idea at the time they were a low-carbon food choice.

"Mussels? Why is that?"

"Mussels, oysters, clams, and scallops don't have to be fed. They are filter feeders, eating plankton in the water column. Plus, their shells," Lisa replied.

Lisa tapped the table with a fingernail, like one might tap the shell of a clam. Another light bulb went off in my head. Of course! To build their shells, mussels and other mollusks with shells absorb carbon dioxide from the atmosphere (dissolved in seawater) and biochemically combine it with calcium and other minerals to create their shells. They encase themselves in a protective layer that is essentially limestone. Short of dropping the shells into a vat of boiling acid, the carbon they had stripped from the atmosphere had essentially permanently become rock. They are the ultimate source of low-carbon animal protein.

Lisa, Tyler, and I wrapped up our conversation, and I stepped back into the misty Monterey Bay afternoon to walk the shoreline and ponder what I'd learned: Greenhouse gas emissions are present in virtually every seafood. Wild-catch fisheries fundamentally depend on fossil fuels to power fishing boats. Both on-ship and onshore fish-processing facilities require power to cool and package seafood, and more fuel to bring the fish to market. And most aquaculture farms carry the extra burden of the carbon footprint of growing the crops or catching the baitfish required to feed the fish.

It isn't difficult to find evidence of the problems aquaculture faces. Atlantic salmon aquaculture exemplifies issues in other parts of the industry. Fishers, scientists, and fishery managers in the North Pacific coastlines have documented evidence that escaped salmon displace native stocks. Diseases present in fish farms disperse to infect native fish populations, and pollution piles insult upon injury that native fish stocks already face from overfishing, other sources of pollution, habitat loss, and changing ocean conditions caused by global warming.[127,128,129] These issues and the fights that ensued led state and provincial governments in the Pacific Northwest of North America to take action to protect wild fisheries. The Canadian province of British Columbia and the US state of Washington began phasing out Atlantic salmon farms in their coastal waters in 2018.[130,131] The state of Alaska bans finfish farming in state waters.[132] In contrast to finfish farming, saltwater shellfish farms that raise oysters, mussels, clams, and scallops enjoy broad public and policy support, contribute to restoring coastal ecosystems, and are proliferating throughout the Pacific Northwest.

> • <

What about the emissions connected to producing the fish feed that Lisa and Tyler from Monterey Bay Aquarium spoke about? Paul Greenberg documented the reduction fishery in his trio of books about the dietary quest for omega-3 oils (*Four Fish*, *American Catch*, and *The Omega Principle*).[133] While seafood is frequently cited as a rich source of omega-3 oils, the fish on our plates do not produce those oils on their own. They come from the foods the fish eat in the wild. The reduction fishery provides the fish meal and fish oil needed to feed farmed fish. Capturing these fishes for the reduction fishery requires equipment, fuel, then processing them into meal, and finally shipping the meal to the aquaculture centers where it is fed to fish. All this generates emissions. And like the fish meal from these reduction fisheries, the carbon footprint of the corn, soybeans, and other crops processed into food for aquaculture gets passed on to the footprint of aquaculture fish. In total, the carbon footprint of aquaculture's feed reaches up to two pounds of CO_2e for every pound of food fed to the fish. This contrasts with the native salmon fishery, where the ocean and coastal ecosystem provides the food the wild salmon eat with no carbon footprint.

To more closely examine the emissions from catching, processing, and shipping fish, I stopped at my local fishmonger one Fourth of July morning and examined the offerings. The ice-lined counter behind the glass held a saltwater cornucopia of shrimp, octopus, oysters, halibut, and clams. Bright-red slabs of salmon filets filled a large portion of the case. A sign shouted the news: "Fresh Bristol Bay Sockeye Salmon! Flown in last night!" I winced at the price, yet my mouth watered a little as I imagined the meal planned for friends that evening. I caught the eye of a white-aproned woman behind the counter and nodded toward the filets. "I'll take one of these."

At home in my kitchen, I laid the filet on the counter next to my laptop. What emissions were produced to catch and process the fish? According to a study done by scientists partnering with Ecotrust,[134] a Portland, Oregon-based nonprofit, the fishers who caught this beauty likely burned enough diesel fuel to create about two pounds of carbon dioxide for every pound of salmon.[135] From the port, it would have been processed, loaded onto a cargo aircraft in an insulated container filled with cold packs, and flown 1,600 miles to Seattle. A distributor there transferred it to another aircraft bound for Denver, where it was trucked to another distributor and then trucked to lay on the ice in my fishmonger's shop. I entered the route into my computer.[136,137]

Whew. The process of flying the fish from King Salmon to Denver doubled the emissions produced by the fishing boat. Add to that the emissions from processing, and for every pound of fresh salmon at the dinner table, it carried a burden of about five pounds of CO_2e.

I put my nose to the filet and inhaled its sweet, meaty, umami scent. I did not want to feel guilty about the meal I was about to make, but the nagging fact of the global warming generated to deliver that salmon wouldn't leave me be. Are there farmed-fish alternatives with lower environmental impacts? I reached out with that question to Dr. Chris Myrick, a fisheries biologist at Colorado State University. A self-professed "fish fanatic," Chris had grown up fishing in California's Sacramento River Delta and was a recognized expert in aquaculture systems.

"If you want to see fish farming done at scale, you really ought to go see the fish farms in the Upper Snake River Valley. Clear Springs Foods is probably one of the best operations in the business," he told me over hot coffee on a snowy Colorado morning. But he cautioned further. "With trout and any inland aquaculture, you have to pay attention to how they are managing the waste. Not everybody is doing as good a job at it as Clear Springs."

And so, in between late-January blizzards, I sprinted through the Rocky Mountains to Buhl, Idaho, to see for myself.

> • <

The sound of rushing water softened the morning air as I stepped from my car onto the trimly manicured campus of Clear Springs Foods (acquired as a division of Riverence since my visit). Over the next several days, it became abundantly clear that the constant rushing stream cascading from the cliffs above is the reason more fish are farmed in the Snake River Valley than almost any inland spot in North America.

A long line of volcanic eruptions along the middle Columbia and Snake River Valleys blanketed a vast region, now known as the Snake River Flood Basalts, with volcanic rock. The porous rock gathers snowmelt and rainfall from thousands of square miles, funneling and concentrating the flows underground until it pours straight out of the cliffs linking the river in places with names like "Thousand Springs." Testimony to the quality of the Snake River as fish habitat is the fact that schools of sockeye, chinook, coho salmon, steelhead trout, and sturgeon once migrated nearly a thousand river miles from the Pacific Ocean, up the Columbia River, and then up the Snake River to spawn in these waters and the tributaries feeding it.

Not surprisingly, the temperature and chemistry of the water in these springs are ideal for farming trout, sturgeon, and other fish adapted to the cold waters of the Snake. Besides the cold-water springs, fish farmers capture water from the abundant hot springs in the area to moderate the cold river water up to temperatures suitable for tilapia, catfish, and in the case of one farmer until recently, alligators.[138]

Jeff Jermunson, the Clear Springs director of operations, and Julie Stadelman, the company's director of quality assurance, led me on a tour of the grounds. The company was founded in 1966 and has a reputation in the industry for organizational efficiency. They currently produce more rainbow trout for the retail consumer market than any other company in the United States. The sustainability watchdog organizations Seafood Watch and FishChoice both certify their operations.

Their Box Canyon facility is the largest trout-production facility in the country. On internet map software, the raceways holding the trout look almost like massive black silicon circuit boards laced with interconnecting wires. The Buhl operation has over 250 interconnected concrete-lined pools, all about three feet deep, twelve feet wide, and seventy-five feet long. Each pool holds more than one hundred thousand trout in groups ranging from one-to-two-inch-long fry up to plate-sized trout ready to harvest. The company produces more than fifty million trout per year at this and other complexes in the region.

Cold water gushing from the underground springs enters the upper pools, and gravity carries it through a series of aerators to lower pools. In total, the water is used in three consecutive, separate pools containing trout before it is filtered to remove uneaten feed and the trout's excrement, and then enters a constructed

A commercial trout farm in the Snake River Canyon at Twin Falls, Idaho. *David R. Frazier / Alamy*

wetlands complex to undergo secondary treatment before flowing into the Snake River. The feces are composted and sold as a
nutrient-rich soil amendment to local farmers.

From a walkway between the upper and middle banks of a set
of raceways, we watched a worker dressed in chest-high waders
slowly working his way down one of the raceways, as a coworker
spotted him from above, pushing a mesh fence through the water
ahead of him and gradually crowding the fish into one end.
"These fish are being moved to harvest today," explained Jeff. As
we moved down the walkway, fish came into view as the silvery
morning glare off the water eased. The fish receptors in my brain
went on full alert as trout swarmed a pool near us: thousands of
ten-inch rainbow trout, with deep-blue-black backs and red and
silver sides with black spots. "They think we have food," remarked
Jeff with a smile.

As we walked along the pools, Jeff and Julie streamed information in a relaxed, practiced conversation. They demonstrated
how the company feeds the trout through automated equipment
to harvestable size in about 435 days (around the same number
of days a beef calf is raised to butchering weight). Dr. Stephen
Reichley, at the time of my visit a fish veterinarian and Clear
Springs director of research and development, described for me
later in the day a proprietary mix largely made up of local grains,
soybeans shipped in from outside the state (Idaho's climate is not
suitable for growing soybeans), minerals, and a proportion of
fish meal delivered from sources he described as sustainability-
certified fisheries. Stephen described their feed-conversion ratio
as less than 1.5. The number represents the pounds of feed it takes

to produce a pound of live, fresh trout over the fish's lifetime and is a big part of the carbon footprint of aquaculture. The lower the feed-conversion ratio, the less feed required to bring the trout to market weight, and therefore the lower the greenhouse gas burden of the end product; a trout filet.

For comparison, the feed-conversion ratio in contemporary US chicken facilities is about 1.6. Pork is about 3.8. For cattle the number is typically 6 or higher. The lower the number, the less feed is required to produce a pound of edible flesh per pound of feed. The lower the number, the lower the carbon footprint.

"It's simple: fish are cold-blooded. They don't have to burn a lot of energy regulating their temperature. They are much more efficient at converting feed to protein, fat, and bone than are birds, pigs, and cows," Chris Myrick explained during our coffee meetup about why feed conversion is so much more efficient in fish.

That explains a lot of why the carbon footprint of many farmed fishes is lower than the meat and dairy products from warm-blooded animals. But it didn't explain other aspects of the carbon footprint, like processing and transportation. While returning to the company's laboratory for the next part of the tour, we passed a fleet of identical, cleanly washed tractor-trailer rigs with the Clear Springs logo.

"These trucks are a point of pride for me," remarked Jeff. The trucks were all outfitted with energy-saving fairings, wind skirts, and low-rolling-resistance tires. "These are some of the most energy-efficient trucks available—and we deliver products only by truck."

Trucks with tandem drivers leave multiple times each week to deliver fish on transcontinental circuits. This saves both the inflated cost and greatly inflated carbon emissions from air freight.

I was curious about alternatives to feeding wild-caught fish like anchovies and sardines to trout, so I asked Stephen about alternatives to fish meal caught for the reduction industry.

"We are constantly looking at alternatives, especially since the availability and price of fish meal is so variable," he said.

"What about insects?"

"Insects are an option. They may be the next big thing in fish food, as it's an excellent food source for trout. After all, insects are their natural prey." I thought of the boxes of flies in my fishing vest at home, nearly all of them imitations of aquatic insects.

"The problem is the cost. We aren't there yet."

"What about algae?" Some growers were raising red algae in bioreactors to dry and process into trout food. Certain species of algae are rich in both the carotene that color the fish's flesh and the omega-3 oils consumers demand.

"Also an option," Stephen replied, "but again, cost at scale is a problem. I think that cost is going to come down, though."

Fish food rations with algae and insects hold promise in reducing the carbon footprint of farmed fish. Insects like black soldier flies are often raised on composting food waste, and leveraging that supply could reduce the pressure on the reduction fishery. Algae for fish food might be grown on-site rather than requiring that grains and other products be shipped in from a distance. Stephen agreed that both are likely to be healthier options for fish than corn and soybeans.

Like the concentrated animal feeding operations on the Great Plains, aquaculture holds large numbers of animals in close proximity. And just as with the animals in dairies, pig farms, chicken farms, and beef feedlots, the fish grown in the raceways have to defecate, and the feces have to go somewhere. Any kind of animal manure can be a real problem downstream if it isn't handled well.

That said, these raceways are still the aquaculture equivalent of the concentrated feeding operations that supply over 90 percent of the beef, pork, and poultry eaten in the United States. Wherever one concentrates animals into small spaces and raises them on rationed feeds, preventing disease and preventing pollution from the feces are paramount. Phosphorus, nitrogen, and other pollutants common in fish feces must be collected and managed carefully. Fish diseases, if not controlled in the raceways, can spread to native fish populations downstream.

I asked Stephen about it. "Every year we beat the standards in our water-quality permits," he replied simply.

Later, I looked up their water-quality standards and permit performance and found that Clear Springs' method for capturing and composting the fish manure and treating the farm waste is considered state of the art. Chris Myrick had mentioned it in our earlier discussions, and scientists from Clear Springs, the US Agricultural Research Service, and Idaho State University had published a peer-reviewed paper describing their method and its advantages.[139]

These are serious concerns that require attention. Evidence that Clear Springs is taking those issues seriously is what led external observers to certify their operations.

After donning a cap, white lab coat, and latex shoe coverings, Julie, the company's QA director, toured us through the butchering facility. It is a large, insulated building about the size of a modern supermarket, filled with automated equipment. Over the course of a few hours, workers operating machines process thousands of live fish into fish filets. After being killed, fish stream down narrow stainless-steel chutes into devices that separate each fish's edible and inedible portions in less than a second. Filets stream into neat racks that are wheeled into coolers and later into ice-cold tractor-trailer rigs. Hampers filled with the remains (entrails, skeletons, fins, and heads) go into separate coolers, their contents destined to become pet food and other products. As I walked out into the sunlight that had driven back the morning fog, a fully loaded tractor-trailer rig loaded that morning crept around the building. The driver smiled and waved from his high perch in the cab as he eased onto the highway.

I thought back to the fish-processing benches I'd seen in fish camps in remote Alaskan villages. Residents hauled fish from riverbank nets or boats to process and dry their catch on wooden racks through the long arctic days. Along the coast, boats pulled in from the open ocean and used cranes to unload pallets of fish onto docks, until they disappeared into cavernous processing facilities. Whether in automated facilities at Buhl or along remote arctic rivers, the process is essentially the same. The difference is that Clear Springs operates twelve months out of the year, and fish were transported perhaps a hundred yards from the raceways into the processing facility. Salmon caught in or near salt water are only available a few months out of the year, and require trawlers, nets, diesel fuel, a part-time processing facility, and a transportation network at least a thousand miles longer than the one from Buhl, Idaho.

Which approach offers seafood with the lowest emissions and least environmental footprint? There are trade-offs.

Trout raised at Clear Springs are the product of a highly engineered system, delivering food to market with minimized emissions from transportation. The carbon footprint ranges between about three and seven pounds of CO_2e per pound of fish, comparable to the carbon footprint of chicken. The emissions are dominated by those required to produce the feed. Risks of pollution and disease downstream from the fish feces have to be carefully managed and controlled. The same issues and a comparable carbon footprint apply to farm-raised salmon, char, and freshwater fish like catfish.

The emissions from comparable wild-caught salmon, caught on the open ocean, average about half that of farm-raised trout, char, and salmon. The carbon footprint of frozen, wild-caught salmon, transported by boat and truck, remains low. If flown to market, the emissions are about the same as farmed trout, char, and salmon. In contrast to farmed trout, however, the emissions are dominated by the fuel required to catch and process the fish and deliver it on longer supply chains to market. The wild fisheries have to be carefully managed to reduce impacts on bycatch, marine mammals, and the ocean ecosystem that sustain the fish.

Are there ways to sustainably increase the Pacific salmon fishery? South of British Columbia, salmon populations are currently at just 6 to 7 percent of the stocks that flooded the rivers of Washington,

Oregon, and California before fish-killing dams and water pollution sent them into a downward spiral.[140] Restoring that salmon habitat to its previous potential could increase North Pacific salmon catch by perhaps 10 percent,[141] which would help to fulfill a backlog of unkept treaty obligations to Indigenous peoples who historically relied on salmon, while increasing the commercially viable catch in the region. Restoring the salmon pump that historically fertilized the forests lining the spawning streams with the nutrients in the salmon bodies would help maintain and restore declining forests in the region that are losing carbon to the atmosphere.

The only other way to increase the salmon and trout supply in supermarkets appears to be farming fish, with the associated risks to coastal and inland ecosystems if it is not done well.

But what about the low-carbon shellfish the Seafood Carbon Emissions Tool had described?

A cold call to a prominent California supplier led to the opportunity to learn more. Terry Sawyer, one of the founders of the Hog Island Oyster Company north of San Francisco, phoned me right back and offered a farm tour. My colleague Amy Swan and I swung by during a work trip in the region, and when we stepped out of the car, we were delighted to find Terry, a fit-looking man in jeans and a T-shirt with a salt-and-pepper beard, sitting in the shade with two friends of ours. We had worked with John Wick from the Marin Carbon Project and Lynette Niebrugge, then an ecologist at the Marin Resource Conservation District (Marin RCD),[142] for nearly a decade on various projects. After hugs with John and Lynette, and a warm handshake from Terry, Amy and I looked at the group inquisitively.

"You three know each other?"

"John and I are both on the board of the Marin RCD. I thought it would be fun to give him and Lynette the tour along with you two," said Terry.

The network of resource conservation districts in California plays a central role in lowering the carbon footprint of agriculture throughout the state and has become a model for conservation and carbon sequestration across the United States. Lynette, now working with the Carbon Cycle Institute, has helped dozens of farmers and ranchers implement carbon farm plans throughout the country. With the help of these plans, producers modify their growing practices, plant trees, and adjust crop and livestock management to shift the greenhouse gas balance of their enterprises from being net emitters to net carbon storers in soils and trees.

We followed Terry into a covered area occupied by rows of tanks filled with bubbling water. Banks of solar panels framed the view beyond. There, he gave us a primer in the life cycle of an oyster, which began with a primer on climate change.

"We grow four species of oysters, clams, and mussels, and they all start with spawn. Spawn are free-swimming animals, like little fish, that grow into these things." Terry lifted a netted bag of oysters from a tank of bubbling water. "But we are on the east coast of the Pacific Ocean, which is ground zero for the problems fishermen are worried about. It is getting harder and harder to grow the spat [immature oysters] because of ocean acidification and warming water temperatures."

Raising oysters begins with mature males and females that are collected and stimulated to release eggs and sperm into a tank

Workers maintain oyster baskets at an oyster farm. Hog Island Oyster Co., Tomales Bay, California. *Remy Anthes / Hog Island Oyster Co.*

when they are ready to spawn. The sperm fertilize the eggs, and the embryonic oysters continue to divide and grow in a controlled environment, with fresh influxes of salt water from the ocean, until they form free-swimming larvae and begin eating the microorganisms in the salt water. They grow for several weeks until they form an eyespot and a muscular foot, and they are ready to settle and begin growing a shell. They attach themselves to ground oyster shells placed in the bottom of the tank, at which point they become known as spat. Terry explained that this was the most sensitive and critical time in the life cycle of an oyster.

"We're experiencing rising acidity and warmer water. Some growers lost 100 percent of their [oyster] spat at their hatcheries because the animals were so stressed by the conditions, they died of disease." He paused and looked out onto the surface of the bay that made up their farm. "We've been hit hard, too, but we are doing okay now."

Acidity and warming water were themes I would hear repeatedly from Terry and other shellfish farmers. Terry continued to worry out loud about it as he led us into a small building at the edge of the cement platform where the tanks lay bubbling and opened the door into a crowded space with a window facing out to the bay. It was crammed with electronic equipment like in our laboratory at the Colorado State University campus.

"This is our Burkolator," he said with reverence, sweeping his arm across the banks of equipment, dials, and computers filling the space. I asked for an explanation.

The equipment housed in the building was connected via cellular phone networks to sensors installed out in the bay, in an innovative collection matching those in fourteen other locations up and down the Pacific Coast. They are part of a network of sensors and analytical equipment monitored by scientists at the University of California, designed to collect and analyze data on changing ocean conditions driven by the climate crisis.

A pile of printouts lay next to the keyboard, and Terry selected one showing ocean water acidity at sites up and down the coast.

"It was a complete no-brainer that we would get one of these installed here once the network was announced," he said. "We are doing okay so far. The waters in Tomales Bay haven't acidified or warmed as much as other parts of the Pacific. Our oysters and mussels don't seem to be too stressed for the time being. But we have no idea how long that will last." Terry's voice was calm, but his expression intense.

The guy I'd met an hour earlier in his jeans and flip-flops seemed at the time like he'd just stowed his surfboard after coming off the beach. Now he seemed like a different man.

"It is an open question whether my daughter will be able to make a living in this place in the future, doing what I am doing," he said.

I'd heard other shellfish farmers up and down the coast worry aloud about the same question. Sea level rise, changing water temperatures, and ocean acidification all threatened their livelihood's future. It reminded me of a cattle farmer in Colorado who questioned whether the climate forecasted for the region could support his grandchildren living in that place. Livestock are livestock, apparently, whether they are covered with feathers, fur, or shells, and the consequences of global warming weigh heavily on the minds of their tenders.

Terry led us out of the building and back to the tanks at the far end of the platform. The fine scent of cold salt water came off the bubbling surface.

"We harvested these this morning," he said, raising a mesh bag holding several dozen oysters. The tanks were running cold, oxygenated, and clean salt water from Tomales Bay through the live, harvested oysters stacked in the tank. "They will be shipped to market over the next couple of days."

"How will you ship them?" asked Amy.

"We pretty much ship only by truck," he said with a nod to John and Lynette. The work of the Marin RCD had helped them assess and minimize their carbon emissions.

"Shipping by air makes some clients feel better, but these critters don't have to be rushed to market." He gestured to the tank of oysters. "They will do just fine for up to three weeks if they are just kept cool and moist." Then he raised an eyebrow. "That is, if the people driving the trucks know what they are doing."

Our conversation had run far longer than we'd planned and the late-afternoon light off Tomales Bay revealed the hour. Amy and I wanted to enjoy the oyster bar before it closed, so we thanked Terry and said goodbye to John and Lynette.

Amy stopped me on the way to the counter and lowered her voice to a conspiratorial tone.

"Mark, I've never eaten a raw oyster before."

The uncertainty on Amy's face reflected my own shocked expression. She and I have had innumerable food adventures in work travel around the world. I've learned to trust her food instincts implicitly and never regretted following her lead. Suddenly the role

was reversed. This adventurous colleague who'd grown up ranching livestock in South Dakota, and had eaten all parts of the animals they'd raised, was asking me to lead us on a new food adventure.

Which is how we found ourselves a short time later seated with two crisp lagers and a dozen oysters on a tray. A burly, bearded bartender instructed in animated tones how to hold the oyster, how to lay the shucking knife into the shell, and how to twist the knife and pop open the hinge without spilling "the liquor," which is the succulent, briny liquid cradling the oyster within the shell. He deftly sliced the oyster's foot free from the shell, laid the oyster on our tray, and then moved on to the next table before we could ask any questions. We sat before the pile, a little lost.

"You go first," she said.

I took a pull from my beer, donned the shucking glove, and clumsily tried to reproduce the bartender's motions. In the process, I cracked the lip of the shell, spilled the liquor, and sliced the oyster inside in half. Pieces of shell lay on the oyster parts.

"I'll take this one!" I said.

I removed the glove and pondered the rocklike consistency of the shell. There was close to a half a pound of atmospheric carbon dioxide the oysters had absorbed and locked up in the shells on the platter before us.

Amy picked up her own shucking glove and the knife, and deliberately placed an oyster in the glove's palm. Then in slow motion, she perfectly shucked the oyster, cut it free of the shell,

A dozen oysters like these remove about a half pound of carbon dioxide from the atmosphere to build their shells. *Amy Kumler*

175

and looked at me, a little blank-faced. By then I'd finished removing the shell fragments from my own oyster. It was my turn to be chagrined. Hers lay in the shell, clean and shimmering a little in the liquid.

"Like this," I set the shell of my oyster against my lips, tipped it slightly, and sipped. The oyster pieces slid onto my tongue, where I savored the brine. It was the taste of Tomales Bay. I tilted my head and let the oyster slide down my throat. Amy lifted the oyster to her mouth and did the same, and I tried hard to not stare. She subtly mouthed the oyster for a few moments, then swallowed.

"My gosh, it tastes so clean."

She paused. We sat quietly for several moments while she absorbed the flavors. "Delicious!" she concluded.

Yes! We slapped a high-five, and then settled into the feast.

> • <

What will it take to inspire the nations of the world to collaborate on solutions to the climate crisis? The mounting risks we face on every continent threaten every person on the planet in some capacity. Millions have already died from the direct and indirect effects of the climate crisis.[143] Millions more are likely to become casualties to the dangerously heating climate.[144] Can we join forces to right the ship of humanity in danger of sinking?

Perhaps nowhere in the food system is this more imperative than with seafood. Fifty years ago, humanity passed the limits of what our oceans could provide. Attempting to extract more will only lead to further competition and conflict. Oceans, and fish, do not respect international boundaries.

It's ironic that in the rush to clear-cut mangroves and degrade coastal wetlands to create shrimp and fish farms, while harvesting diminishing baitfish stocks to feed a continually expanding catch in those farms, there are fewer wild fish left in the oceans, with an increasing carbon footprint per serving. Developing the world's coastlines to farm fish parallels the chronic push to clear-cut the world's life-giving forests to create pasture for livestock. Humanity and the world's oceans are facing a problem common to so many crisis points in human history. In one corner are highly desirable, but declining wild fish stocks, requiring increasingly more energy to find, harvest, process, and transport to market. In the other corner are abundant, inexpensive farmed-fish products raised in increasingly unsustainable ways contributing to the decline in the wild fish stocks they aim to supplement, but in the end may supplant.

It appears to be a race to the bottom.

The best practices emerging in the aquaculture industry focus on recirculating, land-based tanks that capture and filter waste to make into soil-building fertilizers much like other animal manures, powered by sustainable, low-carbon energy.[145,146] Fish populations in the tanks must be maintained at levels that don't require the use of antibiotic chemicals that risk degrading ecosystems nearby if tanks are flushed or creating antibiotic-resistant superbugs. Sustainable alternatives to baitfish and bycatch must be expanded to feed the seafoods requiring other animal products in their diet.

In the meantime, I'll renew my love affair with shellfish, eat sustainably managed, wild-caught seafood whenever I can, and make my seafood choices based on the advice of watchdog organizations like Seafood Watch.

The Corn Eaters

In some respects, it was just another idyllic April tropical evening. The rainy season was trailing off, and the temperatures oscillated between the balmy days and lovely, cool nights that define the weather of tropical Pacific islands. Despite their lush surroundings, however, the people of Sumbawa must have been worried. The supervolcano known as Tambora on the island's flank had begun erupting in earnest five days earlier. Ash clouds, pyroclastic flows, and earthquakes surged from the 14,100-foot peak, one of the highest rimming the Pacific Ring of Fire at the time, and one of the largest volcanoes in the world. Many people had already lost homes, some had died in mudslides. Residents who had the means had fled to nearby islands. Those who stayed couldn't have predicted the extent of naked geologic violence that would soon be visited upon them.

The land beneath them would heave and tumble. Earthborn glass and debris would fly through the air at supersonic speeds.

Previous spread: Corn tortilla tacos. *Thomas J. Story*

The land would be buried under feet of ash. Tambora's violence and the end of the Sumbawa residents' world would, like a gigantic butterfly flapping its wings, set off a chain of events culminating in nitrogen and corn (also known to much of the world as "maize") dominating the Earth's and the climate's future in countless ways, both seen and unseen.

> • <

On the evening of April 10, 1815, Tambora blew its top. The facts of history record that the city of Tambora was destroyed by extreme heat and a shock wave of gas, ash, and shards of volcanic glass that killed ten thousand people within minutes. At least sixty thousand more died in the region from tsunamis, suffocation, heat, and starvation in the days and weeks that followed. The massive explosion was clearly heard in places over a thousand miles away.

Having evacuated the earth beneath itself like some geologic bowel cleansing, the peak then collapsed upon itself like a giant, exhausted animal, losing a mile of its height. There it has lain ever since, occasionally rumbling, largely sleeping, a cogent reminder of the Earth's capacity for violent overthrow.

One might think that would be the end of the story. A volcano erupts, wipes out the residents on its lush Pacific island, upends lives in the region, and cloaks the surrounding earth in ash. And when the rains return, the microbes, insects, birds, plants, and animals colonize the ash flows. And eventually so do humans. People rebuild, and life continues.

But that simply wasn't the case. The volcano shot so much material so high into the Earth's atmosphere that skies throughout the Northern Hemisphere became colored for years in animated reds, purples, yellows, and greens. Ash and chemicals created low-altitude fogs that shrouded the world in deep grays so thick that many of the most active seaports in the world closed because navigation became treacherous.

People coined 1816, the year following the eruption, as "The Year Without a Summer," and "Eighteen Hundred and Froze to Death." For years afterward, deadly frosts and snow fell throughout what was normally the growing season, and the Northern Hemisphere winter that followed the eruption was so bitterly cold it surpassed that of human memory. The Indian Ocean monsoons failed to arrive for three years in a row. The emotionless agronomic term for what occurred those years is "crop failure." The historic term was "famine." In the following years, throughout the Northern Hemisphere, millions of people starved to death or succumbed to disease in their weakened states. It must have been a miserable time to be alive.[147]

Livestock died or were butchered in droves as forage crops and pastures froze. Shortages of cereals and hay meant that horses became astronomically expensive to feed. The sheer absence of horses inspired Karl von Drais in Germany to develop what became the first prototype of a bicycle. Mary Shelley wrote the novel *Frankenstein* during the peak of the famine and published it in January of 1818 to a despondent Europe after three long, dreary, hungry years. It became a sensation, perhaps at least partially because everybody who read it could relate to the ghostly story it told.

Since the eruption, historians and scientists have reconstructed what happened beneath Tambora. During the three-hour eruption, the volcano ejected about thirty-eight cubic miles of molten rock from the Earth's core. Under the unique conditions beneath Tambora, it came out not as bubbly, viscous red magma, but as an explosive event equaling the simultaneous detonation of dozens of the largest thermonuclear warheads. On the severity scale geophysicists have developed to describe observed and reconstructed volcanic eruptions, running from one being small to eight being the largest scientifically imaginable, the Mount St. Helens eruption of 1982 was just barely a five. The eruption scale is exponential, meaning that an eruption ranked a two is ten times greater than an eruption ranked a one. Science ranks Tambora at seven, meaning it was one hundred times greater than the Mount St. Helens eruption. The cataclysm that formed the Yellowstone Caldera is calculated to be an eight, which was ten times greater than Tambora. Only three other documented or scientifically reconstructed eruptions are believed to have matched Tambora's sheer scale.

Tambora shot an almost unfathomable quantity of gas, atomized magma, sulfur, and other materials straight into the stratosphere. Superheated sulfur reacted with atmospheric oxygen to produce a vast amount of tiny sulfate aerosol particles. The aerosols spread throughout most of the Northern Hemisphere. And this is where Tambora's eruption intersected with the climate in such a consequential way.

Aerosolized sulfate turns out to be excellent sunblock. The ejecta from the volcano reflected enough sunlight back into space to cool the planet dramatically, bringing summer snow events even to regions like the Sahara Desert. July and August temperatures alternated between summer heat and winter cold in the space

of less than twenty-four hours. Famine, the grim reaper's unsparing cousin, spawned a rapid cycle of evolution between host and pathogen so that cholera quickly evolved and leapt from being a localized, chronic disease to a pathogen capable of widespread, deadly epidemics, sweeping through the region now known as Bangladesh. Typhus and other diseases took hold in many parts of Asia and Eastern Europe.[148] No exact numbers are known; however, millions are believed to have died there from disease alone.

The geographer Clive Oppenheimer calculated that Tambora's eruption cooled the Northern Hemisphere temperature in 1816 by 0.4 to 0.7 degrees Fahrenheit—surprising that such a seemingly small drop in temperature brought such calamity. At the time of this writing, the Earth's global average temperature has risen about 1.1 degrees Celsius (1.8 degrees Fahrenheit) due to the burning of fossil fuels since the Industrial Revolution began, around the time of Tambora's eruption. The volume of material Tambora blew into the atmosphere equals about 40 percent of the volume of coal, oil, and gas humans have burned since the Industrial Age began. Though the chemistry and physics of Tambora's eruption are different from those of burning fossil fuels, this simple fact implies that if a volcano can, in a single eruption, throw enough stuff into the atmosphere to wreck the climate, then humanity burning fossil fuels over a century and a half could certainly wreak similar havoc.

Ash eruption at Kīlauea Volcano in March 2008, the first since 1924. Major volcanic eruptions have both cooled and warmed the Earth with their emissions. Island of Hawai'i, Hawai'i. *Stephen & Donna O'Meara / Science Source*

Chapter 4

Imagine a time when the only thing to eat, for years at a stretch, might be rye bread and a few meager greens, or occasionally the meat from a stringy cow, chicken, or horse. Weather and crop yields did not approach previously typical levels for four years. During the famine, scientific societies turned their attention to this unprecedented event. Many scientists became consumed by questions about how to grow more food.

Two scientists who would shape the world's future came of age in the decades of recovery after Tambora. One was the English agronomist and inventor John Bennet Lawes, who was a toddler living with his family at Rothamsted Manor in central England when Tambora erupted. The other was German scientist Justus von Liebig, whose adolescence was defined by those three starving years following the eruption. Their ambitions, formed in part from those years as youths with the world collectively under Tambora's thumb, catapulted the two men later in life into a scientific collision that would alter the course of history. Liebig reportedly said those hungry times in Germany motivated him to study agricultural chemistry and develop chemical fertilizers, and so finally put to rest the idea that anybody, anywhere, should ever go hungry again.

› • ‹

My first introduction to Rothamsted Manor came through a stone sitting on the windowsill in the office of my scientific mentor, Dr. Keith Paustian. I worked in Keith's research group for more than two decades, and I've come to know that like many scientists, Keith maintained his office as a time capsule of mementos from his work around the world. Within arm's reach of his computer lay an oblong, pale-brown stone that I first thought could be a fossilized dinosaur turd. Shortly after I came to work for Keith, I stood in his office and posed a question.

"Is that a coprolite?" I pointed to the stone resting on the windowsill, hoping to sound properly scientific.

I hadn't worked for Keith for very long at the time, and was concerned he might be a little too serious. But suddenly he laughed out loud, snatched the stone from the sill, and lobbed it across the room at me. I dropped my notebook and scrambled to catch it, worried about the presumed artifact's value.

"It's a flint nodule! From the Broadbalk experiment at Rothamsted!" he exclaimed.

He then put his feet up on his desk, leaned back, and launched into an expansive description of the longest-running ecological experiment known to science. It was a project he loved and had collaborated on for years before I'd come to work in his group. Not very long after that I was walking with Keith through the fields at Rothamsted Manor, learning firsthand about Sir John Lawes's and Sir Joseph Gilbert's inspiration, touring the grounds with Keith and Pete Falloon, a graduate student studying there for his PhD.

Pete led us through the methodical grid of large rectangular plots that grew food and animal forage crops in an evolving set of experimental treatments designed to answer the basic question that every farmer or home gardener has asked themselves: How can I grow the most food, forage, and flowers in the soil and weather at my home? How can I produce the most bushels of wheat, the largest tomatoes, or the deepest-green alfalfa? Farmers may be the greatest innovators in the world, and the field at Broadbalk was rife with experimentation begun in the mind of Lawes, and expanded upon with his scientific partner, Joseph Henry Gilbert.

After an aborted Oxford education, Lawes returned to Rothamsted to live the life of a post-Renaissance English nobleman. He indulged a love of chemistry, experimenting with soil supplements designed to improve crop yields. The science of modern chemistry had been fermenting, and new findings about the elements on the periodic chart—the basic stuff that we are made of—were beginning to emerge. Certain groups of chemicals were becoming known to be important for growing crops. The burning questions at the time were which chemicals were most important, in what quantity, and why? And could they be added to fields to boost yields?

In the years before he first laid out the plots at Broadbalk, Lawes experimented with chemistry in a laboratory installed in one of the manor's bedrooms. He understood that bones were rich in phosphate, as was the ash left over after plants had been burned. He speculated that plants needed to absorb phosphorus from the soil through their roots, and manufacturing a chemical that made it quickly available to crops might boost yields. He eventually perfected a recipe wherein he mixed ground bones with sulfuric acid to produce a product he called "superphosphate." When applied to soil, the product dissolved into the soil, making the phosphorus quickly available to crops. The effects on plants grown in pots in the manor's greenhouse were immediate. Those grown with superphosphate grew greener, more vigorous, and were larger and hardier.

The effects of the first synthetic fertilizers on wheat yields in an experiment at Rothamsted Manor. The leftmost sheaf came from an unfertilized plot. The others show the effects of synthetic fertilizer. Harpenden, England. *The Bookworm Collection / Alamy*

Huzzah! It was 1842, and the first manufactured, synthetic fertilizer came into being. The age of modern agriculture had begun.

Lawes gathered investors, built a superphosphate factory, and quickly developed a brisk business selling superphosphate to growers. Over time he refined the process and the raw materials and developed ways to manufacture other chemicals useful in agriculture, called "manures" in the lexicon of the time. Whenever I am in my local garden nursery, I make a point to walk the fertilizer aisle and ponder his legacy. There among the diverse sacks, jars, and tubes of different chemical fertilizers and soil amendments will lay bags of superphosphate. Read the labels on the other products, and many contain superphosphate. The local farmers' supply co-op sells it by the ton. The chemical is as ubiquitous in farming today as seed, tractors, and diesel fuel. The millions of tons manufactured every year now come from phosphate-rich rock (also a discovery of Lawes) that's mined on every continent except Antarctica.[149]

As valuable as superphosphate was to farmers, it was not quite the lynchpin Lawes originally thought it might be. Crop yields improved after it was added to fields that were low in phosphorus or where animal manure had not been added to the soil. But the increase was not to the extent that many had hoped for. Was there some other basic limitation at play? Were other chemicals needed to facilitate the benefits of superphosphate? Questions like these led Lawes to hire Dr. Joseph Henry Gilbert to help him fine-tune and expand his experiments in 1843, the year after he patented superphosphate. Gilbert had studied under Liebig, who had become one of the most prominent scientists of the time. Liebig had devoted his life to understanding and developing chemical fertilizers. Lawes was well aware of Liebig's interest in chemical fertilizers, and he actually had a beef with Liebig's ideas about manures; this would grow into a full-blown scientific kerfuffle.

Chemists like Liebig studied what plants were made of and how they derived their nutrients. Some of the most advanced work involved burning the grain, roots, and stems of different crops, analyzing them, and applying the chemicals found in the ash to the soil. They wanted to know how the roots took up chemicals in the soil, what defined the limits of plant growth, and how farmers could deliver key ingredients to plants to get them to grow as quickly as possible. They had lived through the lean years following Tambora's explosion and were motivated by the memory of that physical hunger. Famine today is known to most in the developed world only through news media reports of crop losses in remote regions. We think of famine as something resolved with planeloads and shiploads of rice, wheat, and powdered milk. In the early- and mid-nineteenth century, famine was both a recent memory and a clear and present danger to the majority of the world's people.

Liebig had co-opted from his colleague Carl Sprengel—apparently without attribution—a biophysical notion that he popularized as "the law of the minimum." Simply put, it meant that plant growth is always limited by some factor in the ecosystem, whether in a tropical forest, or field of wheat, or algae in the oceans. The limiting factor could be any number of things—lack of moisture, too much (or too little) heat or cold, the timing of spring or fall frosts, or basic nutrients the plants needed for growth.[150]

Before Lawes invented superphosphate, Liebig promoted the idea that plants received directly from the atmosphere all the nitrogen (referred to as ammonia at that time) they needed. In Liebig's view, nitrogen was not a limiting factor. Lawes wasn't so sure. They began a very public argument on this question in the scientific literature. Their philosophical dispute had the best possible outcome: Highly innovative scientific inquiries emerged from the debate.

Lawes and Gilbert designed an experiment in which crops received doses of chemicals chemically isolated from plants: salts and other compounds of nitrogen, phosphorus, potassium, sulfur, and magnesium. Lawes's genius lay in the questions he raised,

Gilbert's in the innovative, methodical experiments he designed to answer them. Gilbert invented novel statistical advances that allowed them to demonstrate the relative effects of the different experiments they ran. Their beginnings at Rothamsted evolved into one of the longest-known collaborations in scientific history, spanning five decades and ending only when the two men died within a year of each other.

What was the principal element that limited plant growth more than all others? Clues arose after Broadbalk's first harvest. One chemical immediately began to stand out alone and in combination with the others as producing a spike in crop yields. One can imagine an excitable Lawes practically bursting to shout their findings to the world, only to hear a steadfast Gilbert advising they accumulate irrefutable proof that would put Liebig's claims to rest. Gilbert knew Liebig well, and both understood their finding's importance and the scrutiny it would bear. So they collected several years of data before presenting the results to the Royal Agricultural Society in London.

Just as Lawes had originally suspected (and farmers with whom Lawes worked were advocating), it was indeed nitrogen.

When added to the soil as sodium nitrate,[151] alone or combined with other nutrients, nitrogen led to unambiguous yield increases well above any other agricultural practice known at the time besides adding farmyard manure or irrigating crops grown in dry climates. The other amendments (sulfur, magnesium, phosphorus, potassium) helped increase yields, but not to the extent that nitrogen did. Lawes was correct. Liebig was wrong.[152] And so began humanity's race to secure nitrogen fertilizers.

Understanding the role that nitrogen played in growing crops stimulated a race to develop nitrogen deposits that would change the world. Farmers firmly understood how manure in general, and bird manure in particular, boosted crop yields. Deposits of bird guano quickly became the focus of a worldwide rush. Seabird rookeries the world over were razed as sailors stripped them of centuries of guano deposits to be sold as fertilizer. Saltpeter mines in remote parts of the world, particularly Chile, gained strategic importance. And the quest to manufacture fertilizers led to the deaths of thousands of people killed in accidental detonations that cratered ammonia factories around the world. The fate of combatants in two world wars was tied to breakneck manufacturing of fertilizers-cum-explosives. Today, we live with the seemingly sleepy but insidious consequences of a world literally soaked in what scientists call "reactive nitrogen," consisting largely of the sister chemicals known as ammonia, nitrogen oxides (including the fertilizer known as nitrate), and the extremely potent greenhouse gas nitrous oxide.

Used judiciously, they can accomplish miracles. Used carelessly, they kill.

> • <

A decade after my first trip to Rothamsted, I found myself in a van filled with students and colleagues approaching the Dyno Nobel factory complex outside Cheyenne, Wyoming. As the network of pipes, holding tanks, and metal columns came into view, I turned and looked back toward Cheyenne—which was miles behind us, and for good reason. As the blast berms came into view and we pulled into the parking lot, a student in the van remarked, "If this place blows, it would be one giant hole in the ground." Nitrogen's awesome power suddenly came into very precise focus.

Modern fertilizer factories are a baffling maze of metal towers, tanks, scaffolding, wires, and pipes. The complex outside Cheyenne is one of dozens of factories around North America, and hundreds around the world, built to satisfy the global demand for ammonia, nitrate, nitric acid, and their chemical cousins, all known as "reactive nitrogen." These chemicals play innumerable roles in agriculture, manufacturing, the cleaning industry, mining, modern warfare, and countless other pursuits. The Dyno Nobel plant, built in 1965, has the capacity to manufacture 178,000 metric tons of ammonia per year.[153] If all that ammonia were used to grow corn, it could fertilize about 1.6 million acres per year.[154]

Through video and slide presentations, our hosts at the plant explained the chemical process in terms they assumed a State University audience would appreciate, but none of us clearly understood. We were either too polite or too bewildered to ask for clarification, but in the end we were all astonished at the scale and organization of the facility. Before touring the grounds, we received an extensive safety briefing, which could be summed up simply as this: "If anything goes wrong, stay calm but get the hell away through whatever means possible. Fast!"

They suited us up in fireproof suits, industrial helmets, and steel-toed boots and then loaded us into a van that drove slowly through the factory grounds while a communications specialist read from a tour script. It was a blustery winter day, the temperature well below freezing. The van rocked in the omnipresent

The Nutrien Redwater Fertilizer plant near Fort Saskatchewan, Alberta, Canada. Thousands of facilities like this manufacture fertilizers from fossil fuels and mined minerals to sell into a market worth about $200 billion in 2023. *Todd Korol / REUTERS*

Wyoming wind as it crept along. We sat in awed silence as we peered through the van's windows at the network of steel and concrete, tanks and towers.

What came to my mind was how the entire manufacturing process was bookended by fossil fuels. Methane from fracked natural gas piped from distant parts of Wyoming provided the hydrogen atoms needed for the chemical reaction. Most of the product from this factory would become explosives used in the coal mines of the Cheyenne and Powder River drainages to the north. Train-car loads of ammonium nitrate would be packaged and laid down, then combined with diesel fuel and detonated to explode away the rock and topsoil covering vast Paleocene coal deposits. Thoughts of Timothy McVeigh and Oklahoma City came to mind when that factoid emerged.

At one point in the tour, we were invited into a small building near the perimeter of the complex. "But please, no photographs inside this building," instructed the tour guide. The wind tugged at the hard hat on my head as I stepped from the van and climbed a short flight of stairs into a large, open space lined with computer monitors staffed by half a dozen men. A network of large screens mapped out the status of the factory's processes in dynamic, color-coded, graphic engineering terms and symbols. One of the men seated near the display pivoted his chair to us and gave us a kind smile.

"Are you the CSU crew?"

"Yes, that's us," I replied. I think we all felt a little self-conscious standing there in our oversized fire suits, the boots that felt gigantic on our feet, and the unfamiliar hard hats.

"Welcome," he said, and smiled the smile of a competent individual who likes to explain things.

"Can you explain what we are seeing?"

He turned to the screen and pointed with a finger. "In a nutshell, it is this. Natural gas comes in here." We saw what seemed like an entry point in the process, with color-coded statistics adjacent to it.

"We clean the gas and separate out the methane, and then separate nitrogen from the atmosphere and add it here." He pointed to another part of the diagram. "The rest of this is too complicated to explain, as I've only got a minute and I need to stay focused." Having read histories of fertilizer plant explosions,[155,156] I was grateful for that.

"But the short version is we combine nitrogen and methane under high heat and pressure to produce ammonia and nitric acid, and the end products come out here." He pointed to another part of the screen. "In this list we have the various products we produce." He pointed to another screen and rattled off the names of a half dozen chemicals I recognized from the jargon of modern agronomy.

"And that is about it." He smiled over his shoulder, we thanked him in unison, and he casually waved goodbye as he turned back to his computer monitor. After a few moments, our tour guide shepherded us back into the van. We chatted excitedly about the monitoring technology as the van crept back to the factory entrance, where we traded the safety gear for the clothing we'd left, thanked our hosts, and climbed into our own van for the drive home.

As I pondered the enormous investment made to build that fertilizer and explosives factory and others like it around the world, a question arose in my mind. When combined, the greenhouse gas emissions from facilities like that around the world produced more emissions than the total impact of the sixty-five lowest-emitting countries in the world, most of them among the world's poorest.[157]

I wondered at the time and still wonder today if all of it was completely necessary.

> • <

More than fifty years after the experiments at Broadbalk were brought to light, the world continued to struggle with questions of food security. The Industrial Revolution led to an expanding human population, and evidence emerged that agriculture was not keeping up with the increasing demand for food. Despite the burgeoning understanding about the role of fertilizers, population growth was outpacing worldwide crop yields. Other problems emerged. When amended to soils, mined nitrogen fertilizer (known as "saltpeter") led to salt buildup in soils and contaminated aquifers, causing crop yields to drop if applied to fields for very long. The economically accessible guano deposits worldwide had been used up. The scientific and agronomic community approached a consensus that a method to manufacture nitrogen fertilizer was increasingly necessary to keep pace with food demand. The seats of political power also understood that whoever invented such a method could manufacture explosive munitions without relying on long, vulnerable supply lines to saltpeter (the raw material for explosives at the time) mines around the world.

Ammonia had dozens of potential industrial, agricultural, and military uses. Scientists in laboratories around the world were racing to be the first to fabricate ammonia in the lab and take it to scale. In 1909, Fritz Haber and his assistant Robert Le Rossignol became the first to achieve it in the laboratory by combining methane with atmospheric nitrogen at high pressure and temperatures in the presence of a catalyst. The company BASF bought the technology and immediately tasked the industrial chemist Carl Bosch with taking it to scale. Bosch succeeded the following year, inventing a scalable manufacturing method the world now knows as the Haber-Bosch process. The Austro-Hungarian Empire tapped its investment network to construct an ammonia factory at Ludwigshafen, Germany, and in 1913 began manufacturing ammonia at a rate of twenty tons per day to feed Germany's munitions plants and agriculture. Because Germany had no nitrate mines, the ability to create ammonia dramatically destabilized the balance of political power at the time.

In addition to military and agricultural uses, the promise of electrification led to an exponentially growing demand for mining explosives. New turbines capable of generating electricity from steam heated by burning coal had led to a demand for explosives for the coal mining industry. The sudden availability of reactive nitrogen spawned new industries. In the end, Haber (in 1918) and Bosch (in 1933) received Nobel Prizes in Chemistry for their work.[158] So auspicious was their invention that one of the principal articles in the Treaty of Versailles (signed on June 28, 1919, concluding World War I) addressed this technology directly:

Workers nap on piles of fertilizer shipped from China on the banks of the Yalu River near the North Korean town of Sinuiju.
Jacky Chen / REUTERS

Within a period of three months from the coming into force of the present Treaty, the German Government will disclose to the Governments of the Principal Allied and Associated Powers the nature and mode of manufacture of all explosives, toxic substances or other like chemical preparations used by them in the war or prepared by them for the purpose of being so used.

After the war, the allies quickly adopted the Haber-Bosch process in plants built throughout the Western world. And though it has only been available for a century, reactive nitrogen dominates the manufacturing world today through the many new industrial processes spawned to produce and distribute it. Many of the ubiquitous plastics, pharmaceuticals, fibers, chemical dyes, and agricultural chemicals known today owe their beginning to reactive nitrogen. I can find no fault in the motivations of innovators like Liebig, Lawes, and Gilbert, and though chemical fertilizers have improved the lives of millions over the past century and a half, like so many human innovations, their helpful inventions birthed destructive cousins.

The Haber-Bosch process made possible the materials Fritz Haber used to create the very first modern ammonia-based explosives, along with mustard gas—the first mass-manufactured chemical weapon. Haber directly supervised the first use of mustard gas on the battlefield in 1915 against French and Canadian troops at Ypres.[159] His exuberance for chemical weapons led his pacifist colleague, Albert Einstein, to denounce Haber.

Science has learned over the years that in the case of reactive nitrogen, there can definitely be too much of a good thing. The overuse of modern chemical fertilizers, especially nitrogen, underpins a host of troubling problems. Overapplication of nitrogen fertilizers contributes to ocean and lake dead zones downstream and leads to enormous methane emissions from the oxygen-depleted depths of eutrophic (nutrient-rich) water bodies. Fertilizer ammonia contributes to ozone formation in the lower atmosphere and dangerous particulate pollution. There is also the fact that ammonia factories and their products have a tendency to catch fire and explode.

Since 1916, accidents in at least nine fertilizer factories created fireballs that killed thousands of people and injured tens of thousands more.[160] Dozens more major accidents away from factories, but involving ammonium nitrate or its chemical antecedents, have killed and injured an unknown number of others. The earliest prominent example occurred in 1921 at Ludwigshafen, now known as the Oppau disaster. The explosion completely destroyed the factory, killed at least 560 people, and injured thousands more. Residents 180 miles away in Munich heard the explosion, and the shock wave destroyed glass windows for miles around, ripped the roofs off buildings up to fifteen miles away, and toppled trolleys from their tracks. The United States experienced a similar accident at Nixon Nitration Works in Nixon, New Jersey. The most recent explosions were in Bryan, Texas (2009), and West, Texas (2013), where fires spawned explosions killing more than a dozen people, injuring hundreds, and destroying buildings surrounding the plant.

The use of nitrogen fertilizers contributes about two billion metric tons of CO_2e annually to the atmosphere, or about 4 percent of the world's total carbon footprint, and about one-sixth of food's carbon footprint. Farmers apply more fertilizer to corn worldwide than any other crop.[161,162] Corn dominates the developed world's diet, as well as that of much of the developing world. The animals producing meat, dairy, or egg products are fed diets rich in corn. Examine food product labels and you will likely see corn starch, corn syrup, and corn oil, along with derivative products like xanthan gum, ascorbic acid, maltodextrin, and vanilla extract produced from corn.[163] In fact, corn is so much a part of our diet that if archaeologists discover our bodies millennia from now and chemically examine the remains, they will be able to detect corn's chemical signature in our bones, teeth, and hair fragments.

Corn belongs to a class of plants, called C4 plants, that evolved an extra chemical pathway to take up carbon dioxide from the atmosphere, giving them a competitive advantage to photosynthesize more and hence grow faster and larger than their neighbors. For reasons scientists can't yet explain, that extra pathway takes up an extra dose of carbon dioxide with heavy carbon isotopes. Those heavy carbon isotopes have an atomic number of 13, rather than 12, due to an extra neutron in the atom's nucleus. Examine the isotope ratio in a corn plant compared with a geranium, for example, which is not a C4 plant, and a radically larger number of stable isotopes appear in the corn plant than in the geranium. Because we eat so much corn, combined with the animals (or their products like eggs and milk) we eat that ate so much corn, the heavy carbon isotopes persist in our muscles, fat, neurons, bones, and hair. Archaeologists of the future, perhaps lacking a clear name for our civilization, very well could label us "The Corn Eaters."

› • ‹

To learn more about corn, nitrogen, and its climate-warming effects, I visited Dr. Steve DelGrosso at his research plots at the Colorado State University Agricultural Research, Development and Education Center (or ARDEC). The sprawling complex hosts a regional seat for agricultural education, extension work, and nearly fifty different ongoing agricultural experiments. Steve wrote his PhD dissertation as a student in the research group where I worked at Colorado State University, and after graduating he made the leap to the US Department of Agriculture's Agricultural Research Service (ARS), where he has become one of the world's leading experts researching nitrous oxide in agriculture. Early one July morning I joined Steve and his crew as they measured the nitrous oxide emissions from soil in one of ARDEC's corn fields.

Soil microbes consume nitrogen fertilizer and give off nitrous oxide whenever fertilizer is applied and soil oxygen levels fall after rain, snow, or irrigation, facilitating one of the most significant earth-atmosphere exchanges on the planet. Unfortunately, the scientific community hasn't yet been able to put a precise number on how high that number is. Nor can science recommend the best way to reduce soil nitrous oxide emissions beyond simply lowering the quantity of fertilizers used or carefully managing when and how they are applied. Conventional practice today is to apply far more nitrogen fertilizer than crops need, with the excess treated as just the cost of doing business. That excess nitrogen volatilizes into the air or washes into groundwater and waterways, creating trouble downwind and downstream.[164]

Nitrous oxide's sheer power to warm the climate critically underscores how important it is to better understand how and why it comes from soil. How do we reduce nitrous oxide emissions that come from fertilizer use? Or how do we grow crops using less fertilizer? Can we apply the fertilizers differently, in different forms, or at different times to reduce the damage? DelGrosso is part of a research network trying to provide answers to these desperately important, but aggravatingly difficult-to-answer questions.

An athletic, perpetually smiling scientist, with a shaved head and one of the best beards in the field of ecology, Steve doesn't own an automobile. He and his wife live in downtown Fort Collins and get around on foot, bicycle, and bus. On this morning, he and his crew were in Carhartt pants and work boots, long-sleeved shirts, and big floppy hats to protect against the sun, with water bottles clipped to their belts. They were measuring soil nitrous oxide as part of an experiment to see how emissions changed in response to different synthetic fertilizer rates and types, and whether the soil was tilled. The amount of nitrogen fertilizer applied on this experiment ranged from none to three hundred kilograms of nitrogen per hectare (267 pounds per acre).[165] Some of the research plots were plowed every year, some received a light tilling, and some were never tilled. For comparison, the norm to grow corn in Colorado's Front Range east of the Rocky Mountains is heavy tillage and about two hundred pounds of nitrogen per acre every year.

"It rained pretty hard last night, and we could see a big pulse of N_2O today," Steve remarked as the crew set up. A classic line of thunderstorms had brought nearly constant lightning, hail, and more than an inch of rain and had drawn me to my bedroom window hours earlier. As the water percolated down through the soil, it had the potential to drive the soil into and out of conditions that could cause nitrous oxide emissions to peak.

DelGrosso and his crew strode directly down the rows of seven-foot-tall corn stalks, carrying boxes filled with equipment and a cooler filled with blue ice packs as they searched for the first research plot. I chased after the crew through the dense canopy, but immediately lost sight of them, though I could hear their mutterings through the rustle of corn leaves. My world suddenly was confined to the corn plants' sweet smell, the moist and herby aroma from the soil, and the leaves' sharp edges nicking my skin.

"Here it is!" DelGrosso's call yanked me from my isolation. I staggered in his direction, and a few moments later I fell over him, nearly breaking some of his equipment in the process.

The other crew members arrived and began staging the gear to collect a nitrous oxide sample. A large, white plastic collar buried in the soil marked a spot where the crew had taken previous samples, measurements that they would repeat that day. Steve carefully wiped the collar clean and covered it with a sealed, airtight lid, and a team member immediately started a timer. Then the crew prepared the sampling syringes while waiting for nitrous oxide and other trace gases to accumulate in the chamber. When the timer's alarm sounded, they connected a large plastic syringe to a tube emerging from the collar's cover, opened a valve partway down the tube, and drew a set quantity of air from inside the chamber. They then closed the valve, sealed the syringe, fastened the plunger in place with tape, and labeled it with the plot number, date, and time. A team member placed the sample on ice while the crew headed to the next plot.

Back in his laboratory, Steve's crew members ran the samples through an instrument known as a gas chromatograph to measure the concentration of nitrous oxide, methane, and carbon dioxide. The methane concentrations are typically zero in corn fields like this one, but nitrous oxide measurements spiked up and down erratically. DelGrosso and his team aggregated the measurements over the course of the growing season into a total nitrous oxide budget for the year. Over the course of the growing season, the emissions from the research plot that received typical tillage and fertilizer levels for a corn crop on Colorado's Front Range exceeded a half metric ton CO_2e per acre, per year—equivalent to the emissions from a typical American automobile produced in about three months.

The perplexing thing with nitrous oxide is that measurements are frequently higher, or lower, than expected, or the peaks appear at unexpected times. They can be exceptionally difficult to predict. It's those pesky microbes.

Soil microbes have evolved biochemical strategies to live in the highly variable conditions within soil. An adaptation allows them to live through the peaks and valleys of oxygen concentrations found in soil. In a typical cube of soil at the ARDEC, about half of the space is occupied by the mineral and rock fragments and organic matter that make up soil. Billions of tiny spaces take up the other half, filled with roots, soil organisms, water in solution with soil minerals, and atmospheric gases. Soil scientists call this the pore space. As water falls on the soil surface and percolates into the soil, it absorbs or displaces gases present in the soil, including oxygen, but as the soil pores fill to capacity with water after a heavy rain or major irrigation event, oxygen movement slows. Oxygen is necessary for many soil organisms' metabolism, and as the trillions of microbes present in a single cubic meter of soil use up the free oxygen gas in the pore space, many shift to a different strategy to keep their metabolism churning.

Whereas humans and other mammals take in oxygen for respiration through their lungs, microbes in the soil absorb it directly from the air or the soil-water solution. When oxygen levels in the soil drop, the microbes chemically strip oxygen from nitrate (NO_3) molecules in the soil solution through a process known by the term *denitrification*. Doing so costs them extra energy, but it works in a pinch. Most of the waste product from the microbes executing this process is stable nitrogen gas (N_2); however, a small amount of nitrous oxide (N_2O) leaks from the process. A small amount of nitrous oxide goes a very long way.

A similar process, known by the term *nitrification*, occurs somewhat in reverse as plant roots take up the water in the soil while gravity inexorably draws the water slowly downward. Oxygen infiltrates into the soil once again, and as it becomes available, the microbes convert free ammonia in the soil solution

A tractor applies anhydrous ammonia fertilizer to a cornfield in Marion, Colorado. *Daybreak Imagery / Alamy*

and air space back into nitrite (NO$_2$) and then to nitrate (NO$_3$). Like with denitrification's leaky process, a small amount of nitrous oxide results. Why microbes developed this capacity is not entirely clear, though evolution may explain at least some of it. Ammonium ions are highly reactive and are toxic to plant roots. The soil microbes, which have co-evolved with plants to depend upon each other in myriad ways, may have developed this ability to convert ammonia to improve living conditions for the plants they depend upon for food.[166]

In this way, we find the microbes going about their daily lives in crop fields and pastures around the world are responsible every year for about two billion tons of global warming effect. About 2,500,000,000,000,000,000,000,000,000,000,000,000,000 (twenty-five followed by thirty-eight zeros) individual microbial interactions with nitrate and ammonia molecules lead to these emissions. An international scientific unit for this proposed by Andre Joyce is 2.5 "treda" interactions.[167] Bill Watterson's Calvin of *Calvin and Hobbes* cartoon fame might call a number of that size a gazillion gazillion.[168]

The microbes are exploiting an evolutionary strategy developed over hundreds of millions, perhaps billions, of years, which is playing out in the historically and evolutionarily unprecedented conditions that occur in soils today. Farmers and ranchers literally soak their fields and pastures with reactive nitrogen from the Haber-Bosch process as a risk-hedging measure. The conditions that lead to these collectively enormous nitrous oxide emissions occur on hundreds of millions to perhaps billions of acres of soil every year. Is there a way to fix it? Yes. But solutions lie in natural ecosystem processes that are not quite what scientists had previously thought.

> • ‹

I gained some insight into those solutions through an unexpected meeting. While attending a workshop on soil health in Central California, I noticed a quiet, dignified man sitting in the back of the room, occasionally taking notes, but listening in a focused way to everything that was being said. I hadn't caught his name during the introductions, so during a break I introduced myself. "My name is Jim Moseley," he said. "I'm from Indiana." His name struck a chord, but I couldn't quite place it. Later that day, over a cup of coffee during an interlude, we spoke about our mutual interest in soil health, carbon sequestration, and soil conservation until a softly ringing bell announced the end of the break.

I learned more about Jim's history later through a colleague. Jim had been the US Deputy Secretary of Agriculture from 2001 to 2005, serving under George W. Bush. Before that he had been Assistant Secretary of Agriculture from 1990 to 1991 under George H. W. Bush, overseeing both the Forest Service and the Natural Resources Conservation Service during that administration. Jim had founded critical, bulwark soil-conservation programs administered by the NRCS under both administrations. In collaboration with NRCS Chief Bruce Knight, they had introduced the term "soil health" to the national conservation lexicon.

We got to know each other a little over the next couple of days in the workshop. Jim described his own soil-health innovations and lessons learned and those of his neighbors in his west-central

Indiana farm watershed. Raising crops without tilling the soil, growing cover crops in between the main crops of corn and soybeans, reducing fertilizer use, and carefully applying manure at appropriate times were all part of his system. They were the foundations of the programs he had authored while at USDA. From the CSU research team's work, I understood these to be critical practices to mitigate global warming; however, I didn't know any growers in our area who combined these practices. So, when I had the opportunity to take an early spring-break trip, I made a phone call.

"Jim, would it work for me to come visit, see your farm, and learn more about your efforts?"

"Yes, surely, but I'd rather you met some of the younger growers doing good work in our area. They are the future, and I'd be happy to connect you with them." Not long afterward, Jim and I rendezvoused in rural, west-central Indiana before heading out to meet Dan DeSutter.

Colleagues of mine and I had heard about Dan's work through the grapevine, and Jim briefed me during the drive. "Dan has taken a business approach to conservation that has him focusing not just on crop yields, like most farmers do, but on his net profitability and how that is linked directly to water quality, air quality, and avoiding soil erosion. He has cut out nearly all his herbicide and pesticide use. He is transitioning to organic without having to till his fields at all, on several thousand acres of land," he informed me.

The organic cropping system he described, achieved without tilling the soil for weed control, is the gold standard for conservation in the Corn Belt. I had no reason to doubt Jim, but I could hardly believe it was true. Our research team hadn't heard of anybody outside the Rodale Institute's research plots who was taking these kinds of practices to scale and making it profitable.

After an interval, Jim said, "Turn left up here. That is Dan's place, and these are some of his fields." I slowed and looked out the window at the soil in the fields we passed. To be more precise, what I saw was a bumpy carpet of green replacing the monochrome brown soil that had been tilled and exposed to the sky in every other field we passed. It was early April, and Dan's fields were already a bright green after a cold, wet winter. Cover crops planted the previous fall came back to life as the soil thawed.

If it weren't for his beefy hands and forearms, I'd have guessed Dan was a banker rather than a farmer, dressed in his neat turtleneck and clean blue jeans. He offered us a cup of coffee and invited us into his tidy, brightly lit farm office, where he and Jim launched into a conversation about farm bill policy. "The crop insurance program is really bugging me. I'm not sure how I can transition to organic and still keep my crops insured!" I listened to the two of them catalog the program's inconsistencies as I scanned Dan's bookshelves. Books by soil-conservation and farm-innovation heroes shared shelf space with those on investment strategy, accounting, and financial management. As I examined the shelves, Jim and Dan carried on a diverse, literary conversation that included references to the *New York Times*, the local newspaper, quotes from Wendell Berry, and corn futures prices.

"Have you read Charles Massy's *Call of the Reed Warbler*?"

Farmers are reviving cover crops to protect soil and increase yields.
Dan DeSutter has been experimenting with cover crops for over two
decades. Attica, Indiana. *David Kasnic / The New York Times / Redux*

I turned to see Dan standing next to me. It was a new title at the time about the regenerative agriculture transformation of a depleted farm in Australia. "No, but it's on my list," I replied. We sat down with our steaming mugs and I took the chance to ask Dan how he got his start in farming.

"I grew up on this farm, but I studied finance in college, and worked in finance before my dad had a heart attack and I returned home to help." His reply reminded me of Jim's comments about Dan's approach to conservation finance.

"My dad's approach to farming his whole life has been about soil conservation. We switched to ridge tillage [a form of soil tillage easier on soil than plowing] in 1983. It was just the way my dad worked. Then he and I went to a no-tillage farming demonstration, and on the way home I convinced my dad to try no-till."

No-till farming is basically what it sounds like: growing crops without the use of a plow or any other implements to break up the soil. The only impact from implements is when a tractor pulls a seeder through the soil at the start of the growing season, a sprayer distributes fertilizer or other chemicals, and a harvester like a combine comes at the end of the growing season. That's it. Seeds are planted directly into the soil through the stubble left over from the previous crop. No-till was started in the 1970s by farmers who were frustrated by the erosion that plows caused and began manufacturing their own seeding equipment. Implement companies and university researchers collaborated with the growers to help develop better seeding equipment and techniques for growing more and more crops with no-till techniques. Today in the United States, no-till agriculture is practiced on about 25 percent of row crops and about 10 percent of all cropland, and is among the fastest-growing sectors in carbon-farming innovation.[169] Under the right conditions with the right crops, no-till practices can lead to large increases in carbon in the soil because by leaving the soil intact and undisturbed, organic matter from the roots and crop residues left after crop harvest can build up quickly.

By adopting no-till more than two decades earlier, Dan and his father had been on the front line of that innovation. But I was also curious about another innovation I'd seen during the drive to his place. I mentioned the cover crops on his fields, and asked Dan about them.

"We had switched to no-tillage, and things were going okay. We were building soil carbon; we weren't having to use as much fertilizer after we worked out the initial kinks. But we still occasionally had some soil-compaction problems that we felt we might have to break out some steel and a tractor to deal with. Then one day I was repairing a drainage pipe. I was working with a shovel and had dug a hole four or five feet down, trying to get to the source of the problem. I had finally dug my way there, and I saw all of these plant roots way down at the bottom of the hole. I suddenly realized that the plants could do more to mitigate soil compaction and other problems on my fields than any piece of steel could ever do. That was my 'aha' moment." I saw Jim nod firmly in agreement. "I realized that there was probably no agronomic problem I couldn't solve with plants. At the next opportunity, I planted cover crops."

I thought of a presentation I'd seen by Wes Jackson, the founder of The Land Institute in Salina, Kansas, during which he unrolled a fourteen-foot-long photograph of plant roots of Kernza®, a variety of perennial wheat his organization had developed.

"Ending tillage was just a beginning," Dan added. "That plant community has been out there all the time, waiting to be utilized. That is the most important thing. But it didn't happen overnight. It started with my dad, ridge tillage, then no tillage, then cover crops."

Dan looked at the field immediately outside his office window. "And now we are adding in cattle."

"Can we go look at some of your soil?"

"Yes, let's go."

We climbed into Dan's pickup and set out, passing a wide piece of tractor-pulled equipment known as a roller-crimper that lay in his driveway. It was a round tube of steel about two feet in diameter, covered with alternating rows

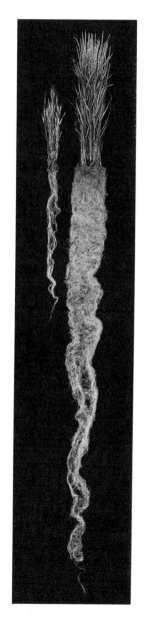

Ten-foot-long perennial Kernza plant roots compared to the three-foot-long roots of an annual wheat plant. The deep Kernza roots stabilize soil, gather water and nutrients from deep in the soil, and sequester greater amounts of carbon than comparable annual crops. *The Land Institute*

of blunt steel blades set at angles roughly parallel to the tube. Developed at the Rodale Institute in Kutztown, Pennsylvania— pioneers of organic farming—the implement has become a mainstay of the regenerative farming movement, with open-source plans freely available to the public. The roller-crimper is replacing tillage implements to knock down thick mats of cover crops and establish a mulching layer before planting new crops into the fields, with minimum soil disturbance. The cover crop and resulting thick mulch layer prove to be effective weed controls, reducing, or in the case of the DeSutters, largely eliminating, reliance on herbicides to control weeds. Herbicides are commonly used by both no-till and conventional farmers to control weeds, and avoiding them completely can be difficult. Eliminating use of herbicides is an active area of research in agriculture today.[170] Cover crops can effectively control weeds biologically rather than chemically, whether or not systems are tilled.[171,172,173]

A short distance from his house, Dan pulled the truck over to the side of the road and we stepped into a field they had spent the last ten years converting to his uniquely blended system of no tillage, highly diverse cover crops, and cattle grazing. Dan grabbed a shovel out of the pickup bed and we walked some distance into the field. He handed me the shovel and I pushed it into the soil. It sliced in evenly, and I turned the shovelful out onto the soil surface.

A menagerie of soil critters sped for safety. "Look at all the worms!" exclaimed Dan. It was still early spring, and the soil had thawed only a couple of weeks earlier, but despite the cold conditions, red and orange earthworms wriggled through the complex of clods and roots spanning the dark matrix. Coils of segmented worms lay scattered throughout. A millipede emerged, climbed to the top of the pile, and waved its antennae threateningly at us before racing off and under a mass of green cereal rye. I knelt, scooped up a double handful into my palms, and buried my nose into it. It smelled like the grocery store produce section—clean, almost citrusy, of earth and growing plants and moisture. It smelled of carbon.

Dan's soil sat in stark contrast to soil I'd seen the day before on a tilled field that had never had cover crops rooting in its depths. Rodney Rulon, who farmed with his brother Ken near Indianapolis, Indiana, had taken me onto a series of cover crop trials they ran in collaboration with Dr. Eileen Kladivko from Purdue University. The plots ran in long, narrow strips remarkably similar to the Rothamsted Broadbalk experiments. An adjacent corn field had been tilled every year, and to Rodney's knowledge, had never seen a cover crop. As we stepped from the lawn-like green cover crop surface onto the tilled soil, I felt my boots smear into the noticeably muddier conditions. Rodney and I dug a shovelful. We could see no worms. No root tendrils threaded the soil matrix. I took a sniff. The soil smelled like a dark, wet basement. Standing there in Dan's field, I realized those were the same conditions in Dan's soil before he began regenerative farming.

"What is the organic matter concentration of this field?"

"It's at about 3.5 percent, up from about 2 percent when we adopted regenerative ag techniques on this field a decade ago. Yields are way up, my costs are down, and we are building soil."

At the time of European colonization, the soils in Dan's fields likely held organic matter concentrations of 5 percent or more in the top foot of the soil, with similar concentrations extending down and tapering off to zero several meters below the soil surface. That soil and the organic matter it held would have developed over many thousands of years under a forested grassland known as a savanna, with frequent fires. Trees, shrubs, and perennial grasses and herbs would have dominated the ecosystem. Before the first European immigrants farmed it, that thin layer of soil held about forty-two tons of carbon per acre, equaling the amount of carbon in about 840 one-hundred-pound wheelbarrow loads of charcoal briquettes. The organic matter concentration in his field when he took it over—2 percent—was typical of most of the soils in the county where Dan farmed.

Achieving such a dramatic soil organic matter increase signaled a host of winning prospects for Dan's operation. Nearly doubling the organic matter had captured more than thirty metric tons of CO_2 per acre, equal to the yearly tailpipe emissions from about six typical American automobiles. That is a huge win. But the other big win comes from the nitrogen the soil holds with the carbon, and the amount of nutrients the additional organic matter feeds to the crops in the field. The more organic matter soil holds, the more nitrogen and other critical nutrients the microbial community can efficiently cycle to their plant partners. Studies from around the world support this notion, and work by Dr. Louise Jackson from the University of California, Davis,[174] added concrete scientific evidence. Increasing soil organic matter made for healthier, more productive crops and higher yields, achieved with far less fertilizer.

We walked back to the pickup truck and continued the tour. Dan pointed to a hillock about a hundred yards away.

"The topsoil had been completely lost from the hilltops here when I was a kid. But regenerative practices," he said, pointing to the cover crops emerging from the winter deep freeze, "turned it all around. After decades of tillage, this soil was sterile. It was gray and greasy whenever it rained. Weeds couldn't even grow there. Now the soil is black again, and we are getting two hundred-plus bushels of corn and seventy-plus bushels of soybeans from those same spots, which is more than twice the yield we got when we began farming the field." He paused. "Using a lot less fertilizer, all of it organic. This occurred in one generation, a blip in time in soil terms."

He paused the truck at a point closest to the hill. I could not see the soil through the heavy green cover crop. I let the impact of his point soak in. Dan and his family were growing crops by leveraging innovations that yielded grain harvests at or above the average his neighbors produced with conventional farming, but with far less help from the Haber-Bosch process.[175]

"And it costs less than when we first started farming," he said. "Less fuel, less fertilizer. We don't have to rely on herbicides, fungicides, or pesticides, except for spot applications in rare circumstances."

Before synthetic fertilizers became widely available, cover crops and livestock were mainstream components of agriculture. Farmers planted cover crops in the shoulder seasons between their cash or food crops to capture nutrients, stabilize soils, add organic matter, and capture nitrogen from the atmosphere through nitrogen fixation by legume crops. In a chapter titled "The Use of Cover and Green-Manure Crops," A. J. Pieters and Roland McKee contributed this section in the United States Department of Agriculture's *Soils and Men: Yearbook of Agriculture 1938*:[176]

> *The Greeks turned under broadbeans* (Vicia faba *L.*) *300 years before the time of Christ, and the planting of lupines and beans* (Phaseolus *spp.*) *for soil improvement was a common practice in the early years of the Roman Republic. The Chinese wrote about the fertilizing value of grass and weeds several hundred years before our era.*

I ran some computer simulations back at the lab that confirmed Dan's carbon accumulations. But that was only half the story of the greenhouse gas reductions associated with his regenerative agriculture techniques. The soybeans in his crop rotation, combined with the nitrogen-fixing cover crops he grew in the shoulder season and the modicum of chicken manure he spread on the soil before he grew the corn, provided all the nutrients his crops needed. Having the cattle graze down the cover crops returned about three-quarters of the nitrogen in the plants back to the soil in their manure and urine, along with a large mass of carbohydrates and partially decomposed plant parts in the manure as food for the microbes responsible for cycling the nutrients for the crops.

Separate research studies conducted by Drs. Tim Bowles, Louise Jackson, Kerri Steenwerth, Xia Zhu-Barker, and Will

Dryland cover crop being flattened by a roller-crimper at the Sayles farm. Knocking down cover crops this way helps feed soil, control weeds, and hold water in the soil for the next crop. Seibert, Colorado. *Curtis Sayles*

Horwath at the University of California, Davis, confirmed that in agricultural systems with high soil-organic-matter levels, low soil disturbance, and careful nutrient applications in the form of organic matter like chicken manure or compost, nitrogen quickly ties to organic matter in the soil, bypassing processes that cause nitrogen loss and climate-heating nitrous oxide. Soil microbes surrounding the uncountable miles of threads of hair roots of plants in the soil (called the rhizosphere) cycle nutrients like nitrogen very tightly with plants. The process is very efficient compared with conventional agriculture, in which more than half of the applied fertilizer is leached or eroded from the soil and known scientifically as "poor nitrogen use efficiency." Dan described it as "lost profits."

What does this mean for the climate? Dan's farming innovations help him avoid more than a ton of CO_2e per acre of climate-heating emissions from manufacturing, transporting, and applying synthetic fertilizers and farm chemicals. That one innovation, spread across the roughly two thousand acres that Dan and his family farm, was equivalent to removing four hundred American cars from the road. Combined with the nitrous oxide emissions the soil microbes never produced, because of the health of the ecosystem underfoot, systems like this can do a great deal to mitigate the climate crisis.

As Dan drove us around the farm to see other fields and his son's cattle herd, our conversation returned to the policy issues we'd begun the day with. The federal government had been talking about soil conservation in wonky and sterile terms since the Dust Bowl; however, when Jim Moseley and his colleagues got the NRCS to begin talking about soil health, farmers began to adopt soil-conservation practices at a much higher rate. Surveys indicate that farmers adopting cover crops and ending tillage remained at low percentages for more than two decades after the NRCS began promoting the practices.[177] When "soil health" became the mantra, farmers took up soil-friendly practices more quickly. I thought back to a conversation I'd had with Jim at the workshop where we'd first met.

"A farm demonstration held by NRCS and farm consultants on reducing tillage might bring six or eight people, and most of them came only for the donuts. Then the world started talking about soil health, and suddenly two hundred people started showing up for the same demonstrations. You can't find a farm magazine today that doesn't have an article about soil health in it."[178]

Then Jim added a detail that clarified for me what I'd obliquely heard in conversations with farmers around the country but hadn't heard voiced so succinctly.

"'Soil health' has become the surrogate for 'soil carbon.' That change of term relieved farmers of the burden of talking about global warming at a time when they felt under attack as being solely responsible. Politically, the other responsible industries needed someone to blame and deflect the need for answers to their own challenges. Farming was an easy target."

Then he shared what I think has become a closing argument for many in the agricultural community.

"Soil health has become a central organizing theme for a lot of people in the farming community. It has drawn people out to share their experiences and learn from each other. Dan is a real standout in the region, and a lot of people are paying attention to what he is doing, but he isn't the only one. Dan openly shares just about everything he learns. The fact that he is achieving such soil-conservation gains, improving yields, and improving his bottom line at the same time has people's attention."

I asked Jim about a remark he and Dan had made earlier in the day about breaking farmers' reliance on chemicals and seed from large agribusiness companies.

"A lot of people, including me, would like to see farmers regain some independence. The fertilizer- and farm-input community has written almost all the present recipes for nutrients and pest controls they market for growing a crop. I believe all these soil-health innovations can and will help growers get further down that road [to independence]."

This reflects a common refrain within farmer circles. Seeds, synthetic fertilizers, and farm chemicals are essentially locked into expensive package prescriptions that make up the majority of a farmer's financial budget. Improving soil health can unlock the ecosystem's potential to do more, without expensive soil amendments.

Can these carbon-friendly farming practices be taken to scale? Dan's example may be at the pinnacle in this particular farming innovation, yet he is one of thousands of farmers learning to grow high-yield corn and soybean crops with less fertilizer and less reliance on farm chemicals, on millions of acres throughout the world.

After visiting Dan's farm, I traveled to Washington County, Iowa, which has some of the highest proportions of farms under regenerative agriculture practices in the country. NRCS soil conservationists Tony Maxwell and Tanya Dideriksen spent a day introducing me to innovative growers they knew. All of them had been growing corn and soybeans with cover crops and without tilling soil for at least five years, some for far longer. All reported they'd reduced their fertilizer and farm chemicals applied by at least half, some even more. And without exception, all of them led with the story that their soil organic matter had increased markedly, plus they were making more money than before.

That final point—making more money—seems likely to sell this particular version of carbon farming more than any other factor, though supply-chain issues, cost of seed, and the added complexity of adding cover crops into a cropping system remain barriers to some growers.[179]

What does this mean across the country? Within the next decade or two, an airline flight over the Corn Belt in early spring, before planting season, could yield a far different scene from the one today. Rather than the patchwork of eroding, carbon-losing, tilled brown fields showing soil laid bare, we would see the same fields quilted in various shades of green where cover crops held and fed the soil. Rather than the occasional patch of green cover crops we see today, the rare patch of dark brown where a farmer had tilled his or her field would be the exception. And if we could examine this earth in profile and see the carbon and nitrogen moving between earth and sky, we'd see a dramatic and noticeable flux of carbon downward into the soil, rather than upward, contributing to a cooler, more stable climate.

Steve's Peaches

To awaken in an orchard on a Rocky Mountain spring morning is a singular pleasure, even after just a few hours of sleep. Such vital experiences have a way of marking us, and though that emotional tattoo is still with me some years later, it never occurred to me at the time that future opportunities like that might someday vanish, and more importantly, that the glorious fruit from the orchard around me, and the carbon the orchard held, might one day disappear.

I'd arrived at Ela Family Farms the night before in a caravan with about thirty others, sated and sleepy after lingering at a local farm-to-table restaurant long after a sumptuous dinner. We donned headlamps and laid out tents and sleeping bags under the orchard's canopy. Now it was early morning, and the light slowly came into focus. Shadows of leaves dappled the tent's translucent nylon walls, which expanded and contracted like the abdomen of a gently breathing beast. A rooster crowed, and other sleepers

Previous spread: Peach galette. *Cavan Images*

around me began to murmur. I crept out of the tent, dressed, and walked among the trees.

Robins and house finches flitted on determined yet seemingly spastic routes through the branches. Warblers enthusiastically attacked unseen but apparently delicious insects. A flicker hammered up breakfast nearby. *How come that doesn't hurt?* I wondered for the ten-thousandth time, imagining the bird's head pounding the wood like an avian jackhammer. Honeybees flew by on their way to some choice nectar cup. A bumblebee bounced noisily through the cover crop before disappearing into its nest in the soil. The scent of moist earth and bark permeated everything. The orchard was soaked in carbon—in the trees and leaves, in the cover crops, in the roots, deep in the soil, carbon vectored on a pathway straight from the atmosphere into the ecosystem. And amidst it all, tiny fruits hung from the branches, summer's promise holding forth. It was about as fine a start to a day as I could imagine.

Running through my mind during this morning walk was the realization that no orchard lasted forever. What would be the fate of all that carbon the trees had fixed into their trunks, limbs, and roots after the trees stopped producing fruit, or after a storm or severe cold killed the trees? I didn't know it at the time, but over the next several seasons, I would learn through visits, conversations, and personal experience the risks that the rapidly changing climate posed for the future of fruit growers like the Elas, and the role the carbon in the trees could play in moving us into a future with a stable climate.

> • <

Steve Ela, his wife, Regan Choi, his family, and their employees grow fifty-five varieties of organic peaches, apples, pears, plums, cherries, and apricots on 180 acres of high-elevation soil in the valley of the North Fork of the Gunnison River, near Hotchkiss, Colorado. "Home of the 'Oh My God' Peach," proclaim the signs and brochures. Wine lovers call it *terroir*. Steve Ela calls it the North Fork Valley. The scientist in me wants to just call it healthy soil. Whatever we call it, the peaches are outrageously good.

It is my considered opinion that a great peach, eaten fresh at the peak of flavor and condition, ranks as a culinary experience equal to a great bottle of wine, a fresh Dungeness crab, or a spring salad plucked from a garden just minutes before. I'd met Steve and his son the previous summer in Fort Collins when we had struck up a conversation at their booth at the Saturday morning Fort Collins Farmers Market. It was early in the season, and baskets of fine yellow apricots and perfect, intensely flavored cherries flowed steadily into the hands of buyers. Steve, who stands almost a head above his workers and most shoppers (including me), is the image of a perpetual-motion machine. I bought a passel of their fruit, introduced myself, and launched into a conversation, ignoring my worries about distracting him from the business at hand.

Orchard farming methods were at the center of a new project in our research lab at Colorado State University, and we were looking for farmers to instruct us on their methods. Steve chaired the board of the Organic Farming Research Foundation, a national organization focused on advancing organic farming methods through scientific research. I asked him if we could chat for a few minutes. We found a shady spot near the booth and snacked on cherries, his young son holding his hand at his side, while I described our work. I worried aloud at how busy he must be, to take the time to talk with me.

"I was ready for a break," he reassured me. At the end of my pitch, he immediately agreed to get involved.

"I love working in science. I'll come see you after the holidays," he said with a grin that I have since learned seems to always occupy his face. "I've got a lot going on until then." Then he launched himself back into the market fray.

One snowy February morning, Steve dropped by the university to talk with our research group for "an hour or so," and generously ended up staying most of the day. Snow fell outside the windows all day long while we talked over coffee and donuts, then a late lunch, and then afternoon snacks, as Steve walked us through the farm's calendar year. The conference room's whiteboard filled with multi-colored diagrams of soil profiles, pear trees, root hair cross sections, chemical formulas. It was an almost perfect day for our team—the opportunity to learn from a dedicated, informed practitioner. Among the day's many lessons, one in particular from Steve stood out. "I think farming is all about building healthy soil," he said. We ended the day understanding that two themes—infectious enthusiasm and healthy soil—are Steve's trademarks.

Despite the delightful exchange throughout the day, a rumbling, worried thread resurfaced at intervals in the conversation—how would climate change affect operations like the Ela family's orchards? We couldn't say at the time. But I was determined to see the family's operation on the ground. After his visit, I signed up for their farm-to-table tour of the North Fork Valley, which is how I found myself waking up in the orchard that fine spring morning. And during the tour and conversations that followed, I learned how the Ela family was able to grow fruit with the lowest carbon footprint I had seen anywhere

After breakfast about fifty people gathered near the orchard's fruit-packing shed. A diversity of shoes described the group— Chaco sandals, muddy boots, lawyer's oxfords, loafers. For the next three hours, Steve described a typical farming year as he walked us first through the buildings, then through the leafy blocks of trees. We learned that winter pruning and equipment repairs keep the farm crew occupied through the cold months. The critical, and sometimes frenetic, task of protecting spring-time blossoms from frost typically cranks up in April, followed by a whirlwind of summer tasks: irrigation, dealing with pests, seeding, mowing cover crops, and spreading compost and organic fertilizer all leads up to the chaotic picking, packing, and process-ing season. The harvest begins with cherries and apricots in July, continues into the peach and plum season in August, and ends in October with pears and apples. In November the crew collapses with their families to take a few weeks off.

"I sleep for a while. Then I spend the winter skiing." Steve's grin brought a barrage of laughter from the crowd.

"Don't believe him!" shouted a friendly neighbor standing nearby.

I complain occasionally about the grant-writing treadmill of a scientist's life, the withering barrage of conferences, meetings, workshops, and the constant, but necessary, dialogue with colleagues. But I became exhausted just hearing about an orchardist's workload. My own little micro-orchard and garden pale in comparison to the life of somebody making an actual living from growing food for others. My desk and office suddenly seemed quite comfortable in comparison.

Unlike most orchards and vineyards in the region, the soil surface under the Elas' orchards was lush with cover crops. Most orchardists drag a tillage implement called a disk through their orchard several times each year to kill weeds and direct all their irrigation water and fertilizer to the trees. On the Elas' farm, they don't till the soil at all, other than to run a rotary rake close to the tree trunks to keep down the vegetative growth there.

The cover crops include a mix of annual and perennial grasses and forbs, some of them legumes, to keep nutrients in the soil, build organic matter, and fix nitrogen from the air so Steve doesn't have to fertilize as much. Legumes, such as clover, form a symbiotic bond with bacteria in the soil to capture nitrogen from the atmosphere and convert it to a form that plants can use. Nitrogen is a critical nutrient essential for plants to build proteins.

"We want most of the nutrients to be available to the trees early to mid-season, then taper off as we get close to harvest," Steve explained. "The fruit quality is best that way. It's tricky getting the nutrients to the trees with cover crops since most of the [cover crop] plant growth is in the middle and late season. So, we mow the cover crops often in the spring and early summer to release the nutrients and let the microbes decompose them into the soil for the trees to use."

Steve supplements what the cover crops add with organic fertilizer applications based on chicken manure.

Summer rainfall in the Rocky Mountains can be unpredictable, therefore most orchards rely on irrigation water. Running down each line of trees in the family's orchards are irrigation lines dotted with tiny micro-emitters that efficiently ration water to each tree. Steve plunged into that topic with gusto.

"We get our irrigation water off Grand Mesa, to the north. The water is generally available, but in dry years we don't always have as much as we'd like to have. Improving the soil helps the trees be more resilient during a drought. The missing part of the picture with cover crops is that a lot of growers don't realize they are the best way to build organic matter in the soil. You get better water infiltration and better water storage in soil that is not tilled." Extensive research validates Steve's observations.[180]

Steve ended the tour at one of the wind machines as we were starting to think about lunch. Scattered throughout the orchards are a series of forty-foot-tall tubular towers fitted at the top with what look like aircraft propellers. Steve opened a control panel and fiddled with some electronics until a propane-fired engine coughed, sputtered, and then roared. The blades topping the tower began to spin rapidly, producing a chaotic wind all around us.

"These wind machines save our bacon every spring," Steve shouted over the engine's roar. After a minute, he shut off the engine, and the propeller spun to a halt. A relieved silence settled on the crowd for a moment after the engine's deafening roar.

Steve continued, "Whenever a frost threatens the blossoms, we run these wind machines to mix warmer air aloft with cold air at

A peach orchard with a wind machine. Wind machines circulate warmer air into the orchard canopy when frost threatens a crop, a practice increasingly needed as the Earth's climate heats. Ela Family Farms, Hotchkiss, Colorado. *Regan Choi*

the surface. They raise the temperature and keep the air moving so the frost doesn't form."

Somebody asked him how often he ran the wind machines.

"Some years we just run them once or twice. Usually, though, we run them three to five times each year, sometime during early-morning hours on a few frosty days."

After a round of enthusiastic applause for our tour and guide, we all headed back to a picnic lunch of fried chicken and potato salad at the packing shed, where the Ela kids sold cases of the farm's pear jam, peach preserves, and applesauce. It felt like being at the county fair. We loaded up with cases of the Elas' goodies, hugged Steve and his family and the new friends we'd made, and began the drive through the mountains back to Fort Collins.

> • <

During the tour I'd noticed gaps and stumps in the orchard rows, where individual trees had been removed. One stretch of orchard was entirely new (or renewed, in orchardist parlance), with whiplike saplings planted into laser-straight rows. *What happened to the wood in the trees that had been removed?* I had wondered. Piles of wood chips and rows of wood-chip mulch in places partially answered the question, but I was pretty sure that didn't tell the entire story. I asked Steve what had happened to the wood.

"If the trees aren't diseased, we chip them into mulch or sell them to our neighbors for firewood. We sell any diseased wood for firewood." Leaving wood chips from diseased trees could risk spreading the disease to other parts of the orchard.

Cycling the wood waste through the local energy economy clearly made sense, but it was actually rare. Steve's answer was a refreshing change from a scene I'd witnessed the previous winter during a farm tour in California. I was visiting ranchers and farmers to learn about carbon-farming methods, and during a tour, I had driven through a choking plume of smoke coming from an almond orchard that was being renewed. Acres upon acres of trees had been bulldozed and packed into piles along the orchard edge. Thousands of tons burned in blazing bonfires. I imagined the scorched soil underneath each of the piles and all the carbon in the smoke. I asked my colleague Dr. Kerri Steenwerth about the practice. Kerri is a research soil scientist with the USDA Agricultural Research Service (ARS) in Davis, California, and has worked most of her career studying the ecology of vineyard and orchard systems.

"It used to be a lot more common, but permits to burn are getting harder and harder to get these days because of air quality problems," she responded. "More and more people are chipping them for mulch, or leaving them to pile up, or shipping them to electricity plants that burn the wood to create electricity."

We wondered aloud about the climate consequences of burning the wood (what the scientific community calls biomass) in open bonfires, compared with chipping it for mulch or composting, or burning it for energy. I was surprised at what the research shows.

In California, less and less of the wood from renewed or pruned orchards is used to produce energy every year. Dozens of small electricity plants that burned biomass were scattered around the state but have been shutting down over time as the less-costly fossil fuel natural gas takes over as the fuel of choice. Nationwide, less than 5 percent of US energy came from biomass in 2016, the most recent year for which data appeared to be available.[181] Much of that energy came from the leftover by-products of plantation forests after trees were harvested for paper or lumber.

Controversial questions have emerged from the research into bioenergy—can it truly be renewable? And if we can call it renewable, how do we decide when it is, and when it isn't?

The issue revolves around a key fact: Burning biomass produces greenhouse gases from the carbon and nitrogen in the wood. The majority is carbon dioxide, with a small proportion from the products of incomplete combustion, including the powerful greenhouse gases nitrous oxide and methane, and lesser amounts of carbon monoxide. When farmers grow and harvest bioenergy crops in brief cycles, say one to three years, or when leftover by-products from human food production, as in the case of the Ela family orchards, go to produce energy, the case for the energy being labeled renewable is good. The practices do not sacrifice long-lived ecosystem carbon stored in trees or soils for the sake of electricity or heat for human endeavors.

There are, however, important caveats. One is that taking up cropland to produce a bioenergy crop in today's world could very well cause a food-supply gap elsewhere. Filling that food-supply gap means one of two things: doubling down on fields elsewhere—intensifying crop production on existing fields to grow more food—or clearing forestland or grassland elsewhere to create more cropland acres to grow food crops, or worse, to grow more bioenergy crops. The carbon lost from cleared forests adds more dangerous heat-trapping gases to the atmosphere. Many unfortunate examples have sprung up around the world. This very real problem deserves critical attention.[182]

Consider the relatively short cycle of most orchards and vineyards. The Ela family orchards grow on land that has been farmed for more than a century. The stone fruit orchards (peaches, apricots, cherries, plums) are renewed approximately every fifteen to twenty years, and the pome fruit orchards (apples, pears) are renewed approximately every twenty-five to thirty years. Because a few acres are renewed every year, a relatively continuous supply of wood comes off the operation, carbon that is not of fossil origin. The amount of carbon in the pinyon pine and juniper woodland that grew on the land before is very close to the same amount as in a mature fruit orchard, and the Ela family's soil management has led to higher soil-carbon stocks than the land likely held before. In effect, the carbon pool on the land has not diminished with the orchard.

How much energy can an orchard realistically generate? A typical western Colorado orchard might hold about twenty-five tons of dry wood per acre. An almond or walnut orchard in California might hold twice that amount. The trees had spent the previous twenty-five years cranking out fruit, and accumulating biomass in their trunks, roots, and branches at a rate of about a ton or two of wood per acre, per year. Burning that wood straight into the atmosphere after the orchard was renewed was a waste of the work and potential energy those trees had accumulated for more than two decades. But utilizing that carbon to replace fossil carbon eliminates the need to dig fossil carbon out of the ground for that purpose.

Heaped trees of an apple orchard before they are burned in the open. This orchard's biomass could instead be used to create compost or heat homes in the winter. *Leonid Eremeychuk / Alamy*

When cut into firewood, a single acre of wood in the Ela family orchards would fill about 350 wheelbarrows, enough to heat about three homes in the North Fork Valley if they were heated solely with wood. Heating homes with that wood means fossil carbon from gas, heating oil, or coal isn't required to be burned directly in furnaces or in electrical plants to create the electricity required. Using the wood to heat buildings avoids fossil fuel emissions in a very real way, from a locally renewable resource. It is a powerful option to put carbon in the trees to work reducing greenhouse gas emissions in rural areas where wood smoke doesn't create an air quality problem for the region's residents.

The carbon that a tree holds in its wood is valuable for all kinds of uses—building materials, fibers for clothing, paper, as fuel to heat homes and buildings, or as I learned from a colleague, as a bulking agent for making compost. Later in that visit to California with Kerri Steenwerth, I'd asked Lynette Niebrugge from the Marin Resource Conservation District (RCD) about a composting operation I'd seen in northern Marin County. Long lines of compost extended behind the barns of a dairy that milked several hundred cows. It struck me as odd. Dairy manure can be very difficult to compost. Among a class of material that tends to be very sloppy and wet—manure—dairy manure tends to be about as sloppy and wet as it gets. Composting it safely without creating a water quality-runoff problem is tricky. How did they do it?

"Wood chips from the local orchards and wineries," was the answer.

The Marin RCD had connected local vineyard and orchard operators who had an excess-wood problem with local dairies, who had a wet-manure problem, and out of it had come a new business: the West Marin Compost company. The wood chips absorb the moisture in the manure, resulting in a base raw material that composts relatively easily. The operation produces thousands of tons of compost each year for farmers, ranchers, and gardeners to use to improve their soils and sequester carbon. This book's chapter on composting waste, "The Feast of the Legions," discusses the greenhouse gas benefits from composting. To summarize here, a portion of the wood's carbon is likely sequestered in the soil after it is applied as compost. Diverting that wet, sloppy manure out of storage lagoons and into piles of compost avoids the methane emissions from the lagoons, discussed in this book's chapter on milk, "Cecil's Hands." Applying the compost to fields and pastures replaces the nutrients in chemical fertilizers, also avoiding the emissions from manufacturing those products. The wood chips make that possible.

> • <

Our research team at CSU was curious about the carbon footprint of the Ela family's fruit orchard, and so we entered the characteristics of their operation into a tool named COMET-Farm, a web-based decision support system our team developed to examine how a farmer's practices affect the carbon footprint of their crops.[183] The tool predicts the total system greenhouse gas emissions and subtracts from that the carbon pulled from the atmosphere via photosynthesis and stored in soils as organic matter and in trees. The tool predicted soil organic matter concentration (3.5 percent in the top layers) close to the measurements from the Elas' farm.

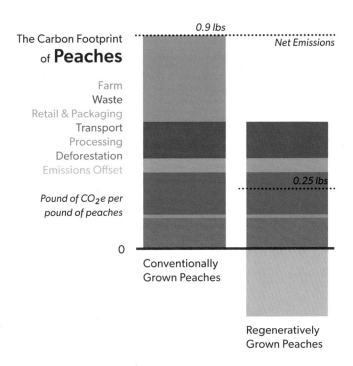

The Carbon Footprint
of **Peaches**

Farm
Waste
Retail & Packaging
Transport
Processing
Deforestation
Emissions Offset

*Pound of CO$_2$e per
pound of peaches*

0.9 lbs

Net Emissions

0.25 lbs

0

Conventionally
Grown Peaches

Regeneratively
Grown Peaches

Wood in fruit trees can be leveraged to reduce fruit's carbon footprint when orchards are renewed. "Farm" is emissions from soil, fertilizer, burning fuel in equipment, and emissions from manufacturing equipment and buildings. "Waste" assumes 40 percent of products are eventually landfilled and become landfill methane CO$_2$e. "Retail and Packaging" includes making containers for products on retail shelves, equipment, fuel, and energy use in retail establishments. "Transport" includes shipping fruit to wholesalers, processors, and retailers. "Processing" refers to manufacturing fruit into shelf-stable food products. "Deforestation" is emissions from clearing forests/ grasslands to grow the fruit. "Emissions Offset" is avoided emissions from utilizing old trees for heating homes or as a bulking agent to compost liquid manure from dairies.

We compared that against a hypothetical scenario of farming the orchard conventionally, tilling the soil through the growing season and using conventional fertilizers, and burning the wood from the renewed orchards in the open. The soil organic matter the tool estimated plunged to less than half that in the Elas' orchard, and other greenhouse gas emissions rose dramatically. When added together, Steve's peaches were almost "carbon neutral," meaning that the carbon stored in the trees and the soil counterbalanced most of the other emissions from the farm. Steve's peaches had a net greenhouse gas balance of less than a twentieth of a pound of CO_2e per pound of fruit. The industry average, according to multiple studies, is about half a pound to a pound of emissions per pound of fresh fruit. Through carbon farming, the Ela family had nearly erased the climate impact of their fruit.

Selling the orchard's wood for firewood contributed about a sixth of their greenhouse gas advantage, as described earlier in this chapter. A relatively small portion of the wood left in root stumps isn't recoverable as firewood, and cannot be safely chipped into mulch, and is the only wood burned in the open. But what about the rest of the carbon footprint advantage the Ela family's farming system offers?

Their orchard holds two to four times the amount of organic matter in their soils as do conventionally farmed orchards. The top foot of a single acre of their soils holds as much extra carbon as would be burned in a single year in about twenty-one American, gasoline-burning automobiles. Growing the crops without tilling soil steadily builds up organic matter. Their cover crops also dramatically increase soil organic matter. This buildup of carbon in the soil, called carbon sequestration, accounts for about two-thirds of the greenhouse gas advantage they have over their peers.

It is important to note here that soil carbon does not increase forever. Soil carbon would reach its highest levels in the first thirty years of Steve's system, then would hold relatively steady. His soil carbon advantage is amortized into the future, assuming the orchard will be managed in future decades like it is now.

How different is that amount compared to the soils if they were still under native vegetation? Soil maps indicate the soils likely held about 1 percent organic matter before the land was converted to an orchard. Irrigation combined with the use of cover crops and compost and manure additions raises the carbon inputs into the soil and therefore its soil organic matter.

Their cover crops and periodic compost applications allow them to apply about a third to half of the fertilizer required by conventional growers. That leads to lower nitrous oxide emissions. Fertilizer made from poultry manure avoids much of the carbon emissions that occur during the energy-intensive manufacturing of chemical fertilizer. This is about one-sixth of the advantage.

The final part of the story comes from how they sell their crop. Once each week during harvest season, and then periodically at winter farmers markets, they pack up to a twenty-ton load in a diesel truck and deliver it to the Front Range, about three hundred miles away. Most produce travels a thousand miles or more before it reaches grocers' shelves. The emissions from those avoided miles add up.

By not tilling the soil, using nitrogen-fixing cover crops, fertil-izing with livestock manure, mulching or selling for firewood the wood from trees they periodically remove, and selling their pro-duce locally, the Elas' carbon-farming techniques have far fewer emissions compared to most other fruit. And the taste of their produce? Well, it causes people to wake up at unreasonable hours and stand in long lines at farmers markets on Colorado's Front Range to make sure they don't miss out.

But potentially missing out on this fruit in the future is a major problem that should concern us all, if the Ela family's experiences with the weather are any indication.

> • <

Steve and I have remained in regular contact since we first met. We see each other in the Fort Collins Farmers Market every sum-mer, and we communicate through email about new research findings. One autumn I phoned to let him know my new partner, Leslie, and I were going to be passing through during an upcoming weekend. "Might we stop by?" I asked. "Please do!" he responded. So, on an almost freakishly balmy November afternoon, we pulled into his driveway. Steve met us outside his lovely stone home, gave us bear hugs, and asked how the snowpack looked up at the pass.

"Thin and bony," Leslie replied.

It was less than half the average depth for that time of year. Steve shook his head and led us inside, where we caught up over steaming mugs of tea. Then he launched into an animated diatribe about the climate.

Steve Ela tends to the orchards. North Fork Valley, Hotchkiss, Colorado. *Regan Choi*

"Our weather the past several years has been so weird! I had to run my wind machines more than twenty times two years ago! I had trees blooming a month early, in March! That's never happened before! We somehow managed to get through the spring—I don't know how—and then it was so warm, and the season was so long that we had a bumper crop."

The growing season had extended by about forty-five days relative to the typical year. It was unheard of.

"One might think—great! Global warming gives us bumper crops! But this year, a similar thing happened, and we got almost no fruit at all. A dry, warm March fooled a lot of the trees into blooming early, but then it started raining in April and we had alternate rain and snow squalls into June. I'd never seen conditions like this before. It killed most of the fruit. We got less than 20 percent of the usual harvest."

We stared at our mugs for a while in silence.

"It's ironic, isn't it?" he observed.

Ironic, indeed, that a hotter climate can lead to frost-damaged crops. Economically, it had been a rough year for the Ela family and their neighbors. Few had income enough to balance their farm's costs. The business of farming aside, watch the Ela family and their workers at a farmers market, or other growers like them, and one sees how their relationship with their customers drives them to grow great produce. It hurt in many ways when they couldn't do this. Their fruit may have one of the best emissions profiles of any fruit grower in North America, yet their operation is on the front line of risk due to climate change.

What does the climate crisis hold for farmers' futures? A group of the nation's top meteorologists and climate scientists meet regularly to assess recent weather and the future of the US climate. In Colorado, the forecast calls for steadily rising temperatures and winter snowfall shifting to rain, yet with no overall change in precipitation. The larger story, though, is likely to be in the peaks and valleys of the weather systems. Snow and rain will likely come harder, faster, and in a greater quantity when it falls. Longer dry periods will prevail between somewhat fewer, more intense storms. The wets will be wetter, the dries drier, the hots hotter, and the cold, while not necessarily colder, will come at inopportune times for growers like the Ela family.

Steve is always innovating, and so I asked if we could see some of his latest work. He walked us into an orchard block where he is experimenting with buried drip-irrigation lines and a new cover crop mix.

"See how few weeds we have where we buried the irrigation lines? I'm irrigating the crop from below," he said. "The diverse cover crops I planted over the buried irrigation lines are doing great, and almost none of the weeds are competing here. Look over here where we irrigated on the surface!"

The ground there was covered with a brown mass of cheatgrass, an invasive weed from Eurasia that has an effect on ecosystems that matches its name. There was little of the desirable clover and other legumes he'd planted. Then I noticed something surprising. None of the season's orchard litter—fruit pits, broken branches, prunings from the previous spring—were present.

"Why aren't there any pruned branches lying around?" I asked.

"They decompose into the soil in just a few weeks," he said, with obvious satisfaction.

Fast decomposition is a clear sign of healthy soil, a diverse population of microbes, insects, and worms going to work as soon as a food source—wood—comes into contact with the soil. Steve had carried a spade into the orchard, and we dug up a shovelful. Insects scattered through the litter as he turned the earth over. Worm tunnels plied the humus-rich loam. The fine white hairs of roots and beneficial mycorrhizal fungi shot through all of it. There were millions of microbes in that little piece of earth, all focused on leveraging a few ounces of carbon, nitrogen, and myriad other nutrients. Tiny ecosystem fragments like these, knitted together across the vast globe, have made the difference between civilization's disaster and prosperity since human agriculture took off nearly ten thousand years ago.

I think of this whenever I tour orchards managed without carbon-farming methods. The dusty bare soil tilled every week or so, the ground alternately rock-solid in one stretch and like a sand dune in others, the near absence of insects and birds. Such places have a barren, almost angry feel to them. In carbon-farming systems the focus is on healthy soil, and as research is beginning to show, the produce from those orchards is higher-quality and usually higher-yielding.

We wandered back to the car. Leslie asked if we could buy some of their pear jam.

"I've only got three cases left. I'm sorry I don't have any more!" He gazed solemnly at the grizzled, old pear trees across the driveway. I felt an involuntary shudder at the loss in revenues and the impact on his bottom line.

Leslie gave a little cry. "No, we're sorry for you!" She then asked him what was up for him the rest of the month.

"I'm off to an organic farming research foundation meeting. Then back home to sleep until Thanksgiving," he said with the perennial Steve Ela grin.

We exchanged goodbye hugs, wished him well, and drove back to the highway toward McClure Pass. The sun sparkled brilliantly off the river that, decades previously, by this time of year would have been burbling through narrow channels of ice, the riverbanks lined with snow. It was early November in the Colorado Rockies, and near the 8,755-foot pass, channels of snowmelt cut through the dark soil of the aspen-studded meadows. We pulled over, stepped out of the car, and stood in silence. To the east, absurd November rain showers obscured our route home over the Continental Divide. To the west, storm clouds piled up in the distance, streaming our way. I suddenly felt like I was part of a company of sentries stationed on the walls of a great, imagined city. Vast and dangerous forces massed at the gate below, and yet nobody listened to our trumpet's warning call.

The Cow in the Room

Society and science are meeting on the playing field of meat, in a debate rivaling some of the greatest science and culture debates in history. No other food item seems to intersect the climate crisis more than meat. Raising meat—and especially meat from cattle, sheep, and goats—creates more emissions by a factor of between ten and fifty than any other food source except shrimp farmed in clear-cut mangrove forests.

Pitched battles rage throughout the culture wars, creating a confusing space where almost anybody can find evidence to support their positions. People feel their livelihoods are threatened. Accusations fly. Motives are questioned.

Questions abound. Is grass-fed meat better for the climate? Can livestock be fed seaweed to reduce their emissions? Should the world give up eating meat altogether?

Previous spread: Grilled striploin steak with arugula salad.
Natalia Lisovskaya / The Picture Pantry

In trying to answer these questions, the scientific community has discovered far more nuance in the story than in almost any other food item. Whereas evidence shows the emissions from producing meat are significant, dealing with the issue does not appear to be as simple as just giving up eating meat.

> • <

How many experiences can we count in our lives where food has defined us and our relationship to place, to family, to loved ones and companions? The most significant moments of life are often marked by food. We meet over meals to talk through difficult relationship issues. Co-workers gather over coffee to solve problems. We gather over food and drinks to propose marriage, to seal business deals, and to mourn losses. We remember the meals at those occasions, and how the food helped us to feel in those moments. And for me, and perhaps for you, the food flavors the emotion.

And perhaps more than any other class of food in America, a dish made with meat is usually at the center of these experiences.

At their core, the foods defined by place and time are cultural and psychological recipes. The tastes these recipes convey can be like a deep time transport straight back to the ancestors from whom many of the recipes originated. The prospect of changing these foods we love—even giving some of them up due to a doctor's prescription—threatens many of us. I know it does me.

Just as doctors prescribe food to treat life-threatening illnesses, ecologists are offering a food prescription to help us to treat the planet's ills. I wonder if there may be more dismay around food, particularly meat, than any of the changes that the climate crisis demands of us.

To better understand our cultural connection to food, and to meat in particular, I proposed a gathering at my home. The year prior I'd traveled to Italy for an extended workshop and stayed on to visit Florence, where I'd enjoyed a meal unlike any I'd ever had. Bistecca is a beacon amongst the many famous lights of Tuscan cuisine. It is a dry-aged steak cut from white Chianina cattle, a heritage breed from Tuscany. Like ribollita, castagnaccio, Chianti, and other mouthwatering dishes and drinks, a meal of bistecca alla fiorentina fuses the experience into a window through which one can view the soul of Tuscan culture. But I'd had the meal alone in a restaurant and felt like I'd missed out on the best part of the experience. I wanted to try to re-create the meal with colleagues and see if it changed how I viewed it. And I wanted to talk with them about meat.

I ordered a dry-aged porterhouse steak from a local butcher, and consulted with my colleague Dr. Shawn Archibeque, an animal scientist whom I trust as an expert on beef, on how to cook it. "Grill it rare, over a hot fire, but not too hot, and salt it lightly just before it comes to the table," he told me. Leslie bought a good bottle of Chianti and some fresh raspberries and gelato for dessert, and we baked a rustic loaf of Tuscan bread. We grilled wild sockeye salmon steaks for anybody who wanted a little surf with their turf. My colleague Amy brought a delicious green salad made from her CSA farm share. Our author friend Laura brought a second, excellent bottle of Chianti. My colleague Francesca, who is from Naples, brought fresh tomatoes, basil, and mozzarella di bufala for a caprese salad. We filled our glasses and sat down to eat.

After savoring the caprese salad, and then Amy's green salad, we opened the second bottle of wine as the sizzling meat and fish came off the grill. "This is excellent," said Amy after the first bite, and the table murmured agreement. I compared it to the steak I'd had in Florence—my American bistecca was less firm on the bite, with far more fat and less of the umami quality than the bistecca alla fiorentina, but it was very good nonetheless. We ate, and we talked, and we drank more wine, and then I asked a question I'd prepared.

"Do you think we can eat less meat to help solve the climate crisis?"

There was a long and thoughtful pause. I was partway through the most delicious beef steak I'd eaten since I was in Florence, and a stunning meal under any circumstances, and despite my forethought about the meal, I realized I was confronted with a major piece of the planet's ills, our attachment to a food we could no longer afford to eat in such abundance, for our future's sake. My meal companions were understandably annoyed with me for bringing it up. These were four of the most thoughtful people I knew, but I also knew I could count on them to be honest. I hadn't meant to set a trap. Suddenly I realized I had.

And in that moment, I wondered if that is how so many other people feel when they are enjoying a hamburger, a steak, or a lamb chop, but are confronted with the news that for personal and planetary reasons, they shouldn't eat so much of it.

Could we eat less beef and lamb to help solve the climate crisis? Amy, who had grown up on a ranch raising sheep and cattle, looked down at her plate, and summed it up beautifully.

"It is going to be hard," she said. "But I think it is going to be necessary."

> • ‹

If we rank the emissions from producing meat, the evidence shows that beef, lamb, and goat top the list. Poultry has the lowest emissions, and pork falls in the middle.

The most comprehensive study about the carbon footprint of beef from a US facility to date indicates the emissions add up to about forty-eight pounds of CO_2e for every pound of beef served on the plate. This includes the emissions from raising a beef animal, finishing it, transporting, slaughtering, processing, and shipping the meat to market, cooking it, and dealing with the leftovers.[184] Deforestation and plowing grasslands to create pasture and grow crops contributes, on average, an additional sixteen pounds of CO_2e to the climate burden of beef.

Conventional pork carries a smaller burden due to pigs' different anatomy. Unlike cattle, sheep, and goats, pigs do not have a rumen, and it takes far less feed to produce a pound of pig flesh than cattle require, though they do emit a small amount of methane as they grow. Methane from storing manure in lagoons contributes significantly to pork's carbon footprint, just like with dairy (as explained in the chapter "Cecil's Hands"). A pound of pork carries a burden of about eight to twelve pounds of CO_2e.

Poultry converts feed to meat and eggs the most efficiently of any land animals that we eat, and conventional chicken, turkey, and other poultry carries the smallest CO_2e burden, at about five and a half to seven and a half pounds per pound of meat. Eggs carry the lowest of any land-based animal product, at about two and a half to four pounds of CO_2e per pound of fresh egg.[185,186]

How does that compare to other foods? Beef carries about twenty-five to one hundred times more emissions on a pound-for-pound basis than a conventionally grown peach, cooked garbanzo beans, a lettuce salad, or a baked potato. It's an extraordinary comparison. To try to understand it myself, I set out to learn about the life of a beef animal.

> • <

Driving across the springtime landscape of the North American Great Plains, or the vast Basin and Range landscape of the Intermountain West, a familiar scene unfolds. Wherever there are green pastures or rangeland, tumble-legged beef-breed calves, just recently born, wobble and bob next to their mothers. Once born, the calves spend their days much like human babies—alternately sleeping, eating, pooping, and bouncing around the confines of their world as they test their muscles and brains. These spring calves, born primarily in the Great Plains and the Mountain West, but also in America's other pasturelands, make up the base of the North American beef industry.[187,188]

Their mothers, who had been born themselves anywhere from two to nine years before, would have been bred by a herd bull or artificially inseminated eight months earlier. Those cows live their lives grazing on rangeland or pasture, or eating hay in the winter months while pregnant. The calves, weighing fifty to seventy-five pounds at birth, spend the next five to seven months nursing and

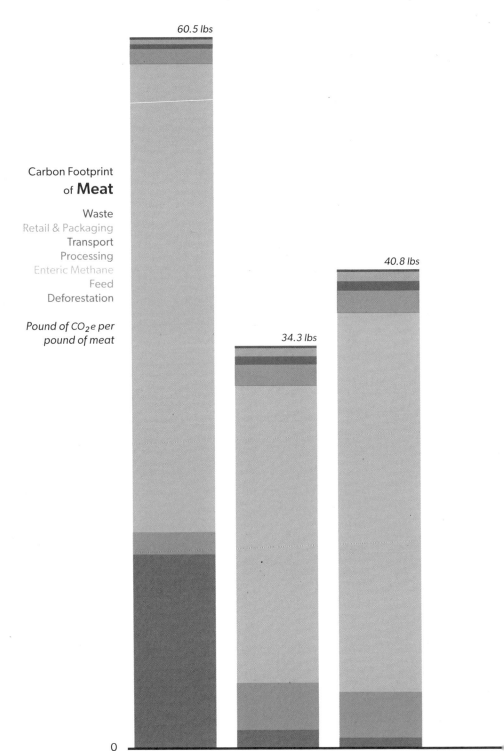

Carbon Footprint
of **Meat**

Waste
Retail & Packaging
Transport
Processing
Enteric Methane
Feed
Deforestation

*Pound of CO₂e per
pound of meat*

60.5 lbs

34.3 lbs

40.8 lbs

Beef: CAFO &
Grass-Fed

Beef: from Dairy
Animals

Lamb & Mutton

learning to eat grass and feed supplements. To be able to eat grass, cattle and other ruminants utilize the symbiotic advantage developed over millions of years of evolution. Their own digestive tract cannot digest the forage directly, but the microbes in their digestive tract can. Those microbes—many of them in the same classes of microbes living in the soil—convert cellulose and other indigestible materials into digestible carbohydrates, fats, and proteins the mother can use. They allow the mother to grow a thick winter

CAFO and grass-fed beef and lamb have the largest footprint because of high enteric methane emissions. Beef from slaughtered dairy animals is somewhat lower because the emissions are split between dairy and beef products. Pork and poultry have little enteric methane emissions and require less feed per unit of meat produced. "Waste" assumes 40 percent of products are landfilled and become landfill methane CO_2e. "Retail and Packaging" includes making containers for products on retail shelves, equipment, fuel, and energy use in retail establishments. "Transport" includes shipping to retailers and food processors. "Processing" is butchering and cooling animal carcasses for retail. "Enteric Methane" is livestock enteric methane and methane and nitrous oxide from manure. "Feed" is emissions to grow and process crops into livestock feed. "Deforestation" includes emissions from forests/grasslands cleared to grow feed for livestock.

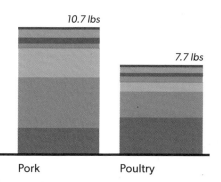

10.7 lbs

7.7 lbs

Pork   Poultry

coat, heat herself through the frigid Great Plains and mountain winters, and grow the calf inside her.

To be precise, it is bacteria, archaea, and fungi in the cow's rumen (her first of five stomachs) that do the heavy lifting for her and every other ruminant animal on the planet. In that dark, warm, wet space, an uncountable community of microbes goes to work on the forage the cow eats. As she grazes, she first cuts, chews, and swallows forage plants into the rumen until it is full, on average about fifty liters of material.

After filling her rumen, the cow rests and "ruminates." Have you ever seen a cow lying down or standing, relaxed, her jaws working in that most cow-like side-by-side grinding action? The cow is chewing her cud. With each wad of cud, she has regurgitated a mouthful of the rumen contents after the microbes have had their way with it. She chews the contents into a sloppy green mash and swallows it back into her reticulum (her second stomach), where it proceeds through the rest of the digestive tract.

We can't see it, but during this process, the cow is regularly belching methane gas from the rumen at a rate that would be the envy of adolescents the world over. Besides the digestible and indigestible by-products of the microbe digestion in the rumen, the microbes, specifically those in an evolutionary branch called the archaea, also produce methane. Humans, pigs, chickens, and other monogastric animals (with just one stomach) mostly produce carbon dioxide as the end waste product from their digestive process and metabolism. Any oxygen that makes it into the cow's rumen, however, is very quickly used up by the microbes. Like animals, microbes require oxygen to completely digest the carbohydrates in the forage down to the waste product carbon dioxide. These microbes can also digest food without oxygen, when oxygen is absent; that digestive pathway ends with the waste product methane, not carbon dioxide. That is what happens in the cow's rumen. It is basically a portable, fifty-liter, anaerobic digester, producing digestible food for the cow, and enough methane from the one cow that, over the course of a year, it could heat an average home in the northern latitudes for a good part of the winter. Scientists have labeled these methane cow belches "enteric methane."

The best prediction models available to us at the time of this writing predict that a cow and calf together (called a cow-calf pair) raised on the Great Plains will produce just shy of half a pound of enteric methane every day, on average, or about 170 pounds of enteric methane per cow-calf pair per year. Bison are believed to produce about the same amount of enteric methane on a pound-per-pound basis as beef cattle if they are fed comparable diets.[189] Sheep and goats produce similar amounts of enteric methane, depending on how they are raised.[190]

It may not sound like much on the face of it, were methane not such a powerful greenhouse gas. That same amount of carbon in grass in the cow's pasture, if left to simply rot and decompose back into the atmosphere at the end of the growing season, would likely decompose into carbon dioxide. Almost no methane would come from the process. Because cows eat it, however, the net effect is to direct a portion of the digested grass to become methane rather than carbon dioxide. When we add it all up, the net increase in the global warming effect is equivalent to adding more than two metric tons (about 2.2 English tons) of CO_2e to the atmosphere each year for every cow-calf pair raised in this example.

About 60 percent of the total emissions over the life of a beef animal raised for slaughter come just from the process of raising the calf to weaning weight (about four hundred to five hundred pounds). After raising, on average, about eight or nine calves over the course of her life, the mother cow is typically slaughtered and the emissions she has produced over her life get attributed to the meat, leather, and other animal products from her carcass.

After weaning, about 10 percent of the calves raised in a given year are kept to become breeding cows and bulls. In the United States, about 95 percent of the remainder gets trucked to be fed to slaughter weight (called "finishing") at a concentrated animal feeding operation (CAFO). The calves eat a diet of concentrated feed, alfalfa hay, and corn or sorghum "silage," all of which carry their own burden of emissions required to grow, process, and deliver the product to the CAFO. Silage, or "ensilage," is corn, sorghum, or other grasses that are harvested green, chopped into small pieces, and fermented in a large pile, then covered and stored in long, tall, linear piles until needed for feeding. The concentrate varies from place to place and year to year, but it can be made up of a cornucopia of different products. Some of the most common ingredients in concentrate include grain corn, ground soybeans, distillers' grains (spent grains left over from fermenting ethanol), and ground canola seeds. Depending on

Hereford bulls feed on silage in a confined feeding operation. More than ninety percent of the beef grown in North America is raised in this manner. *Peggy Greb / USDA*

the region, the concentrate can also contain bakery waste, pulverized almond shells, ground orange peels, avocado pits and skins, and
a host of other agricultural by-products the cattle can digest.

Interestingly enough, the enteric emissions during this time in
the CAFO are actually lower than those from the cow-calf pair living on pasture. The thirty to forty pounds of forage fed daily to the
calves is richer in simple carbohydrates and proteins. It contains
less of the fiber that drives methane production and therefore the
enteric methane emissions are lower. But this dietary transition
carries a new load of emissions into the life of the calf from raising the silage and concentrate, transporting the materials, then
mixing and feeding it to the cattle. The calves get sick if fed too
much of the simple carbohydrates in corn grain or too much protein, like alfalfa hay or soybean meal. Dietary fiber keeps them
healthy. As a result, feeders adjust their mix to get the maximum
weight gain without making the cattle ill.

After 150 to 300 days at the CAFO, the calf reaches a market
weight of about 1,300 pounds. It is slaughtered, and the meat is
cooled, processed, packaged, and shipped to the grocer or restaurant. Greenhouse gas emissions pile up at every step of the way,
in the following manner:

- A little more than half of the emissions come from the cow-
  calf pair. Most of the emissions during this time come from
  enteric methane.

- About one-sixth of the emissions are enteric methane and
  manure emissions while the calf gains weight at the CAFO.

- Another sixth of the emissions come from growing and processing feed and shipping it to the CAFO.

- The final sixth of emissions come from slaughtering, processing, cooling, shipping, cooking the meat, and dealing with the leftovers.

Astonishingly, about a third of the meat is never consumed but goes into landfills, through waste occurring throughout the process from processing to retail to restaurants and home kitchens. This complex combination of emissions makes for a remarkable story, and makes me wonder how it all came about. Examining the operations in a CAFO revealed part of the answer.

› • ‹

Weld County, Colorado, the next county to the east of my home in Fort Collins, has one of the largest agricultural economies in the United States. The town of Greeley, the county seat and once the dream of the utopian entrepreneur and railroad magnate Horace Greeley, sits at the center of more beef cattle than any other US county besides Tulare County, California, near Fresno. The town is constantly saturated with the odor of cattle manure from the hundreds of thousands of cattle raised nearby. But it wasn't always that way.

The first large concentrated animal feeding operations, or CAFOs, came into being in the 1940s, and farmers began growing forage crops to feed the beef and dairy cattle population that rapidly expanded over the ensuing decades. From 1941 to the present day, the number of cattle raised near Greeley quadrupled, and in

2018, more than 590,000 beef cattle were raised in CAFOs, and a smaller number on pasture.[191] Today, more than 95 percent of the meat eaten in the United States—whether it is beef, pork, or poultry—is fattened and finished on a concentrated diet in a CAFO. One of them, Five Rivers Cattle Feeding operation, at four square miles and delivering to slaughter more than a hundred thousand cattle each year, is one of the largest of its kind in the world. At the invitation of the company, I toured the facility one autumn afternoon with a group of colleagues and students from Colorado State University.

As we toured the operation, the cattle moved to a feed trough at one end of their pen as a large truck moved slowly along the trough, piping the feed ration to the herd. The ration, a uniform, custom mix blended for the cattle in that pen, was designed by the company veterinarian to maximize the cattle's growth at their particular size and life stage at that time.

On the south side of the facility, three linear rows of composting manure extended for a third of a mile. A twenty-ton truckload of manure loaded from a pen whose cattle had just gone to slaughter crept slowly down the lane until it disgorged its load onto the end of one of the compost piles. Some distance down the row, a giant piece of equipment approximating an isosceles triangle about twenty feet on a side, with one of the vertices pointing straight up, sat still. When operated, this compost-mixing machine slowly worked its way down the row, mixing water onto the manure and aerating the pile with rotating tines. The manure would be aerated and wetted like this about five times over several months as it sat, while microorganisms decomposed the poop. Semi-tractor loads of the composted manure streamed off the lot in the fall and spring. The vehicles' drivers would spread their loads onto the fields raising the crops that fed the cattle.

Collection lagoons gather runoff from the CAFO paddocks, ranging in color from an unnatural bright red, to an intense green, to a shit brown. Different algae, bacteria, and archaea species dominate the ponds, feasting on the nutrients in the water. The brown ponds are flat expanses layered with a thick slurry of accumulated manure. As we approached one, a semi-tractor towing a trailer supporting a long, oval tank pulled up to a pumping station. It would fill with the nutrient-rich slurry from the pond, then travel to a farm field nearby where the operator would drive the tank across the field, emptying the contents onto the soil to fertilize the crop. These lagoons are a major source of methane, like the manure lagoons discussed in the next chapter, "Cecil's Hands."

Feeding the cattle at Five Rivers requires about a billion pounds of feed[192] and about 265 million gallons of water per year. The net weight of consumable beef products, including meat for human consumption, hide leather, pet food, bone meal, blood meal, and other by-products totals about a hundred million pounds each year. At the time of my visit, the feedlot operators did not maintain statistics on the amount of composted manure and settling pond slurry delivered from the facility. Cattle like those in the facility poop out about fifty-nine pounds of fresh, wet manure each day on average,[193] so besides the beef, a feedlot like this one likely produces about 2.2 billion pounds of fresh manure and a similar amount of urine each year. The CAFO releases air pollutants like

ammonia, particulates, volatile organic compounds, and nitrogen oxides (NOx) as well. An unquantified amount of nitrate, phosphorus, and other pollutants reportedly leak into the waterways and aquifers from CAFOs of this type.[194,195,196,197]

The total process directly emits approximately 340,000 tons of CO_2e per year.[198] Whereas these emissions represent about 15 percent of the total emissions profile from beef, concentrated feeding facilities like Five Rivers are at the center of the entire beef system in North America.

I asked Shawn Archibeque about the incentives to feed beef cattle in CAFOs. Shawn is an internationally known expert on animal nutrition and livestock greenhouse gas emissions, based at the Animal Sciences department at Colorado State University.

"It is all about economic efficiency," he responded. "They are trying to maximize the beef calves' weight gain or dairy cows' milk production while keeping the animal healthy," he added. "Wherever they are located, the growers target an optimum balance of fiber, protein, fats, and carbohydrates."

The Western diet centers on the beef calves raised in modern CAFOs and transformed into hamburgers, hot dogs, steaks, and pot roast. I wanted to learn more about how it actually happens, and Shawn invited me to join him at a CSU research facility to see their herd of fistulated cows.

› • ‹

The Five Rivers Cattle feedlot, one of the largest in the world, holds up to about one hundred thousand cattle. Kersey, Colorado. *Jim West / Alamy*

On a November weekday sometime later, I entered a covered, open-air research facility north of Fort Collins. Dr. Lynne Kesel, a veterinarian, filled buckets with clean, hot water and sanitizing solution while Dr. Terry Engle, another colleague of Shawn's, prepared the data sheets and checked the stanchions that would hold the cattle in place while they were doctored. Shawn gently herded nine black angus calves from a paddock nearby. They all looked like normal cattle, going about their cow lives, but for the rubber caps the size of pie plates fixed to their left side. A cannulated fistula is basically a large port offering an opening from an animal's side into their stomach. A veterinary surgeon anesthetizes the cow and cuts an opening into their side high and behind their last rib. The surgeon opens a corresponding cut into the cow's cavernous first stomach, the rumen, which sits next to the cow's abdominal wall, then fuses the rumen wall to the cow's skin using a sterile implant with a removable, sanitized cover much like a rubber cookie jar lid. Once the animal heals, the fistula makes possible all manner of research into ruminant animal health, digestion, and feeding systems. And methane emissions.

Shawn urged one of the cattle, a black angus steer with a mottled white face, into a stanchion, a large, steel squeeze chute that safely holds animals in place while they are doctored. Terry closed the stanchion and the three of them went to work.

Lynne removed the plug from the gasket on the cow's side and dropped it into a bucket of sanitizing solution. Terry began to scrub the plug clean while Lynne cleaned the gasket in the cow's side and the tissue around it, and reported the tissue and skin health for Shawn to record.

Terry handed her the cleaned plug, and she placed it back into the cow's side, completely sealing the gasket. Terry opened the pneumatic stanchion and released the animal. It stood there for a time, then looked back at Shawn, who got up from his stool and moved around to the animal's side. He put a hand on its shoulder and spoke into the cow's ear. "Come on now, precious." He pointed forward. The steer stepped free of the stanchion and into the holding pen beyond. "Sometimes they just need a little encouragement," he laughed.

The next animal, a heifer, was waiting in line. She moved forward and the process repeated. Doctoring the animals was a routine the three of them did together every week, often with students in tow, and from their practiced manner it was clear they had the routine down.

I tried to stay out of their way, but my curiosity got the best of me. Each time Lynne removed a gasket plug, I peered inside the cow's rumen. In the overhead light and with the aid of the flashlight Lynne carried, the rumen's contents looked like a wet pile of freshly mown grass. I was incredulous.

You are looking directly inside a cow's stomach! I told myself.

What seemed even more improbable is that said bovine, owner of said rumen, just stood there, relaxed, while all the work went on around and inside him or her. I felt a lot like I did in my high school biology class, preparing to dissect a fetal pig. It was a mixture of fascination, absolute wonder, and *ick*.

Shawn related the story of the first known fistulated patient, who happened to be human. "He was a Canadian named Alexis St. Martin, who in 1822 suffered a horrible gunshot injury to the abdomen. Incredibly, the wound healed as a fistula, with a permanent opening into the stomach," he said. The physician who treated him, Dr. William Beaumont, saw the opportunity, and began studying human digestion by dangling different foods into his stomach, attached to a string, and seeing how they changed in the stomach.

Shawn and his colleagues were following in the footsteps of St. Martin and Beaumont by studying ruminant animal nutrition through the gasket, specifically the effects of diet on the amount of methane the animals produced. By feeding the animals in airtight living quarters and monitoring the chemical composition of the gases flowing into and out of the chambers, they were able to measure the amount of methane the animals produced in response to their diet. The fistula allowed them a way to monitor the rumen's contents and record the research progress.

At one point during the morning, Shawn motioned to the opened gasket and said to me, "You can put your hand in there if you want."

"Really?!" I asked.

"Sure," he said, pointing to the box of sanitized gloves on a table nearby.

I donned the gloves and stood near the cow, unsure what to do next. Lynne finished her work on the animal and motioned me to step forward. I tentatively put my hand inside.

"Wow, it is so hot!" I exclaimed, jerking my hand back.

"Yes, about 101 to 102 degrees Fahrenheit," responded Shawn. I glanced over at him, in time to see the three of them all watching me ... and laughing!

I must have looked like one of their undergraduate students does whenever they experience this. I steeled the *ick* factor, reached back into the rumen, and gathered a handful of the contents. I squeezed it, massaged it with my fingers, and looked at the steer. He just stood there, unmoving. My hand felt like it was cooking. I pulled it out and looked at the rumen's contents resting in my palm. It gave off the faint odor I notice when my own gorge rises, but combined with the sweet smell of lawn clippings. I looked back into the rumen as Lynne finished recording her work, then examined the mass of cooling, masticated forage in my hand, and ridiculously asked myself, *Do I just put this back into the cow?* I looked at Shawn, who seemed to know what I was thinking. He nodded with his chin to the paddock outside. After tossing the handful out of the building, I stripped off the gloves, then took a seat on a stool and marveled at the experience.

Not surprisingly, several emerging ventures seek to reduce methane emissions from cattle and sheep, using chemicals that alter the microbial community's metabolism within the rumen. I asked Shawn what he thought of them. As an expert in animal nutrition and enteric methane emissions, Shawn monitors this type of research.

"I think we are years to decades away from having a chemical that *might* be practical," he said, emphasizing the word might. At the time of this writing, several medications and feed supplements aimed at the beef and dairy industry were in the animal trials process, with unclear pathways to a widespread use, and unclear effects on the animals involved.

Some additives appear to reduce the emissions by about a quarter, with no observed short-term effect on the cows, the amount of food the cows eat, or the amount and quality of the meat or milk they produce.[199] Others have little observable impact on the methane produced, or they suppress the activity of the microbes in the cow's rumen for a short time, leading to less digested food and the cows gaining proportionally less weight (and producing proportionally less meat).

Questions still exist about whether ruminants can tolerate these additives in their stomachs over time, or whether the microbial community will simply evolve a mechanism that negates the additives' effects.[200] And since the long-term effects of these additives on the cattle have not yet been determined, it's premature to say how effective feed additives are on reducing enteric methane. In short, the jury is still out.

When I think about this question, I consider the long human history of attempting to manipulate microbes to our advantage. Trying to prevent microbes in a cow's rumen from producing methane alters an evolutionary relationship that literally goes back to the dinosaurs. How would altering the microbes' base metabolism in potentially hundreds of millions of cattle, sheep, and goats play out around the world? How long would it take for the microbes to make an evolutionary end run around and go back to their old ways, cranking out methane again? I'm reminded of the trope "What could possibly go wrong?"

> • <

Do grass-fed and grass-finished meats have a lower carbon footprint than CAFO-fed meat? While there are so many clearer answers to questions like this in other sectors—like low-carbon methods to power automobiles, generate electricity, and heat homes—this question carries a lot more cultural and personal baggage than most. When it comes to impacts other than climate change—like water quality, air quality, acidification potential, animal health and welfare, and human health—the scientific research shows grass-fed and -finished beef has lower total environmental impacts than CAFO-fed.[201] Up to the point the animal leaves its home pasture and enters the slaughterhouse, grass-fed and grass-finished beef likely has the best energy balance (lowest proportion of fossil-carbon emissions), as the animal has not relied on annual crops grown for feed or fossil fuel–supported systems at a CAFO. There is only one clear advantage that CAFO-fed beef has over grass-fed beef: In general, it requires fewer total acres to produce the beef.

Despite its other advantages, grass-fed and grass-finished beef doesn't necessarily have a lower carbon footprint. In some cases yes, in other cases no, and on average, the two systems are comparable.[202]

There are caveats, however. Cattle and other livestock can graze on a wide range of pastures, but we cannot grow human food like lettuce or wheat everywhere. In fact, trying to do so would likely fail and would lead to even higher greenhouse gas emissions. The only type of sustainable agriculture in many parts of the world is grazing livestock. In many places the soils are too erodible, too rocky, too salty, or there is too little rainfall to grow crops. Grass-fed and grass-finished meats and dairy are often the best food choices for people living in those places.

An optimistic story has emerged that grazing livestock can lead to more carbon in the soil. In some cases that is true, but not necessarily everywhere, and the increase in soil carbon does not continue forever.[203] In some pastures, changing the way cattle graze by bringing them onto the pasture for short, intense grazing periods can lead to higher carbon in the soil over a similar period. The clearest examples where livestock have supported increases in soil organic carbon stock have been where they are integrated into grazing systems designed to restore highly degraded eco-systems. Restoring degraded soils, improving plant cover, and rebuilding native plant ecosystems with perennial grasses and forbs, sometimes called "holistic management," all contribute unambiguously to increases in soil organic carbon stock.[204, 205] Livestock can play a role and are often leveraged to help achieve those goals.

Can those gains in soil organic carbon offset the cow belches, the poop, and the urine across the beef industry? Some of it, yes, but all of it? Probably not. And after soil organic carbon stocks settle at a higher level, what scientists call equilibrium, the grazing animals' methane emissions will continue without any associated offset. Restoring pastures to produce the highest quality forage for the grazing livestock helps reduce those methane emissions, but does not eliminate them. That's the rub.

Some practices used to raise livestock for meat are so egregious that governments have outlawed them. One is clearing a forest to plant pasture for grazing livestock or to grow crops to feed live-stock. The other is plowing up a grassland to grow crops to feed to cattle in CAFOs.

Both practices liquidate the ecosystem capital that is the stored carbon, nitrogen, and other nutrients present in the soils and plants. A pine forest in many parts of the world might contain between 50 and 180 metric tons of CO_2e[206] in an acre of trees, and a similar amount of carbon in the soil down to about a meter in depth. Tropical and temperate rain forests have three to four times that amount. Clearing a forest and then plowing the soil to plant pasture or crops means that all the carbon stored in the wood, and a quarter to a third of the carbon stored in the soil, would become carbon dioxide in the atmosphere within a decade. Burning forests like in the Amazon to make space to graze cattle or raise soybeans leads to much higher emissions. All the carbon and much of the nitrogen in the burned trees and degraded topsoil goes straight into the atmosphere as greenhouse gases.

Plowing a grassland has similar effects. Grassland soils hold more carbon than practically any other ecosystem other than Arctic taiga forests and wetlands. On average, they even hold more carbon than tropical rainforests, with a few exceptions.[207] Plowing that soil (like Americans did to the Great Plains) to grow crops to feed livestock in CAFOs carries a very heavy greenhouse gas emissions burden. From the perspective of the climate crisis, we are far better off raising livestock on the remaining intact grasslands, or maintaining said grasslands as natural areas with wildlife, or doing both where wildlife and livestock can coexist.

Destroying forests or intact grasslands to either grow crops or plant pasture means we also lose their climate-cooling effects, their filtered water, their habitat and biodiversity, and the emotional and spiritual benefits that natural landscapes provide. At a time

Bison on well-managed rangeland at a ranch striving to improve soil, sequester carbon, protect wildlife habitat, and responsibly source meat products. Wild Idea Buffalo Company, Cheyenne River Buffalo Ranch, South Dakota. *Jill O'Brien*

when all of these—a stable climate, clean water, wildlife habitat, and spiritual peace—seem to be in short supply, losing even a single acre of intact forests and grasslands is a loss felt directly and indirectly by the entire planet. The scientific evidence indicates we simply won't have enough land available to us in the coming decades to meet expanding consumer demands for ruminants (beef, lamb, goats, bison, water buffalo) while simultaneously reducing greenhouse gas emissions.[208,209,210] Both the planetary and physician's prescription are for much of the world, particularly those in affluent societies, to eat less meat, and especially less from ruminants.

Meeting current and future demand for animal protein means leveraging two core strategies: integrating livestock into croplands and raising livestock on land described as "ecological leftovers." Integrating animals into croplands means grazing them on cover crops during the shoulder seasons between main crops, grazing them on forage crops grown during rest or fallow periods to improve soils, or at times when the main crops can tolerate the livestock, or grazing them on residues and leftover grain left on the fields after harvest. To meet current and future human demands for food while stabilizing the climate, we must devote the most productive agricultural soils to raising food for humans. Raising livestock sustainably in more marginal areas (the ecological leftovers) and on cover crops in the shoulder seasons of human food systems holds promise to protect ecosystem carbon reserves while reducing the overall carbon footprint of the system.

What are the best examples of this if meat is to remain on the table? Part of the answer may lie on Dan DeSutter's farm in west-central Indiana.

> • <

As part of the farm tour given to me by Dan DeSutter and Jim Moseley (described in the chapter on corn and nitrogen, "The Corn Eaters"), we stopped to see some calves that had overwintered on a field planted the previous year with cover crops that doubled as quality livestock forage. About thirty red and black angus steers and heifers, fat with sleek winter coats, began moving slowly away as we got out of Dan's pickup and walked toward them. We stood in the chilly spring sunshine and commented on how good the cattle looked.

"I think bringing livestock back into the fields is key to the future," Dan said.

"I don't see a way to go organic without livestock," added Jim.

Earlier in the day Dan had contrasted how he had cropped two adjacent fields with similar soil and histories. On one of them he'd brought in cattle to graze the winter cover crop before he planted corn. On the other, they'd knocked the cover crop down but had not grazed it before they planted the corn. Both fields achieved above-average yields compared with their conventionally grown counterparts, but the corn crop in the field that had been grazed grew 15 percent more grain than the one that hadn't been grazed. "That one experience cinched it for me. Cattle are now a major part of what we do," he said.

Several years earlier, Dan and his son began collaborating on a farming system that fully integrates livestock into their corn-soybean rotation. "I grow the crops, and my son raises the cattle," Dan explained. "He likes working with cattle, and by dividing the labor, we both get a little more weekend time off."

The term "ecological leftovers" comes to mind when thinking about the DeSutters' farming system. Integrating forage crops and livestock into the shoulder seasons and, as the DeSutters are doing, including a third rest year where they rest the soil and graze livestock, aligns with the principals described in a comprehensive and highly readable report titled "Grazed and Confused" and other research now coming to light.[211, 212] Transferring ruminant livestock like cattle out of CAFOs and integrating them into crop rotations more fully utilizes the resources that ecosystems have to offer, with potential long-term benefits to the climate. In the best systems, like the DeSutters', there is a positive feedback loop. The cattle replace tillage while facilitating the nutrient cycling between soil and plants and shortening the livestock-feed supply chain. Rather than feeding cattle in a CAFO, they are fed directly on the field.

But what about the methane that cattle belch? As positive as systems like the DeSutters' are proving to be, the methane from cow belches would persist in these integrated livestock-cropping systems. Can these systems accommodate all the cattle raised under the beef CAFO model? At the time of this writing, that question has not been answered. I reached out to Dr. Pete Smith at the University of Aberdeen, a respected scientist working in greenhouse gas accounting and co-author of "Grazed and Confused," with the question. "I don't think this method of production would support the numbers of livestock currently produced. So, it is a bandage on the problem rather than a cure," he replied. A positive contribution, yes—a building block in the box of solutions to what ails our overheated planet. But it probably would not meet the sheer volume of beef the world demands today.

Are there other solutions if meat is to remain on the table? Another example in western Colorado involves animals walking on two legs, not four.

> • <

Indian Ridge Farm, about seven thousand feet in elevation and founded by Barclay and Tony Daranyi in 2002, straddles a breezy rise on Wright's Mesa, Colorado, between the grassy pastures, copses of trees, and occasional rock outcrops. They raise an unlikely combination of chickens, cattle, pigs, goats, and vegetables in what seems like an equally unlikely setting for a farm. In a landscape previously devoted to uranium mining and cattle ranching, Barclay and Tony surveyed the economic landscape and realized a different path would be needed if they wanted to live there. Chickens, raised on pasture in a rotation with other two-legged and four-legged grazing partners, have become the center of their livelihood.

Barclay and Tony bring unique credentials to their endeavor. Barclay grew up farming on Caretaker Farm in South Williamstown, Massachusetts, the daughter of Elizabeth and Sam Smith. Elizabeth and Sam are successful growers who helped spearhead the organic farming movement, and whose farm is now permanently protected in an easement that ensures it will continue producing food for the foreseeable future. Tony lived in Chicago, working as a banker on mergers and acquisitions and taking MBA classes at night. The two of them combined a love of land, a deep history in agriculture, and a keen business sense to start their farm.

I visited them on a stunning June morning with the mountains all around retaining their mantles of snow after the largest spring snowpack in recorded history. The landscape practically shouted the word "Green!" wherever I looked. Their border collie met me in a full body wag as I stepped from my car, followed by a smiling Barclay peering through an arbor framing the entrance to their yard. "Hi, Mark!" came her easy, sunny greeting. "Let me go get Tony, and we'll give you a tour. Do you want a cup of coffee?"

When you meet Barclay and Tony they look directly into your eyes and smile. Both have the calloused, muscular hands and fore-arms, tanned faces, and crows-feet eyes of people who farm the land. At over six feet, with sunglasses perched on the bill of his ball cap, Tony moves like the hybrid he is of part-time ski patrol-ler in winter and farmer the rest of his hours. Barclay, who also ran a part-time bakery at the time of my visit, walks with a direct-ness that makes me feel like she likes her life. As with practically every farm family I know, at least one person has a day job to pay for insurance and provide extra income to weather the ups and downs of the farm economy. And like every other farmer I know, though it was only mid-morning, it's obvious they have already been busy and have a lot on their minds for the day. Still, we move deliberately, and I am grateful for the hours they've carved out to show me around.

When they first got started at Wright's Mesa, Barclay and Tony planted windbreaks around a patch of soil that would grow vege-tables, installed high tunnels (inexpensive, passive-heated green-houses) to extend the season, and began growing. "It was a partial disaster," Tony said. A drought pummeled them the first year, and their field was overrun by whitetop, a highly invasive weed. "We learned that we never should have plowed that field," he said. Then they came across the idea of raising chickens and turkeys and read about Joel Salatin's systems for pastured-chicken production.[213, 214] They bought some used equipment, restored their plowed field back to pasture, and began the transition to raising chickens.

Barclay led me toward a pasture with an eight-foot-high fence around it and opened the gate.

"We've just entered our two-acre, pastured-poultry operation," Tony said as we stepped through.

Ahead of us were eleven of the classic Salatin "chicken tractors": rectangular boxes, each about two feet high, eight feet wide, and twelve feet long, roofed with plywood covered by a reflective, waterproof tarp, with mesh wire sides. Each sported an axle supporting two tires at one end, with a trailer hitch on the other. Through the wire mesh we could see the white birds inside. All set in a pasture so lush that I had to high-step over or kick my way through the thick, green forage.

Tony described their grazing system. "When we started, it took us five years of weeding, seeding, and careful grazing to deal with the weeds and get this pasture to where it is now. We use no chemical herbicides." The pasture was a dense, diverse mix of forage grasses and other plants. Soil lab reports put their soil carbon at more than twice the background levels reported by soils maps for the area.

"We grazed our cattle through this pasture early in the season and will graze cattle on the pasture at the season's end as well. In

between we graze the chickens. They start at the far end," Tony
pointed to the west end of the pasture, "and continue in a straight
line to the east end, where we pick them up and move them over
one row onto fresh grass." The chicken tractors lay in rows, like
a disorganized phalanx of giant holiday chocolate boxes. "This
grass is on its third grazing rotation this year, and we move the
tractors daily." The two of them lifted the cover off a corner of
one of the shelters, and bright sunlight streamed in. Each shelter
held fifty birds. A few sat on perches suspended across the shelter,
others dipped for water in pans. Others pecked at the ground. I
watched one take what appeared to be a beetle at the edge of the
wire mesh. Barclay had brought a bucket of feed with her, and she
poured it into feeders attached to the shelter's roof and side. The
birds all crowded in to eat.

"They get about half of their forage from grass and insects in
the pasture," said Tony. At that moment I noticed a small grasshopper nymph bounce onto my trouser leg. "The other half is
from an organic feed mix we buy in Montrose [an agricultural
supply center about seventy-five miles away]. The nutrients in
their droppings are all this pasture gets for fertilizer."

Their pasture is indirectly fertilized by the nutrient leftovers cycled from the feed mix through the chickens, deposited
as manure.

We closed the cover and stepped back to examine the grass from
the previous day's grazing. About half the forage had been grazed
away. The ground was peppered with the grayish-white, black-
edged turds the birds had dropped. I dropped to my knees for a
moment and looked over the pasture from the side, in profile.

Insects that I could not see from above suddenly came into view. I quickly counted what appeared to be more than a dozen different species on the ground or in the air above the grass. The insects, perhaps more than anything, were evidence of thriving ecosystem processes.

"We've had grasshopper problems in the past," Tony said.

"Our first year, which was a drought, they were so bad that they seemed to eat every green thing on the farm," added Barclay. "We found that our turkeys love grasshoppers!" she exclaimed. "The turkeys came out here and like an army, they marched through and ate every single grasshopper!"

We examined the grass in the row as it receded through the succession of days since the most current grazing. "You can see the regrowth already," Tony pointed out; new leaves sprang from grass stems, and new stems emerged from the earth. "More than chickens, we are growing grass."

Barclay and Tony have tightened the food loop by adapting a food system compatible with their ecosystem and selling products into the local economy. Theirs was a clear example of raising livestock in ecosystems too marginal for raising crops—as their experience demonstrated. It is a compelling vision of a diverse food system that, as Tony mentioned to me later, drastically shortens the food miles of the typical plate of North American food.

We'd gathered in the kitchen with the farm's three interns—Caroline, Cory, and Chris—to recap the morning. "I grew up with interns on my parents' farm," Barclay had told me earlier. "We ate three meals a day with them, worked with them all day, and shared our lives together. Though we follow a somewhat different

Tony Daranyi walks among the turkeys grazing on pasture at
Indian Ridge Farm, Wright's Mesa, Colorado. *Barclay Daranyi /
Indian Ridge Farm*

internship model with them here than my parents did, they are a big part of Indian Ridge Farm."

Caroline and Cory were following a similar path to Barclay's and Tony's. A young married couple, they had left their jobs and come to live and work at Indian Ridge to learn how to farm in the Daranyis' model. Chris, a recent college graduate, was exploring a potential life path in agriculture. We discussed the elements of sustainability on Indian Ridge from the perspective of greenhouse gases—improving plant cover, growing ecologically appropriate crops and livestock, increasing soil organic matter, reducing chemical inputs, and reducing fossil fuel use.

Compared with a conventional operation, the meat coming from Indian Ridge is likely to carry a total burden of between three and four pounds of CO_2e per pound of meat, and about 1.5 pounds of CO_2e per pound of egg produced.[215] Indian Ridge Farm had cut their emissions by 30 percent compared with conventional poultry, and by 40 percent in their eggs. On a pound-for-pound basis, the chicken meat carries about one-twelfth, or 8 percent, of the burden of the beef raised in the Nebraska CAFO described earlier. The eggs, about one-thirtieth, or 3 percent, of the burden. Their chickens and eggs carry less of a climate burden in a system that builds and maintains the organic matter in the soil, drastically reduces fuel requirements, and eliminates the need for synthetic farm chemicals.

Chickens, being monogastric, lack the rumen that cattle have co-developed with the microbial community to better digest grass while simultaneously converting a substantial part of it to methane. They still capture a significant portion of the protein, plant nutrients, and complex carbohydrates in the grass, and efficiently process nearly all the insect biomass they eat, but they produce little to no methane. Chickens have the advantage over cattle of being able to convert their feed much more efficiently into meat than ruminants are able to—about three to four times better, besides producing edible eggs. And as I learned on my visit, solar panels power nearly all the farm's electricity, and the distance to market ranges from three to forty-five miles, further reducing the farm's carbon footprint.

And though the system does reduce the amount of grain the chickens may eat, it doesn't eliminate it, and so a portion of the birds' diet is food that humans might eat. About 60 percent of the chickens' feed needs are met with an organic feed mix—corn, wheat, millet, and other grains.

I asked them how to extend the Indian Ridge Farm model to achieve sustainability for the masses. We all thought about it together for a few moments, and Barclay responded first.

"Being accountable to your community is important to us. We work under an open-farm policy, with full transparency. We've developed a system here that works for this place—the soil, the weather, and the animals. The system to grow chickens will be a little different in another part of the world, but ultimately it goes back to Joel Salatin's original idea, and one of the points he makes is that you have to adapt to whatever the conditions are in the place where you live. Chickens and eggs grown here are going to be a little different from chickens and eggs grown in Georgia or California," she said.

Tony chimed in. "One of the issues that we deal with is scale. Consider the food miles question. The founder of an internet food company just announced a plan to farm broiler chickens on a pasture-raised system, and then sell the birds directly to consumers through the internet. Consider the shipping costs! Consider the emissions! The market we sell to is less than a fifty-mile radius."

"People want food with a genuine connection to the land, like the food we raise here, but it is hard," offered Barclay. She thought about it for a moment. "A big piece of the puzzle is how to just have more farmers raising nutritious food."

It was time for me to go, and the five of them had work to do. I had brought with me a cooler containing a block of ice, and so after saying goodbye to the interns and Tony, Barclay and I walked down to the freezer room so I could buy some chickens to take home with me. Even frozen, it was clear that the Daranyis' birds were different from a generic supermarket chicken. They had more structure on the surface, and rather than the round, fatty birds, these were more athletic. The deep orange fat in each chicken's skin was the color of a mandarin orange.

"That's the carotenoids, from the grass," observed Barclay. "Nutritionally, these birds are completely off the charts."[216]

I wrote her a check, thanked her, and set off for home.

That following weekend, Leslie and I roasted one of their chickens for some friends. Compared to conventional and organic supermarket chickens, both we and our dinner guests noted the Indian Ridge Farm chicken was meatier, had more substantial chicken flavor, and had somewhat less of the dominating fat that defines the generic, supermarket chicken.

› • ‹

What can we do about meat's high carbon footprint? There may be no other place in our food system where our evolutionary relationship with microbes impacts us so strongly. Methane belches dominate every plate of food containing beef and lamb.

Technology is coming to the rescue in many parts of our culture where a high carbon footprint confronts our daily lives. Low-carbon energy sources are gradually replacing fossil fuels. Electric vehicles are replacing those that burn fuel. Highly efficient LED lighting has largely replaced the Edison light bulb. Advanced insulation and weather-sealing techniques mean our homes require less energy compared to the past. The list goes on.

In the case of the meat in our diet, technological solutions are limited. Low-carbon energy sources will help reduce the energy burden required to process, ship, and keep meat cool during its journey to our tables. Raising meat differently from the CAFO model can also help. Incorporating grazing livestock into crop rotations, such as at Dan DeSutter's farm, contributes to lower emissions in those crops. Grazing livestock on ecologically appropriate grasslands in ways that improve forage quality and quantity, such as at Indian Creek Farm, can reduce the pressure on croplands where human food can be grown instead of animal forage. Plant-based, manufactured meats may offer alternatives, though the carbon footprint of such products is not clearly better at the time of this writing.

Science does not currently offer a way to mitigate the evolutionary relationship between ruminant animals and microbes that dominates the carbon footprint of beef and lamb. It isn't clear that there will ever be a way to reduce the methane emissions from their rumens in a way that is safe and humane for the animals and safe for the people eating the meat. Demand for meat from ruminant animals outstrips the world's ability to keep pace. Matching the burgeoning demand for meat from a growing, more affluent population requires that we continue to clear the Earth's remaining forests to create grazing land and fields to grow forage.

I do not know anybody who wants to live in a future without forests. It is an open question whether human society could even survive if the forests of the world are lost.

What about pork as an alternative to ruminants? It isn't clear at the time of this writing that there are any lower-carbon alternatives to raising pigs in CAFO systems. Pigs are very hard on soils, and whereas they can be pastured, no evidence currently exists that pigs can help improve degraded soils, maintain healthy soils, and sequester carbon. Demand for soybeans to feed pigs in Europe and elsewhere is driving deforestation in the Amazon and other parts of the world. I and others studying this field would welcome low-carbon pork; however, the only opportunities to reduce pork's carbon footprint appear to be in reducing the carbon-intensity of the energy and transportation emissions in pork's supply chain.

The main opportunity that appears to be left is choice. Just like driving less, or adjusting the thermostat, in order to reduce the emissions from eating animal protein, we are faced with individual decisions that collectively would reduce emissions. These include:

- Eat less meat and replace animal protein in meals with plant-based protein.

- If you eat animal protein, focus on low-carbon seafood or pastured poultry in place of beef, lamb, and pork.

- When eating beef or lamb, try to source the meat from livestock raised on well-managed grasslands, or animals that are integrated into farmers' fields rather than finished in concentrated feeding operations. And ensure the meat you eat is not raised where forests were recently cleared to create pastures or fields to raise the animal forage.

ETOILE
5€
Niortais
6,40€
Bonde
DE GATINE
7€
LINGON
6,80€
Colline
5,60€
Pelardon
3.50€
FRAIS
SUR FEUILLE
6€
Saint
Christophe
FENUGREC
6€80
CHABICHOU
6€
Galletout
5€
Délice
7,50€
PAVÉ DU
8,60€
Galet
Cendré
5€
PELTA
7,60€

Cecil's Hands

My ten-year-old self spilled breathless and excited into the milking parlor. Cecil Laverack, my grandparents' farmhand, sat on a stool near the right-rear flank of the Guernsey cow. He wore a heavy plaid winter coat with a matching winter cap. The cow he was milking was the last of my grandfather's small milking herd, and she and Cecil were iterating on a routine they repeated in the morning and evening of every day. Cecil slowly turned to me and gave me one of the reserved, quiet smiles I knew him for.

"Mornin'."

"Mornin'." I must have smiled back, because he always treated me like a smaller version of a man.

He turned back to face the cow's flank and leaned into her a little. His hands worked steadily through our brief exchange, keeping a steady, alternating stream of milk pouring into the bucket from two of the cow's teats. I wonder if he was expecting me that

Previous spread: A selection of French and Italian cheeses.
Alex Kozlov

morning and had saved the next particular moment of pleasure for when I arrived. He turned his head a little and directed one of the streams at the small swarm of cats rubbing with arched backs and mewing mouths against his and the cow's legs. Daphne, the matriarch, centered her mouth in the stream to get as much as she could. After a time, she stepped out of the way, temporarily sated, and there was a scramble as another took her place.

"Can you hold up the cat bowl for me?"

I lifted the clean metal bowl from its place nearby and held it under the streaming teat while cats rubbed against my legs. Cecil returned the stream to the pail after the bowl held a couple of cups of milk, and I set the bowl down a short distance away amidst a happy cat frenzy. The sound within the parlor instantly went from a din of mews to that of cat mouths urgently lapping the warm liquid. I stood entranced, watching the rhythmic movement of Cecil's hands.

"Do you want to give it a try?" He nodded to the cow's underside. He must have read my mind.

"Can I?"

"You can wash your hands over there." He nodded to a pail of warm water and a bar of soap on a shelf next to the open doorway. I washed my hands in the warm water and dried them on the towel hanging nearby. As I did, Cecil threw some more hay to the cow and topped it with a ration of grain, and then pulled a second stool from the corner. He washed his hands again, then directed me onto the stool he'd been using and sat next to me.

He grasped one of the teats in his right hand, then took my small right hand and placed it over his. His hand began to move, the fingers and palm working in unison. Milk began to stream into the pail just as before. To extract the milk, his index finger and thumb tightened around the teat, then the middle finger, then the ring finger, then his pinky, all in sequence to move milk from the upper part of the teat down to the opening. His palm mirrored the action on the side of the teat opposite his fingers. I focused on absorbing the muscle movements as he repeated the procedure for a while, and then he stopped and placed my hand onto the cow's teat. He wrapped his own hand over mine. The teat felt rubbery, and warm, and full of liquid, and I remember leaning my shoulder and temple into the cow's flank like I had seen Cecil do.

Cecil gently repeated the process, and I attempted to mimic his hands and finger movements as best as I could, watching the milk pour from the teat. After a couple dozen cycles, he took his hand off mine. I tried it on my own. Milk dribbled from the teat. After a few tries, Cecil demonstrated a couple of wordless corrections. I tried again, and the stream strengthened. I took a second teat in my left hand, and awkwardly tried to synchronize the tentative streams falling from the teats like I'd seen him do. After a couple of minutes, I started to get the hang of it. Milk didn't pour into the bucket as it did when Cecil milked, but it flowed steadily into the pail until my hands cramped and I had to stop. I leaned back out of the cow's warmth and traded stools with Cecil, then sat and watched the cats cleaning themselves after their breakfast.

Then the cow's tail suddenly twitched and arched upward. The cats ran for cover, and Cecil immediately stopped milking and pulled the milk pail to the front of the cow. A mass of greenish-brown manure ejected from the Guernsey's backside. After just a few fragrant seconds, several gallons of manure lay steaming on the parlor floor in the December cold. Cecil replaced the pail and resumed the milking, then looked at me, a question on his face. I found the shovel, scraped the manure off the floor, and carried it outside to the manure spreader parked near the milking parlor door.

I came back inside and watched Cecil's hands complete the task. I could not have known then that, fifty years later, I would still remember this moment. There was no way I could have known that one day I would be calculating the differing fates of the carbon and nitrogen molecules shoveled into the wagon versus hosed into a drainpipe and flushed into a lake full of manure. Who could have imagined then how humanity's relationship with manure would change the world the way it did, and shift the world's relationship to milk?

> • <

If you are like me, milk may be such a fundamental part of your life that it would be hard to imagine living without it. Milk may have impacted humans more directly than just about any other type of food. Human creativity, domesticated livestock, micro-climates, and ecosystems have interacted the world over to create a dizzying number of cheeses, yogurts, butters, and other dairy-based foods made by human hands. France alone has more than 350 different registered cheeses! Every country in the world has a dairy tradition that is either native to the culture or was imported with immigrants or entrepreneurs. People around the world milk domestic cows, horses, donkeys, camels, sheep, goats, water buffalo, reindeer, and yaks. We drink the milk raw or pasteurized, ferment it into yogurts and alcoholic drinks, churn the fat from the cream, coagulate the fats and solids into curds and further ferment them into cheeses, precipitate out the whey for food additives; basically, we put every part of the milk to work.

On your next trip to the grocery store, you might walk the dairy aisle and, if you eat dairy products, think about how they are a part of your day. Chances are they have become a conscious or unconscious part of most meals: milk or yogurt on morning cereal, butter on toast, or cream in a morning coffee. Cheese tops millions of sandwiches. Parmesan graces a lunchtime pasta. Perhaps you start some meals with a creamy brie appetizer spread on a crust of bread? Or sprinkle shredded cheese on a burrito or casserole? Imagine finishing a meal with a wedge of buttery apple pie adorned with a slice of melted sharp cheddar or a scoop of ice cream. If you read the ingredients on the food packages you buy or ask the waitstaff what's in the meal you ordered, chances are that dairy is somewhere on the list.

The symbiotic relationship between cattle and humans appears to have begun to develop about eleven thousand years ago, where evidence from the ninth century BCE suggests the first efforts to domesticate cattle were in Southeast Asia.[217] Considering our relationships with animals, whether they're pets, or livestock, or the wildlife that quicken our hearts, it's easy to imagine why people brought cattle, sheep, and goats to live inside their homes. The hard work of daily milking routines like Cecil's have played out an uncountable number of times in the millennia since cattle and then other livestock were first milked. Humanity's relationship with dairy is now literally in our DNA.[218]

That genetic relationship, however, has come at a cost to the climate. When scientists compare the nutrition in milk with the nutrition in other animal-based foods, milk's carbon footprint on a per-calorie or per-gram-of-protein basis is second only to beef, lamb, and goat meat, and greater than pork and chicken meat.[219] Its ubiquitous nature extends that burden throughout our meals wherever ingredients from dairy products find their way onto our plates. Every eight-ounce glass of milk, and the products made from it, carries a burden of just over one pound of CO_2e.

On the face of it, that doesn't sound so bad. Isn't that comparable to bread, beans, or other plant-based foods?

The significance emerges upon a closer look. Milk is more than 90 percent water, meaning it is not as nutrient-dense as a hamburger, for example, which is about 60 percent water. Extract the water to the dry components of the milk—the butterfat, protein, carbohydrates, and minerals (known as "milk solids"), which is the nutrition that really counts in a glass of milk—and compare that against the fats and solids in other foods, and the emissions become starkly clear.

For example, the emissions from an eight-ounce brick of cheddar cheese come in far higher than an eight-ounce cup of milk, even though that cheese is made from milk. This is because the butterfat and milk solids making up that pound of cheddar come from up to four pounds of milk. Typically, about five pounds of emissions come from producing the milk needed for each eight-ounce brick, or about ten pounds of emissions per pound of cheddar cheese. About two additional pounds per brick or four additional pounds of emissions per pound of cheese come from processing, manufacturing, cooling, and shipping the cheese to our tables, including landfill methane emissions from the waste. Each brick of cheddar carries a total footprint of about seven pounds of emissions, or fourteen pounds of CO_2e per pound of cheese.[220, 221] Other dairy products like yogurt and cottage cheese carry about the same burden as milk since little to none of the water has been removed. Drier hard cheeses like parmesan, which have lower water content, have a correspondingly higher carbon footprint.

Another way to think about it is the greenhouse gas burden that comes with the nutrition in milk. For example, a sedentary woman needs a little more than 1.5 ounces (46 grams) of protein per day. A sedentary man needs about 2 ounces (56 grams). Fulfilling that nutritional need with dairy would require a little less than three and a half pounds of milk for a woman, and four pounds of milk for a man. That equals about seven pounds of CO_2e for a woman, and eight pounds for a man. Getting the same amount of protein from beef carries a burden of about sixteen pounds of emissions for a woman, and nineteen pounds for a man. For comparison, about one-third of a pound of emissions come from growing and processing beans to yield the same amount of protein.

Because of this, the dairy industry alone accounts for about 5 percent of the world's total carbon footprint.[222] How can a little butter scraped on toast, or mozzarella on a pizza be such a game changer? Could there possibly be any good news when it comes to dairy's carbon footprint? Fortunately, yes, but the solutions can be complicated, and in some places, it will take a sea change in agricultural policy to bring them about.

> • ‹

Milk's journey from sunlight, air, water, and minerals, through a dairy animal, to the dairy product on our kitchen table can be broken down into four different, roughly equal parts:

Dairy animals are big eaters. On average, a dairy cow eats 80 to 120 pounds of forage each day, with daily caloric demands as high or higher than almost any other four-legged mammal besides elephants, rhinoceros, and hippopotamuses. Producing ten or more gallons of milk each day requires a tremendous amount of energy. The emissions from growing, transporting, and processing the forage to meet that demand add up to about a quarter of the emissions from producing milk.

Transforming that forage into energy, proteins, and fats needed to manufacture the milk in the cow's mammary glands requires a trip through the cow's rumen. Microbes in the rumen digest the normally indigestible complex carbohydrates like cellulose into food the cow can digest. As a result, the cow's rumen is basically a methane factory, and the cows belch it out of their mouths as they chew their cuds. That methane, described in detail in the previous chapter on meat, "The Cow in the Room," makes up another quarter of the emissions from producing milk.

The energy required to run the dairy and milk the cow, cool the milk to safe temperatures, ship it to a processing facility where it is pasteurized, homogenized, cooled again, packaged, and shipped to a retailer, and then deal with the leftovers generates about another quarter of the emissions from producing milk.

The last, but not least, piece of milk's greenhouse gas-emissions story comes with the cow's manure. Because dairy cows are very big eaters, they generate a lot of manure. The typical dairy cow produces about twenty tons of manure every year.[223] The industry produces a thousand pounds of manure each year for every person living in the United States, or just shy of three pounds per person per day. Another way to look at it is that on average in the United States, dairy cows as a sector crank out twice as much fresh manure every day as the US human population does. And today, because of the way most dairies store the manure, the emissions from the manure are about twenty times higher per gallon of milk than they would have been historically. The emissions

---

Dairy animals fed on well-managed pasture produce fewer methane emissions from their manure because far less is held in manure lagoons. Dairies using anaerobic digesters have a lower carbon footprint. "Manure" is methane and nitrous oxide from manure. "Waste" assumes 40 percent of products are eventually landfilled and become landfill methane CO_2e. "Retail and Packaging" includes homogenizing, pasteurizing, and cooling milk; shipping milk products; making containers; and equipment, fuel, and energy used in retail. "Enteric Methane" is livestock enteric methane. "Feed" is emissions to grow and process crops into livestock feed. "Deforestation" is forests/ grasslands converted to create pastures and grow feed for livestock. "Emissions Offset" is the manure methane captured at the dairy and burned to produce heat and electricity, displacing fossil fuel use.

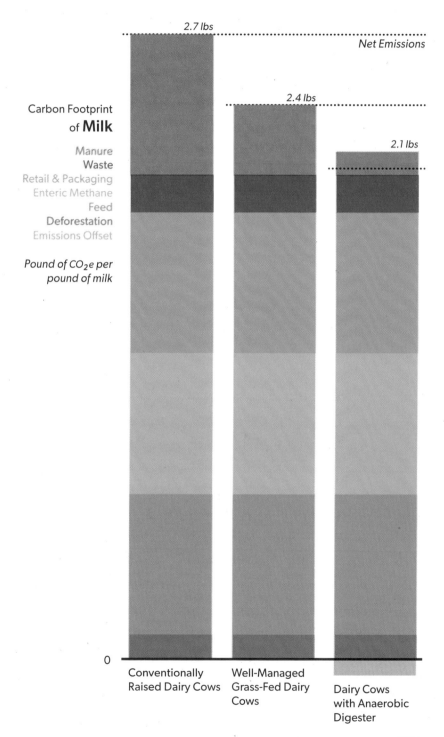

Carbon Footprint
of **Milk**

Manure
Waste
Retail & Packaging
Enteric Methane
Feed
Deforestation
Emissions Offset

*Pound of CO$_2$e per
pound of milk*

2.7 lbs

Net Emissions

2.4 lbs

2.1 lbs

0

Conventionally
Raised Dairy Cows

Well-Managed
Grass-Fed Dairy
Cows

Dairy Cows
with Anaerobic
Digester

from all that manure make up the last quarter of the greenhouse gas emissions from producing milk.

And that's the rub. Dairy manure emissions have been rising since 1992, the year the world first began counting the carbon footprint of livestock. This issue isn't unique to the United States—the problem exists wherever modern dairies operate around the world. Emissions were much smaller before the invention of the dairy concentrated animal feeding operation, or CAFO. And like many other stories of modern agriculture, the greatest emissions come when humans created an ecosystem that was rare before the last century—a lake filled with liquid cow manure.

> • <

What can be done about these emissions? Let's look at the bad news first. As is the case of beef and lamb animals, it is currently unclear whether anything can be done to reduce the enteric methane that dairy animals belch from their stomachs. Because the cow belches are such a significant problem, equaling one of the largest categories of greenhouse gas emissions around the world, scientists and entrepreneurs are actively seeking chemicals and feed additives that reduce the methane that cows belch. At the time of this writing, the evidence from that research may show some promise but is still inconclusive.

What about reducing the emissions from processing milk and bringing it to our tables? Can dairies reduce the energy emissions from cooling, pasteurizing, and processing milk and milk products? There are a lot of good examples of individual dairies doing this, and as energy grids shift to renewable sources, the emissions will drop. This is where the good news comes in. The industry as a whole has not shifted to technologies to resolve this issue; however, progress is being made.

What about the emissions from producing the forage the animals need? The regenerative farming methods described in this book's chapters on corn and grains are already whittling away at feed emissions, with the potential to drop well below current levels, and in some cases to near zero or even below it. This is true for some individual dairies. But again, the industry as a whole has not shifted to the regenerative agricultural methods needed to reduce this emissions class.

That leaves the manure. Why are the emissions so large, and how do we cut the emissions from what comes out of the cow's backside? One of the clearest answers is to change how dairies handle and store the manure. But to understand where the work needs to be done, it helps to understand some of the history behind American dairies, and how manure fits into ecosystems.

> • <

Over the millennia, legions of microbes, insects, and other organisms evolved into a community to efficiently capitalize on the energy and nutrient bonanza that a cow pie represents once it goes splat onto a pasture's surface. Soil ecosystems are particularly attuned to utilizing manure. Whether that manure comes from a cow, a deer, a mouse, or a beetle, all of it represents a bounty for soil organisms. Depending on the season, creatures outside the cow can begin colonizing the pile within seconds. And while processing those nutrients, soil organisms give off greenhouse gases. In the case of dairy cow manure, the main greenhouse gas emissions coming from that cow pie are a nominal amount of nitrous oxide the microbial community produced in digesting the manure's nitrogen. On the basis of pounds of nitrous oxide per pound of dry manure, letting the cow drop the manure on the pasture or field likely results in the least emissions.[224] For millennia, dairy cattle grazed for their forage while distributing their manure around the fields they grazed on. When they lived in shelters during the winter or bad weather, their handlers gathered the manure and spread it on crop and forage fields in largely solid form, as a form of fertilizer, burned it as fuel, or used it as a building material.

The invention of the dairy CAFO changed everything.

During the 1960s, some dairies expanded and switched from grazing dairy cattle on pasture and housing them in barns only temporarily during bad weather, to housing them full-time in barns and feeding them concentrated diets of corn, soybeans, and alfalfa. Automated milking machines along with inexpensive refrigeration equipment made it possible to feed and milk hundreds of cows in a dairy barn, rather than the dozens of cows per dairy that were the norm before 1960.[225] Suddenly a problem emerged—what to do with all that manure the cows dropped inside those buildings.

A modern dairy today milking one thousand cows produces as much manure as a town of sixty thousand people.[226] As dairies expanded, the mass of manure rivaled the sewage-treatment demands on towns and small cities. Somewhere along the line, the practice emerged to simply dig a pond behind the barns, line the bottom with compacted clay or plastic, and put the manure there.[227] Dairies with such lagoons periodically pump the lagoon's contents into trucks that spread the slurry onto nearby pastures and crop fields, or pump the slurry into specialized sprinkler systems that spray the slurry onto fields growing forage for the cows. This practice, while a straightforward approach, requires energy for the pumps and fuel for the trucks, leading to more emissions.

The emissions from pumping and hauling the manure can be significant, but the biggest emissions come from the microbes in the manure. Store the manure as a slurry in a pond or pit, and the microbes shift into the same metabolic pathway as the microbes in the cow's rumen. Any oxygen in the manure is very quickly used up once it enters a lagoon. Without oxygen, the microbes begin to crank out methane, rather than carbon dioxide, as the waste product of their metabolism. It is the same process as in a cow's stomach. They produce so much that the emissions from an equivalent amount of manure stored in a lagoon increase twenty-fold compared with letting the cows crap it all out onto a pasture. It's that big of a deal. Manure lagoons are giant methane factories.

Much of the world today is literally dotted with dairies funneling livestock manure into adjacent lagoons. For every gallon of milk produced at conventional dairies, about four pounds of CO_2e from the manure methane streams into the atmosphere. The US Environmental Protection Agency estimates that emissions from the manure in the dairy industry were almost forty-one million metric tons of CO_2e in 2017, the most recent year it was

A Wisconsin dairy houses thousands of cattle indoors. The buildings include four barns connected to a milking parlor. The manure is stored in lagoons (in the middle right), where it emits large amounts of methane. *BanksPhotos / Getty*

reported.[228] That is the equivalent of the emissions of nearly nine million automobiles in the same year. More than three-quarters of those emissions came from lagoons. The methane emissions from lagoons have more than doubled since 1990, and they continue to increase, despite the number of dairy cattle decreasing over that time. As large as these emissions are currently calculated to be, the news may actually be worse. One recent study indicates the emissions today could be 80 percent higher than currently reported.[229]

In short, manure lagoons lead to three entirely new classes of emissions that would barely exist if cows grazed on pasture instead:

- The lagoons stream tens of millions of metric tons of methane CO_2e into the atmosphere each year.

- Pouring or spraying the manure slurry onto fields and pastures leads to higher emissions compared with letting the cows drop it onto the pastures and fields themselves.

- It takes energy to move that manure around rather than letting the cow do it for us.

So, is the best way to reduce dairy's carbon footprint just to let the cows eat grass and drop it all out on the pasture? The answer appears to be yes, and also no.

A 2022 comparison study[230] of the world's dairy industry showed the lowest emissions came from cattle fed on the best-managed pasture systems in New Zealand, Uruguay, and the Netherlands.

The worst emissions came from cattle fed on less well-managed pastures where farmers tend to have less access to capital, equipment, and materials to improve pastureland, and livestock are frequently grazed under marginal conditions with poorer forage quality. Emissions from concentrated feeding operations were in between those two extremes.

Why is it so complicated?

The issues largely boil down to the types of forage the cows eat, how much milk the cows produce, and what the dairies do with the manure.

Like with beef cattle CAFOs, the cows in a typical dairy CAFO eat a concentrated diet that's rich in grains and other calorie- and protein-rich additives. This diet, typically a lot lower in fiber than the diet cows evolved to eat, means there is less fiber for the microbes in the cow's rumen to digest. Less of that fiber means less methane, and a higher-energy diet means the cows produce more milk than cows eating a grass diet. So, the cows produce more milk and less enteric methane. Nearly all dairy CAFOs, however, store the great majority of the cow's manure in lagoons, leading to much higher manure methane emissions.

In summary, the CAFOs tend to produce more milk per cow, less enteric methane cow belches per cow, and more manure methane.

Contrast this with an organic dairy, where the cows get at least 30 percent of their forage from pastures. Though the pasture-based diet is arguably healthier for the cow in the long term, the cows produce more of the enteric methane cow belches from this diet that's richer in fiber than the typical CAFO diet. The microbes that evolved in the cow's rumen to digest fiber have more fiber to work with. And because the diet tends to be less rich, a cow feeding on pasture and grass tends to produce less milk, averaging six to eight gallons per day compared with the eight to ten at the CAFOs. The manure emissions, however, tend to be lower, because the cows feeding on pasture deposit more of their manure out on the pastures, rather than having it washed from the barn floor into lagoons.

In the end, the answer depends on the individual dairies. Most dairies must address the issue of what to do with the manure, because even in completely pasture- and grass-based systems, the cows have to live indoors and be fed some kind of harvested forage, like hay, for at least part of the year. There are simply times of the year where the pastures have little for the cows to eat, or their compacting hooves would disrupt the soil too much. What this means is that whether the cows feed on pasture for part of the year or are confined the entire year, most large, modern dairies grapple with a manure problem.

Fortunately, there are many good examples of dairies pursuing win-win solutions to cut their manure emissions.

> • <

Early one April morning I found myself standing on a ridge-top pasture above Tomales Bay, California, with Calla Rose Ostrander, John Wick, and Dr. Jeff Creque of the Marin Carbon Project. It was early April and the breeze coming off the bay had broken through the morning fog. It fanned cool, moist salt air that had me, a child of the plains, simultaneously leaning into the Pacific Ocean scent while reaching for my jacket and wool cap.

Albert Straus from Straus Family Creamery had invited our group and a small host of other conservation-minded farmers, ranchers, and agriculture professionals to talk about compost, windbreaks, cow manure, and carbon sequestration. Those gathered had been at the epicenter of work on the West Coast to reduce the carbon footprint of food, combining basic scientific research, on-farm demonstration projects, and civic engagement to explore and define how composting food waste can help solve the climate crisis.

We'd gathered at Straus Family Creamery to talk about carbon; however, all anybody wanted to talk about was the weather. It was 2015 and California was struggling through another extreme drought. Water supplies were dwindling, and the late-February Sierra snowpack was already noodling down toward zero. The long-term forecast predicted no relief. Three months later in May, state officials would make another striking announcement, noting that the usually vast reservoir of snow blanketing the Sierra Nevada range this time of year was completely gone. Nobody had ever seen anything like it. Few seemed to be shocked, considering the warning signs mounting over the previous decades, though everybody seemed to be worried. The Brave New global warming world had settled upon the California psyche like an omnipresent nightmare.

But as alarming as the weather was, the group assembled for the tour managed to refocus on the reason for the gathering and the matters immediately at hand. We chatted quietly with a group of colleagues from resource conservation districts (RCDs) through-out Northern California who'd joined us at the farm. We were standing near a large square of flat ground where we'd parked our cars.

We wandered to another part of the pasture where the forage grew tall and lush. Calla Rose joined me there. "I'm pretty sure this is where Albert put the compost," she said.

I tried to view the pasture as a cow might, and decided that here was where I would want to graze. Coastal Marin and Sonoma Counties were one place that had received highly localized rain while the rest of the region remained devastatingly dry. Two tor-rential storms had dropped nearly an entire winter's worth of moisture in just a few days—and the pasture's diverse grass and forbs grew thick and tall. The rest of the group joined us and wan-dered through the lush growth, marveling at the difference from the rest of the pasture.

"How much has the soil carbon increased?" I asked, wondering if anybody had taken measurements.

"The soil is holding a lot more water than it used to be able to," an anonymous voice answered.

I tried again. "Is anybody measuring nitrous oxide emissions?"

"We are seeing a lot better water infiltration now," came an answer from another voice I didn't recognize. "Albert's soils captured most of the rain in those two storms. There was very little runoff."

It was like a carbon-to-water translator app had been installed into the brains of farm and ranch people throughout the state. Whenever anybody brought up carbon, the conversation always turned to water. Which was okay in the end. Jeff and a host of other researchers throughout the world had learned that increasing soil carbon benefits humans in myriad other ways, including improving the farmlands' resilience to drought. The point of the entire project was to create a strategy that benefited the climate.

One outgrowth of the Marin Carbon Project was the Carbon Cycle Institute (CCI), which was focusing on taking carbon farming to scale. The Institute and Lynette Niebrugge at the Marin County RCD had developed a carbon-farming plan for Straus Family Creamery and were taking steps to reduce its carbon footprint. Albert and his team had applied a layer of compost to the pastures and hay fields, leading to lush growth and an increase in soil carbon. They planted windbreaks and re-established riparian forests along his waterways to reduce erosion, protect livestock in bad weather, and capture carbon from the atmosphere in the woody plants.

"Mark, if you look at that pasture down below us, you can see where we want to put [more] windbreaks," Jeff said.

He pointed down the hill and I recognized the features on the diagrams he had recently shared with me. Green pastures sloped steeply down to the highway below and the bay beyond. The pasture at the base of the hill would be rimmed by a perimeter windbreak. One of Jeff's trademark innovations involves planting native grasses, trees, forbs, and shrubs into pasture borders. The science behind his carbon-farming strategies is made up of equal parts regenerative agriculture, greenhouse gas mitigation, ecosystem recovery, and basic agronomy, all focused on increasing ecosystem carbon stocks in soil and plants.

Dairy cows roam the hills of Marin and Sonoma Counties at the Straus Family Creamery, the first certified organic dairy west of the Mississippi River. Marshall, California. *Shereen Mahnami / Straus Family Creamery*

A bell ringing from the house below broke into our conversations. "Let's head down to the dairy," Calla Rose told the group, and we began working our way down the steep slope toward the milking operation.

Besides the steps Straus Family Creamery was taking to leverage the manure produced on their farm to improve their pastures and sequester carbon, their cattle grazed on pasture whenever the season allowed. Among their many firsts in the dairy industry, the creamery's anaerobic digester captured the manure from the milking parlor and barns where cattle sheltered during bad weather. A thick mat of synthetic material, sealed at the edges, lay over the small slurry pond, capturing the methane the microbes in the lagoon produced, and shunting it to a pipe that led to an engine that burned methane. Albert had paid little or nothing for energy to power his dairy and heat water in more than a decade. After microbes decomposed the manure, workers at the creamery periodically collected the sludge, or biosolids, and remaining liquid from the digester pit and applied them to his fields. Albert was leveraging nature to power the dairy and recycle nutrients back onto the pastures, all while improving the operation's bottom line.

Albert met us in the yard. He'd taken advantage of the clearing weather to don sandals and an ancient fleece jacket. It was a departure from the knee-high rubber boots standard to dairies everywhere. We were visiting between milkings and the cattle were out on pasture, so the farmyard was relatively quiet. The only sound was the muffled roar from the electric generator in a building up the hill. He welcomed us to the farm, gave us a brief introduction to his operation, and then turned to Jeff.

"Why don't you tell them the rest—you know the story here better than I do." Albert smiled as he pointed us up the hill, and Jeff led us up to the rim of the lagoon.

Albert's anaerobic digester was simply a small pond lined with thick plastic liner and covered with a heavy seal. He feeds and milks 350 cattle on this farm, and the manure scraped from the milking parlor and barns flows through a series of pipes and pumps until it rests in the lagoon. The liner ballooned visibly from its load of methane. A crusty brown seep of overflowed manure rested on one corner. Just a few steps away from the lagoon, the generator roared inside an insulated building. The sight of heavy equipment tweaked the latent engineer in me, and I asked if we could look inside. Albert unlocked and pulled back the door. Inside, a giant piston engine powered the pumps, coolers, and lights that make up his dairy while heating the water needed for sanitizing equipment.

After the tour, we headed back toward town, but with a detour to Point Reyes Station. In a renovated barn there, we saw the one-of-a-kind cheeses made by Cowgirl Creamery using Straus Family Creamery milk. Across the room and under a chalkboard menu sat a refrigerated case holding tins of Straus Family Creamery ice cream. It was nearly dinnertime, but I couldn't stop myself from ordering a scoop, along with some cheese to take home with me.

> • <

After Cecil milked my grandparents' cow, he would bring the milk into the mud room of the farmhouse, where my grandmother poured it into jars for Cecil's family, our neighbors, and our own family. What she kept she chilled in a refrigerator and separated out the cream, some of which she churned into butter. The buttermilk left behind went into morning oatmeal or bread. Sometimes she turned the milk into fresh cottage cheese. Most of it our family drank straight away. I realize now that the milk reflected the place and my grandparents' lives as Dust Bowl refugees. It defined a culture from a time when many families in the region either kept a dairy cow or bought or bartered for milk with a family that had one. When I look at how dairies have changed, I'm struck by how my own life spans these poles in the agriculture of milk. And perhaps more than anything, I'm struck by how the emissions profile of milk has changed since my grandparents farmed the land.

Maybe more than in any other place where the climate crisis confronts my own life, I struggle with this uncomfortable fact. Does it matter so much what we eat? Must cheeses, some of which are arguably among the world's greatest culinary achievements, be swept into the climate dustbin? Does a morning latte matter that much? At a time when we are told that time matters, when every little bit helps, when every single pound of methane avoided is a pound of cure, it feels like so much is being demanded of us when our leaders are making such poor choices about our future, and so little is being done in other sectors that increasingly matter. Why should I change what I eat, or be bothered with how my food is produced, since relatively little seems to be done anywhere else?

But then I consider that the Earth's climate may be the world's greatest integrator. It does not give a whit for bullshit rationalizations. And though I'm not a religious person, I sometimes imagine that there may be an especially warm place in hell for greenhouse gas accountants who rationalize away the impacts of their own lives.

So for me, the answer is yes, our choices matter, whether they are as individuals or as a society as a whole.

If we are going to continue to enjoy dairy products, we must accelerate the practices that eliminate the emissions from the energy required to process and transport the milk to our table. We must transform how we handle the manure the cows produce, and we must adopt carbon-friendly farming practices for the forage produced for dairy animals and the soil that underpins the system. The animals must be fed on well-managed pasture for as much of their lives as is possible.

As recently as 1972, some US states still allowed dairies to dump manure into lakes and rivers. The practice remained commonplace in other parts of the world. It wasn't until the Clean Water Act of 1972 that US dairies began investing en masse to line the lagoons, which addressed part of the water-quality problem. The scientific community certainly understood how ecosystems produce methane; however, the burgeoning climate crisis did not spur the scientific discipline defining greenhouse gas inventories for another two decades.

Until that time, the only place where manure became concentrated into such huge amounts was in cities, where it was produced by people, not cows. The Federal Clean Water Act enabled the last few cities and towns in the United States that lacked effective sewage-treatment facilities to get them installed.

Modern sewage-treatment plants that deal with human manure are genuine engineering marvels, and society's collective health and welfare improved immensely with their invention. A problem that had plagued society—what to do with our human manure—was finally resolved at scale. Those improvements have become a model for the developing world.

Today it is unusual to come across what we call "raw sewage," or untreated human manure, in any kind of quantity unless a treatment plant has been overwhelmed by a storm or some other catastrophe. Larger communities like the town where I live, and nearly all US cities, treat human manure much like Albert Straus does at his dairy. The manure gets piped to decompose in anaerobic digesters, generating energy for community needs, degrading and eliminating pathogens, and producing biosolids as an end product. Biosolids can be further composted and/or spread directly onto pastures as a soil amendment as long as they are Type A, as defined by the US Environmental Protection Agency (EPA), and not contaminated with heavy metals or other dangerous pollutants.

Isn't it ironic, then, that just at the point where the United States had largely implemented solutions for safely dealing with human manure, literally entire cities' worth of cow manure began accumulating at thousands of points around the country, with fewer of the health restrictions that we place on human manure? Dairies in other parts of the world quickly followed suit.[231, 232] If stored in a lagoon, the manure from a relatively typical industrial dairy of one thousand cows produces the same emissions in a year as more than forty-five hundred typical American cars.[233, 234]

The greenhouse gas consequences of this novel new ecosystem, a veritable lake full of dairy cow manure, beg for a better solution for what to do with it all.

Fortunately, innovators like Straus Family Creamery, with the support of organizations like the Carbon Cycle Institute and the regional conservation districts, are creating alternatives that others can build on. Dairies can produce milk with much lower impacts, and reduced cost, by grazing animals on well-managed pastures integrated with crop rotations on land that doesn't compete with growing human food. Innovative dairies around the world are demonstrating how to grow highly nutritious, productive mixtures of perennial and annual forages that cattle can graze in place, relieving growers of the emissions-intensive task of growing, processing, and importing feed to CAFOs. Feeding cattle on pastures dramatically cuts the manure greenhouse gas emissions, with equally important benefits to water and air resources when managed well. Letting nature do the work by collaborating with cows and the soil ecosystem won't erase all the emissions in producing milk, but it will be a strong contribution to a more sustainable future.

The Feast of the Legions

Standing on a gigantic pile of garbage can be a strange experience. Dan Matsch and I were on the summit of the Front Range Landfill in Erie, Colorado, elevated a modest Denver skyscraper's height above the retired coal mine beneath us. Dan directs the Center for Hard to Recycle Materials (CHaRM) in Boulder, Colorado, and we were on the final leg of a daylong *tour-de-garbage* he'd invited me to join him on.

We were each lost in our individual thoughts there at the summit, experiencing the place in all senses. There was the unlikely view of the Indian Peaks Wilderness within the Colorado Front Range to the west. The uneven, spongey-pokey surface felt through my boot soles left me with a queasy, in-between feeling that both invited and prevented me from imagining what lay beneath. I could hear the engine of a garbage truck disgorging its contents into a pile while an enormous diesel-engine landfill compactor screamed nearby. An American flag flew high and stiff in the

Previous spread: Fresh vegetables in an organic garden. *Pedro Gomes*

breeze above the cab as it quickly spread and leveled the garbage truck's putrid contents, while another truck backed into place to drop its load. The smell was an acrid mix of moldy carpet layered with the heavy stink universally known as "wet garbage." Even though the day was cool and bright, the odor lay upon us like a scratchy wool blanket.

Dan turned my way and called out above the din, "This place looks and smells like a giant pile of lost opportunities!"

I nodded. That was exactly how it felt.

We could not see it at the time, but tons of methane were streaming from the pile below into the atmosphere around us. That daily plume, when compounded yearly, added up to slightly more than 211,000 tons of fossil fuel emissions each year, equal to the tailpipe emissions from about forty-seven thousand typical gasoline-powered automobiles per year.[235] The thought of those emissions was overwhelming. Especially since they could be avoided.

> • <

A few weeks earlier, I'd raced home from work on my bicycle, changed clothes, and set to work harvesting my garden as snow began piling up. Snow could fall at my home in Colorado any time after Labor Day, and here I was, three days after the autumnal equinox, kicking myself for not wrapping up this garden task the day before. I stumbled through the blizzard, collecting every vegetable I could find. Tomatoes, peppers, eggplants, melons, squash, and beans went into the boxes. Root vegetables would survive in the ground until they could be harvested after a burst of Indian summer melted off the snow. Tender herbs went into paper sacks to dry in the garage. The harvest sprint ended with a final bag of rescued basil leaves destined to become pesto.

On my way into the house, I stopped and surveyed what just the day before had been our green garden oasis. It now lay under a deepening layer of white. Whereas the commercial growers in my area would survive the storm just fine, and their cold-hardy produce would grace the market shelves for months to come, my wife Leslie's and my gardening season was now essentially over. I kicked the snow from my boots before going inside.

I started some onions browning for a fresh tomato pasta sauce, then began sorting my harvest. Over the next few weeks, we would make more pasta sauces, soups, and side dishes as the veggies gradually ripened in the boxes we stored in a cool, dry corner. After the tender produce was gone, the winter squash would go into lasagna, soups, or pies. Much to my chagrin, however, a portion of these vegetables would never make it to the table.

Some were already showing spots of mold or late-season rot, and I salvaged what I could from them and tossed them into the pot with the onions. Some would turn black in the boxes, others would get moldy along the edges, some would wilt, and one or two would rot wholesale. In an earlier time in our lives, rotten produce like this went into the garbage can and then off to the landfill. But not now. With the help and guidance of people like Dan Matsch, we've joined the ranks of recycling's final frontier,[236] and now compost everything that doesn't get eaten.

What is compost? In short, it is the fully rotted remains from our kitchens, restaurants, and gardens. Food leftovers are

The author's and his wife's final fall harvest from their garden in
Fort Collins, Colorado. *Mark Easter*

combined with animal manure and/or yard waste like leaves, grass clippings, and wood chips to rot down into a humus-y mix that is a highly sought-after soil amendment. Compost may be the ultimate in recycling. It can be made at home or in local communities into a product that can be used at home or sold back to farmers, ranchers, or other gardeners to build their soil and replace commercial fertilizers. Almost anybody can do it, making it perhaps the epitome of the circular economy, where useful products and waste cycle continuously. And, compost has a key role in a climate-smart food future.

I think about all the human effort it takes to raise food—planting the seeds, fertilizing and amending the soil, irrigating when necessary, removing weeds, harvesting the goods, and putting the beds to rest at the end of the growing season. It's a ton of work! The plants themselves, having leveraged the evolutionary miracle of photosynthesis, had built a vibrant green canopy through the season. They held a panoply of nutrients that, even when the food couldn't be eaten, were extremely valuable. They didn't need to be condemned to the landfill just because they were past their immediate usefulness as human food. Throw them away? It makes no more sense to bury food waste in a landfill than it does to commit a car we no longer drive to the same fate. I couldn't do that when I considered the labor, materials, time, sun, and water that went into growing them. They still had a useful purpose, but after being remanufactured into something directly useful again.

As it turns out, taking this simple step to divert the food into compost, rather than throwing it into the landfill, is one of the most straightforward climate-cooling actions a person can take.

Food that is thrown away is subject to the microbes that consume the waste in the oxygen-free depths of the landfill, resulting in copious methane emissions. Those emissions are about three-tenths of a pound of CO_2e for every pound of food that goes into the landfill.[237,238] We avoid those emissions in the same way as when we reduce the miles driven in our gasoline- or diesel-powered automobiles, turn down the thermostat in our homes, or get our electricity from wind turbines and solar panels rather than coal or fracked natural gas.

As is the case with most of the stories in this book, the microscopic legions beneath our feet play the central role. Feeding the soil's shadow fauna is central to a cooler climate and a sustainable future.

> • ‹

One afternoon the previous spring, Leslie and I stood before a steaming pile of garbage in a field near our home. It had been raining and snowing off-and-on all day, and we raced out to finish a chore when the weather broke. Thunderstorms rimmed the horizon on all sides, and a cumulus cloud upwind dropped a squall curtain into the gathering breeze as we got to work. We were part of the compost rangers, a team of neighborhood volunteers sharing tasks to transform neighborhood food waste into compost. That day it was our turn to pull the wheeled carts from their collection points in the neighborhood to the compost pile and add the week's food waste to the main compost bins.

The bins were a long row of three-sided compartments open to the soil below, constructed from discarded pallets. Each could

Neighborhood compost bins. Fort Collins, Colorado. *Leslie Brown*

hold the contents of about a dozen wheelbarrows. The rightmost bin held the freshest material and was nearly full of still-recognizable food items, combined with a little hay and some leaves. It stank lightly of rotting food. The leftmost bin was about half-full of a dark-brown mix of fine particles interspersed with what looked like small chunks of rotted wood. It smelled like soil. The three bins in between contained materials in various stages of rot as the soil organisms did their work. Once a month a few strong volunteers emptied the leftmost bin into a pile of fresh compost for the gardeners in the neighborhood. Then they shoveled the contents from the bin immediately to the right of that one into the now-empty leftmost bin, aerating and watering the contents to stimulate a last round of microbial activity, and then proceeded down the bins from left to right. They were duplicating, by hand, the aerating equipment that commercial composters use.

We removed the discarded table that served as the cover for the rightmost of the bins. Leslie tilted the two-wheeled cart that held the kitchen and yard scraps while I shoveled and scraped the contents into the bin. The carts normally sit covered at their stations, and during the week our neighbors dump their plant-based food scraps into them. Meat, dairy products, woody yard waste, and eggshells go into a dumpster that is collected every few days by a commercial composting company, which will hot-compost the material into a product they sell back to farmers, ranchers, and the community at large.

That part of the chore done, I poked the probe of a thirty-inch-long compost thermometer into the leftmost pile. The outside air temperature was about forty-five degrees Fahrenheit. After a few moments to let the thermometer dial settle, Leslie read aloud the pile's internal temperature.

"One hundred and five degrees."

"It's still cooking," I replied.

Microbes generate heat as they eat the rotting produce. When the temperature inside the pile drops to near the air temperature, the microbes have finished their work. All that will be left is a brown, crumbly substance with the texture and scent of healthy soil. But although it looks like soil, and smells like soil, compost isn't soil. It is the myriad living and dead bodies of bacteria, archaea, fungi, protozoans, arthropods, annelids, and other organisms, and their waste products. When added to gardens, farm fields, and pastures, it has the potential to take degraded soils to new levels of productivity, yielding produce and animal products far higher in nutrition than their conventionally grown counterparts.

Why go to all this trouble? The compost is a soil amendment par excellence. Almost nothing beats it for feeding soil. And if the emissions from all the food dumped into landfills were its own country, it would have the third largest greenhouse gas emissions of all the world's countries. The only countries having more emissions would be China (number 1) and the United States (number 2). Avoiding those emissions, growing nutritious food, and restoring health to degraded soil begins with the simple act of dropping our leftover food into a bin slated for the compost pile, rather than into the trash headed to the landfill.

> • <

Modern agriculture is arguably the most mechanized, industrialized, and productive food engine the world has ever seen.[239] Farmers today consistently produce mountains of food.[240] And for the last four decades, throughout the world we have consistently thrown 40 percent of it away every year.[241, 242] Dana Gunders shared this incredible story in the landmark 2012 report (and updated with Jonathan Bloom in 2017) "Wasted: How America is Losing up to 40 Percent of Its Food from Farm to Fork to Landfill." The report's first paragraph contains this chilling concept:

> *If the United States went grocery shopping, we would leave the store with five bags and drop two in the parking lot. And leave them there. Seems crazy, but we do it every day.*

This story is remarkably consistent throughout the developed world, a stark metaphor for food that takes such an extraordinary effort to create and then is never consumed. Fortunately, communities are beginning to gain ground in preventing the food from being wasted in the first place. Food that is beyond regulatory labeling dates but still safe is being collected and distributed through local and regional programs throughout the world. Yet it's inevitable that some food will go bad before we can finish it.

The science of carbon emissions is making it increasingly clear that burying those leftovers in the landfill is literally a waste. Recycling the nutrients back to farm fields through compost prevents the need to mine and manufacture more agricultural fertilizers, some of which are projected to become increasingly scarce.[243]

Yet only about a third of food and other compostable waste in North America, Europe, and Asia outside of China is diverted from landfills. Some of it is incinerated, and some goes into municipal anaerobic digesters. Only about a fifth is composted.[244,245,246] Clearly there is a lot more that the developed world can do to first reduce food waste, and then to recycle the remainder in responsible ways. For a growing fraction of communities, composting has become the method of choice.

Though statistics on food waste in China are difficult to consolidate, the majority of food waste there is believed to be landfilled.[247] Remarkably, a land shortage crisis in South Korea led the country to create programs to extend the lives of its landfills. They built food-redistribution systems to minimize food waste, and whatever food cannot be used is diverted into making compost, into anaerobic digesters to produce biogas, and to feed livestock.[248]

I could grasp composting at home, but I'd never seen how it was done at the industrial scale. To understand the barriers to reclaiming the lost tons of potent farm fertilizer, I turned to Dan Matsch. He understands the ins and outs of composting better than anybody I know, so when he offered to arrange a tour of a commercial composting facility near my home, I jumped at the chance.

I'd describe Dan as an environmental entrepreneur. In his late fifties, with a slim build, a full head of hair, and a quiet, measured

Compost is used to feed and improve soil, provide essential nutrients to crops, sequester carbon, retain moisture, and reduce the need for chemical fertilizers. Weld County, Colorado. *Beau Barkley / Veteran Move Media* way of speaking, he leads a team of workers running CHaRM in Boulder, Colorado. It is part of Eco-Cycle, a public-private partnership in Boulder that is organized around a unique mission: to create a circular economy within their community that can help get them as close to zero waste as possible. Whatever item we might think of as garbage—be it electronics, building materials, appliances, furniture, toys, packaging—Eco-Cycle tries to put the item back into use, by either selling it to the public after a cleanup or repair or breaking it down into recyclable components.

A decade earlier, Dan had convinced Eco-Cycle to expand their recycling services to include a composting program. He explained it was a natural fit for CHaRM and for him, considering his former life as a farmer for whom composting defined a major part of his livelihood. I asked Dan when his focus on composting began. He explained that he became interested after hearing a presentation by John Wick about the Marin Carbon Project in California.

"The story John shared that day changed me and the work I was doing, and things have never been quite the same," said Dan. "Hearing John's story made me think we could do something positive with compost here in Boulder County."

Dan's career turn, and passion, have inspired a community movement that is reducing the region's carbon footprint while helping to drive a subtle but critical change in the local agricultural economy and municipal waste management.

A retired architectural project manager, Wick had experienced an epiphany one day while moving cattle between pastures on his ranch. He tells his story this way: The pastures on his ranch were in rough shape after decades of poor grazing practices by the previous owners. Invasive, shallow-rooted annual grasses had taken over from the diverse mix of native annuals and deeper-rooted, perennial plants that made up the foundation of the ecosystem before Spanish settlers introduced range cattle in the 1850s. He wasn't sure what to do about it until he hired Dr. Jeff Creque, an ecologist who specialized in restoring the health and productivity of agricultural ecosystems through a process known as carbon farming. Jeff advised John to spread compost on his degraded pastures and change the grazing patterns of the cattle to be lighter on the land. The pair created two one-acre test plots on some of the poorest soil on his ranch. They spread compost on the plots and commercial fertilizer with equivalent amounts of nutrients on nearby control plots.

Within the year, the soil where they'd applied compost bore lush new growth that was clearly different from the control plots. Over time, desirable native perennial grasses and forbs, formerly rare, began to reappear where the compost had been spread, and eventually restored their dominance over the invasive annual plants in John's degraded pastures. The year after beginning the experiment, John noticed that his cattle focused their grazing where the compost had been laid down. Lab tests showed that samples of the forage from the composted plots had markedly higher concentrations of protein, micronutrients, and other compounds known to be healthy for cows.

That finding inspired John, his wife, Peggy Rathmann, and Jeff to create an initiative they called the Marin Carbon Project. The goal was to further study what they had observed while replicating Jeff's technique on other farms and ranches, and ultimately to explore the climate-mitigation opportunities of diverting food waste from landfills and creating compost for use on pastures and farm fields. They hired Calla Rose Ostrander to implement the project, and over the course of a decade they conducted research, set up test trials, and established pilot composting projects based on the lessons learned. They concluded that a large chunk of our human carbon footprint could be reduced, and a substantial part of it offset by carbon sequestration, through the simple action of diverting food from landfills, transforming it into compost, and returning that compost to the agricultural pastures and fields used to grow human food.[249, 250]

> • <

During our drive that day I learned that Dan had taken John's story to heart. He seemed to know everything about compost in Colorado—potential feed stocks, hauling costs, compost facility siting issues, regulatory barriers. He ran through a litany of them during the drive.

"There are myriad reasons why composting has not become as widespread as recycling aluminum cans," he said. "Waste management companies are very influential in the state legislature and have created regulatory barriers. People are worried about the smell. There are examples where the US EPA and state regulatory agencies have undercounted groundwater contamination from waste management sites. And perhaps the biggest obstacle is that food waste is treated just like it sounds—as waste, something to be thrown away, rather than treating it as valuable raw materials for an important agricultural amendment."

The last mile of the drive took us down a narrow asphalt road, with sagebrush crowding in from the sand dunes lining the route. Suddenly the aroma of rotting organic matter hit us.

Dan grinned. "Smells like we're here."

We popped over a rise and turned into the staging yard for the flagship composting facility of A1 Organics, near Keenesburg, Colorado.

At first the place looked like a farmyard, with its heavy equipment, steel buildings, and the ubiquitous barking dog trotting up to greet us. Then I saw the long, linear piles of dark-brown material up to twenty feet high and a hundred yards long stretching past us on three sides. The piles literally ran out of sight.

Bob Yost, a man many in the region know as Mister Compost, greeted us and ushered us into his pickup. Dan and Bob had worked together for years, and Bob serves as vice president and chief technical officer for A1. Bob is a likable, energetic, and fit man in his sixties, over six feet tall, quick with a smile and a joke. He drove us straight to a pile of material at the far end of a loading yard, beginning what for the next hour would be a steady stream of keen observations, commentary, and self-deprecating humor about anything and everything having do with compost. A heavily bearded truck driver had backed up his rig to the pile and was tilting the truck bed to empty it.

"Looks like he has a load of food waste," said Bob.

The driver jerked the truck into a stop and the load swept down the truck bed in a mad rush. A worker from A1 moved up and circled the pile slowly, inspecting it for contaminants.

"From time to time a hauler sends a load of complete garbage here. And I mean *garbage*," Bob told us. "We send them right back out of here. No plastic bags, no plywood, no furniture, no metal. None of that will compost."

After a time, satisfied, the inspector waved the driver off, and a giant yellow front loader pulled in and started moving the material into a pile near a grinding machine that was the size of a small house.

"Mind if I get out and take a closer look?"

Bob nodded and I jumped out to step through the muddy yard up to the pile. It was an astonishing mass of waste. Twenty tons arrived in this one load from Denver. A1 Organics receives several such loads each day, and it was a small fraction of the leftover food, leaves, lawn clippings, and tree branches produced each day in Colorado's largest metropolitan area.

According to a study of my own community, Fort Collins, each resident produces about nine hundred pounds of compostable organic waste every year. Compostable organic waste includes anything made from plants (food, leftovers, cooking oils, wood, paper without additives or plastic coatings, leaves, garden waste, etc.) or animals (meat, bones, fat, hides, organs, feathers). Compostable raw materials must not be contaminated with plastic, metals, chemicals, dyes, synthetic additives, or other materials that won't decompose. Four out of every ten pounds of waste we generate is material that could be recycled into compost. On a monthly basis, that is about enough raw material to fill one hefty

This leftover produce from grocery stores will be ground and mixed with wood chips to become compost. If buried in landfills instead, it produces climate-heating methane emissions. Keenesburg, Colorado. *Clinton T. Sander / A1 Organics*

wheelbarrow load for each citizen. If composted, that monthly wheelbarrow load of kitchen and yard leftovers would become enough compost to fill about two five-gallon buckets full of the crumbly goodness craved by many gardeners and farmers.

I returned to the pickup. Bob spun the wheel, gunned the motor a little, and stopped next to a giant machine a short distance away. It was fantastically loud as it took in tons of food waste by the minute from the front loader and ground it to a gray-brown mash destined for the compost piles. Bob gunned the engine again and we moved past piles of ground-up wood chips and shredded paper to a series of uniformly long rows of brown compost in the making. "This is our EcoGro product. We mix food waste, wood chips, paper if it is available, and an inoculant [an accelerator] together into these long piles, and then aerate it about five times over the course of a few weeks. Then we cover it with this sealant and let it cook until it is done."

The compost pile aerator was out of sight at the moment, but it was a unique invention the shape of an upright, equal-sided triangle on wheels that traversed the length of the pile. The machine stirred the contents to create a uniform mix while blending in oxygen and moisture to support the microbes within.

We scanned the rows of piles before us. Each was about the height of a single-story house and spaced just far enough apart that a truck could move between them. To the left, the freshest piles stood tallest and looked a little ragged. Steam rose from them in places. The interiors were hot as the waste heat from microbe digestion built up in the pile, much like our own bodies warm from the heat generated by metabolism in our muscles and organs. Bob explained the composting process in detail, and I recalled a bread metaphor that my home-composting mentor liked to use.

Bob selected from a slate of raw ingredients: inoculum (a mix of microbes, analogous to a sourdough starter), water, and a mixing cycle tied to the type of ingredients and wetness of the blend to reach a desired goal several weeks in the future. Attributes like carbon and nutrient content define how compost is used. Gardeners and farmers growing organic vegetables and fruit often seek out compost high in nitrogen, phosphorus, and micronutrients. A rancher seeking to boost the water-holding capacity in pastures might seek a more carbon-rich product. Park and golf course turf managers tend to request products in between the two.

Green products (like lawn clippings, green leaves, and food waste) launch the compost into a fast and hot decomposition cycle that yields a product rich in nutrients important for plant growth. Livestock manure has much the same effect when added to the mix. Conversely, products high in fiber and low in nutrients—like wood chips, shredded paperboard food containers, dried autumn leaves, and ground wheat straw—decompose more slowly, with less heat and with a product rich in organic matter but lower in other nutrients. Commercial composters such as Al blend the high-nitrogen and high-fiber materials much like commercial bakers blend ingredients with an end product in mind. Manure from carnivorous pets like dogs and cats have too much potential to spread disease to humans, and therefore are prohibited from the composting recipe.

The more oxygen the pile holds, the higher the potential for rapid composting and the more the ecosystem inside the compost pile favors single-celled organisms like certain bacteria, archaea, and protozoan (amoeba) species as well as multi-celled organisms like arthropods (spiders and mites) and annelids (worms). Less oxygen favors a somewhat different mix of those same organisms, but more fungi. A wetter mix drives the process in a different direction, favoring other organisms, but if the pile is too wet, it "increases the stink factor," as Bob described it.

The oldest compost piles in the A1 yard were smaller and homogenous. They had lost about half of their volume as the microbes consumed the sugars, fats, and proteins present in the waste, burning it into dead microbe bodies. About half of the carbon would be consumed and released into the atmosphere in the end. Most of that carbon would become carbon dioxide, its end fate if it had been left to rot out in the open. A small portion would become the greenhouse gas methane, but much less of it than had it been dumped into the landfill. Whereas most of the remaining nitrogen and other nutrients would remain and be stabilized in the organic matter, a portion of the nitrogen would be lost in decomposition. Of that portion, most would become nitrogen gas; however, some would come off the piles as the air pollutants ammonia and nitrogen oxides, or NOx. A smaller but significant amount would become nitrous oxide. The nitrous oxide emissions are approximately the same as would be emitted if the garbage were left to rot out in the open.

Besides achieving certain end-product attributes, the composting process is designed to minimize emissions. When composting proceeds slowly, the piles are cooler, as the microbes quickly deplete the oxygen, leading to more methane emissions. When the piles compost quickly, they are hotter, and far less methane results, but more nitrous oxide is produced. Studies show that the net emissions from these two pathways are different. The cooler piles that compost more slowly produce more net emissions compared to the hot-composted piles. But in the end, those emissions are substantially less than if the food had been buried in the landfill, where much of it would decompose into methane in a process that can continue for decades. Interestingly, the greenhouse gas emissions and air pollutants can be substantially reduced if the decomposing piles are covered with a layer of finished compost several inches thick. The layer acts like a filter, in which microbes consume pollutants as they seep through.

Bob drove us to a finished mound of compost ready to be loaded, shipped, and sold. Suddenly, his face soured as he noticed a bright-yellow plastic label from a banana peel resting on the compost pile. He leapt from the driver's seat, darted to the pile, and plucked it from the surface. Dan and I piled out of the pickup and joined him. Bob held it out to us to inspect, and then hurled it into the breeze in great irritation.

"These GD things," he said. "They will be the death of me."

"Can't they make them out of PLA?" Dan moaned. PLA is polylactic acid, made from corn starch, and often referred to as bioplastic. It is fully compostable in operations like those at A1.

"Unfortunately, some people didn't get the memo!"

I asked Bob to clarify.

"Plastic doesn't decompose—period. We get way more plastic than we'd like!" he lamented.

A1 Organics lays their compost in 500-foot rows and produces over 500,000 tons of it annually. Keenesburg, Colorado. *Clinton T. Sander / A1 Organics*

I recalled a visit I'd made with my colleague Amy Swan to California's Salinas Valley. Scientists were studying how combining cover crops with compost affected organic broccoli and strawberry crops. For years the researchers had applied compost made from food waste. The soil was sparsely littered with plastic labels and small pieces of plastic bags everywhere we looked in the plots. The scientist giving us the tour speculated there were hundreds of pounds of plastic per acre in the field.

People who throw their label-ridden food waste into compost bins are committing those plastic bits to accumulate in agricultural fields and gardens. As the vegetables rot, the labels and the bags remain intact, or slowly break apart into the dangerous microplastics becoming ubiquitous throughout ecosystems where humans live, even accumulating in our bodies.[251]

We got back into the truck as Dan and Bob talked about label litter. "I hope it doesn't take us twenty years of education to get people to deal with these things right, like it is taking with recycling," Dan commented. Most of the effort he and his colleagues put in at CHaRM is devoted to educating the public about what can and cannot be composted and recycled, and what is truly landfill trash.

We pulled up to another apparently finished pile waiting to be loaded and sold.

"This is our BioComp product," Bob said.

"It's the most beautiful stuff! Everybody wants it!" Dan enthused.

I got out of the truck for a closer look. I saw no plastic. The material was uniform, clean, and fine-grained. Like at the other pile, I felt a faint warmth on my face while standing near it, and imagined layering it into my garden. I stripped off my jacket and plunged my arm into the pile. I pulled out a handful and squeezed it. As had been the case with the other compost, this was warm, and indeed beautiful in a deeply agronomic way.

"Yeah, put your hand into that stuff!" Dan enthused. Bob and Dan were both looking at me, their faces lit.

I glanced down at the pile in my hand, and the word *BioComp* suddenly came back into focus in my mind. The word was close to biosolids. I looked at the two of them and ventured a tentative question. "What's this made of?"

"Biodigest. The sludge from sewage treatment plants," Bob replied.

My hand froze.

"It's composted human poop," Bob continued.

"It's beautiful stuff!" Dan added.

I glanced down at my hand and squeezed it once again, then released the material in the most nonchalant way I could manage. I had seen on their website that A1 produced a high-grade compost from sewage sludge, but the thought had slipped my mind until now. Then Dan stepped up to the pile and took a handful like mine, still smiling. I felt only marginally better.

"It's okay, it's safe," Bob said. "Farmers love this stuff! It's super-high in nutrients. We compost it in a way that kills the pathogens. But you two should probably wash your hands when we get back to the office."[252]

Bob was going on a family trip the next day, and had work to do before leaving, so he took us back to the office where I washed my hands. We then shook hands, I thanked him, and Dan and

I departed for our appointment at the Front Range Landfill in Erie, Colorado.

Which is how we found ourselves standing on the largest pile of garbage I'd ever seen.

> • <

Dan and I were there as guests of the landfill's sustainability coordinator, a thoughtful, efficient, young civil engineer in his early thirties. We met him at the entrance, where we donned hard hats and lime green safety vests before he drove us on a circuitous route through the garbage pile toward the summit, introducing us to his work en route. Despite the surroundings and the omnipresent odor, his focus was not on the garbage. His vision was entirely upon the network of pipes and pumps running into, across, and just beneath the skin of the garbage pile. His job was to capture as much as possible of the methane that had been created within the pile by the microbes digesting the food and yard leftovers underfoot and turn that methane into electricity.

A latticework of perforated pipe ran across and below the landfill's surface. A series of pumps created a negative pressure, or partial vacuum, within the pipes drawing air from the landfill into the pipes' perforations before separating the methane from the carbon dioxide and other impurities dominating the gas from the pile. Pumps concentrated and moved the gas to a noisy building located on the northeast boundary property, which contained two massive internal combustion engines connected to generators to create electricity—along with by-products of heat, carbon dioxide, nitrogen oxides (NOx), and other trace pollutants—from the methane.

From the landfill summit we could hear the engine's roar during a brief interlude when the roaring trash compactor was briefly out of earshot. The methane was burned in generators to produce electricity the same way that Albert Straus's generator burns the methane from his manure lagoon, as described in the dairy chapter, "Cecil's Hands."

We asked the engineer why composting was difficult to introduce to operations like this landfill. His answer mirrored that of core studies conducted by the EPA and others.[253,254,255] People threw their waste into one bin that haulers picked up regularly and carried to a single destination, completing the job simply, and in the minds of municipal managers, efficiently. It was a straightforward system, replicated tens of thousands of times across the country by an industry worth $70 billion in the United States and $422 billion worldwide in 2021.[256] And whereas there is no question that removing waste from people's homes and neighborhoods has almost uncountable public health benefits, that oversimplified model is now coming under scrutiny.

For decades, the US waste management industry has faced increasing consumer and municipal demands for solid waste recycling. Recycling creates a need for at least two waste diversion streams with their separate receptacles. Municipal composting requires a third diversion stream, along with the need to educate consumers about what can be composted versus what is trash. Composting requires land for the operations, along with equipment and operators. It requires a change to a more complicated business model in a well-established industry that is already highly profitable.

In summary, the Front Range Landfill, and the waste management industry in general, simply hadn't geared itself up to remanufacture and sell back to consumers a portion of the material it collected. The industry had defined efficiency in terms that, in the end, pushed onto others the burden of the dispersed network of thousands of giant methane factories—landfills—that their business model relies upon.

Those consequences can be clearly seen in a map of methane emissions from landfills produced by Climate TRACE, a nonprofit organization devoted to mapping major sources of greenhouse gas emissions around the world. Scientists at Climate TRACE leveraged data from satellite-based sensors designed to detect point-sources of dangerous climate-heating gases.[257] In late 2022, Climate TRACE estimated 440,000 metric tons of CO_2e emissions from the Front Range Landfill,[258] ranking it in the worst 11 percent worldwide for landfill methane emissions (531st out of about 4,500 landfills). That is the equivalent yearly carbon emissions from around 95,000 cars, or roughly equal to a third of the total year 2022 automobile emissions in Weld County, Colorado, where the landfill is located.

According to the *Inventory of US Greenhouse Gas Emissions and Sinks* compiled by the US Environmental Protection Agency (EPA), methane from landfills like the Front Range Landfill accounts for just short of 2 percent of the US carbon footprint. Two percent may not seem like a big deal, until one considers that the US carbon footprint is the second largest in the world.

Two percent of such a large value is greater than the carbon footprint of more than two-thirds of the other countries in the world. The emissions from US food and yard waste alone eclipse the national emissions from all sources (energy, transportation, heating, etc.) emitted by individual countries like Chile, Israel, Greece, and Austria.[259]

As large as those numbers are, recent evidence suggests the emissions are substantially higher. Climate TRACE's satellite-based inventory of emissions estimates the emissions from landfills are twice as large as reported by the EPA.[260] The EPA's emissions estimate for the Front Range Landfill was half that detected by Climate TRACE, in keeping with overall emissions estimates. Methane capture reported to the EPA by the Front Range Landfill's operators in 2021 indicated that less than 20 percent of the EPA's estimate of the methane from the landfill (less than 10 percent of the Climate TRACE estimate) had been diverted by the methane-capture system to produce electricity.[261] These methane emissions could be largely avoided if compostable raw materials were diverted into a compost-remanufacturing stream to create locally usable agricultural amendments.

Information provided by the generator operators indicates the two generators at the landfill produce enough electricity to power three thousand homes, or approximately half of the homes in the nearby town of Erie, Colorado, which sponsored the project. Thousands of facilities like this one dot the landscape at landfills around the world. Emissions from most landfills are still not regulated. EPA studies indicate that about 40 percent of total landfill methane emissions in the United States come from landfills where methane-capturing equipment is not required. The remaining 60 percent come from sites that attempt to capture methane.

What if all the food and yard waste were diverted from the Front Range Landfill and used to make compost? Enough compost could be created yearly from the waste at the Front Range Landfill to apply to about a fifth of the cropland in the three-county region that utilizes the landfill.[262] Considering the four landfills in the region that are a comparable size, imagine the possibilities.

As Dan had cogently described it, here lies a mountain of lost opportunities. In the meantime, the raw materials at our disposal are making the Earth burn.

> • <

The best use of food waste may vary from place to place; however, composting has emerged as a clearly positive solution.[263] The research laboratory where I worked at Colorado State University once partnered with Boulder County and the City of Boulder, Colorado, to study the advantages and barriers farmers face in utilizing compost in their fields and pastures. As part of that study, we worked with a father-and-son farming team[264] who were integrating composting into a carbon-farming program on a field of irrigated cropland they leased from Boulder County. Later that spring they intended to plant corn contracted to feed cattle at a dairy nearby, and they were planting a cover crop to build organic matter and capture nutrients in the crop before establishing the corn. A late harvest, combined with wet and muddy conditions the previous autumn, had prevented them from planting the cover crop at that more typical time; however, late in February a weather window opened that allowed them to get out into the field.

The day before I arrived, they had spread a nutrient-rich layer of A1 Organics EcoGro compost. During my visit they filled the bin of their high-tech, GPS-enabled planter with the seeds of the cover crops and sped across the field, seeding the hundred-acre field in less than an hour. They could plant the cover crops in precise rows in the field and later plant the corn crop in between the rows of the cover crop to reduce the competition between them. The cover crop would stabilize the soil, capture nutrients for the corn crop from the air and soil, and sequester carbon from the atmosphere through the biomass it created, as described in the chapter on corn and nitrogen, "The Corn Eaters."

The EcoGro compost, combined with the cover crop, would feed and improve the soil community, boost crop yields, and reduce the net greenhouse gas emissions from growing the corn. As John Wick had found in his pastures, the corn grown on plots with the compost and cover crops produced markedly higher yields, with higher nutritional value for the livestock it would feed. Corn grown conventionally, without the aid of cover crops and compost, produced net emissions of about one metric ton of CO_2e per acre per year. Combining the use of compost and cover crops reversed that flow of carbon, turning the pastures from a source of carbon pollution into the atmosphere to a net sink of

This corn has been planted directly through a cereal rye cover crop. Wisconsin. *Erin Silva / Center for Integrated Agricultural Systems*

carbon into the soil. The amount of the sink was stunning—three and a half metric tons of CO_2e per acre per year were sequestered in the soil. As the project progressed, and as has been seen in multiple studies elsewhere, the health of the soil has improved in ways that lead to myriad other benefits.

Impressive as these local reductions are, what impact would there be if many more farmers, ranchers, landfill managers, and consumers were engaged in the compost cycle? Project Drawdown, a nonprofit committed to identifying and implementing strategies to eliminate carbon pollution, calculated the greenhouse gas reductions from composting just 38 percent of compostable waste in developing countries, and 57 percent in developed countries. These relatively modest actions would reduce greenhouse gas emissions every year by 2.1 billion metric tons of CO_2e, or about 5 percent of the world's total carbon footprint. That's about one-fifth of the total carbon footprint of our food system.[265] Achieving that remarkable reduction assumes only about half of the compostable waste worldwide would be recycled back onto cropland and pastures. Going "all-in" globally, following South Korea's example, could effectively cut the total emissions coming from our food system by somewhere between a third and a half.

It's remarkable that such a simple step—keeping our food out of the trash—has such a dramatic ripple effect.

The Carbon Footprint of **Food Waste**

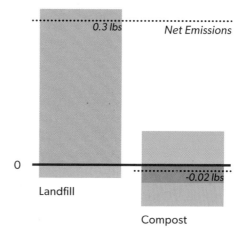

Methane
Fertilizer Offset
Carbon Capture
Composting Emissions

*Pound of CO$_2$e per
pound of waste*

0.3 lbs   *Net Emissions*

0

Landfill

-0.02 lbs

Compost

Composting food waste and applying it to fields and pastures leads to a net carbon offset through the avoided emissions from synthetic fertilizers for crop nutrients, as well as a soil carbon sequestration from the compost application. "Methane" includes emissions from food decomposed by anaerobic microbes. "Fertilizer Offset" includes the emissions from manufactured synthetic fertilizers avoided by the application of compost. "Carbon Capture" includes the portion of food waste that is not decomposed in landfills (plant fibers that cannot be anaerobically digested by microbes) as well as carbon sequestration in soils when compost is applied to fields and pastures. "Composting Emissions" is the methane and nitrous oxide emissions and the fuel burned in composting food waste.

The Blue Plate

Can we eat our way out of the climate crisis?

I pondered the question that opened this book on a bluebird autumn morning where I found myself on a pilgrimage of sorts, standing next to a sturdy white pine tree that had experienced an unlikely life. Surprising as the tree's presence was, the tree was not the only unlikely part of the scene. The small cabin before me, the sunlit meadow awash in goldenrod beyond, the bald eagle that had just flown overhead toward the Wisconsin River in the distance—their presence that day were made possible because of decisions made a century earlier, followed by decades of steadfast work. Had the decisions been otherwise, or the hands been diverted elsewhere, the scene before us would have been entirely different.

Leslie and I had traveled with two lifelong friends to the Aldo Leopold Legacy Center outside of Baraboo, Wisconsin, and were

Previous spread: A backyard feast. *Greg Balkin*

on the land that had inspired the essays in Aldo's stalwart literary classic, *A Sand County Almanac*. As we circled the shack, a former chicken coop that Aldo and Estella Leopold had reconstructed into living quarters amidst the forest they restored from played out, eroded farmland, we pondered the stories from this land that anchored the Leopold family conservation legacy and have inspired millions to take similar steps in their own lives.

Aldo and Estella had bought the 140-acre farm for eight dollars an acre. They immediately set to restoring the forest. The Leopolds and their children planted an average of three thousand trees each year on their land and some of their neighbors' property over the next two decades. During dry periods, they hand-watered the most at-risk seedlings from buckets they carried into the fields. The white pine that towered over me and their neighbors all around were the sweat equity from their labor. Like the forest, the bald eagle that had just flown overhead would probably not have been there had a larger community of conservation-minded people not made the decision five decades earlier to protect the dwindling population of at-risk birds from chemical pollutants and execute on a long-term plan to restore their habitat.

Success stories like the Leopolds' stand out in a world where we seem determined to consume the very planet that sustains us. Aldo did not survive to see the first photographs of the Earth from space taken by astronauts in the Apollo missions. I still remember how the first images of that lovely, blue marble floating in space affected me. I immediately recognized it as *home*, and I was not alone in that experience. This Earth, in all its complexity, is heartbreakingly beautiful.

If we could ask the Leopolds, "Can we eat our way out of the climate crisis?" I can't help but think that they would celebrate the carbon-farming pioneers profiled in this book, but caution us to not lean too hard on the land to get us out of the problem we find ourselves in. Both carbon sequestration and reducing carbon emissions in the food system pivot upon the decisions made one farmer at a time, one field at a time, one herd of livestock at a time, the entire world over. The complexities of each individual field, soil, and cropping and grazing system can be daunting. Perhaps most importantly, nobody wants to be in a situation where solving one environmental problem creates another one.

The term "moon shot" comes to mind when I think about what the Leopolds accomplished. They began a task of unknown duration and uncertain promise of success. They were not certain they could even acquire the tree seedlings necessary for the effort. But they thought it was worth doing. They put their shoulders to the wheel, and the forest, the native prairie flowers, the eagles nesting on the land, and all the carbon the system now holds are testimony to their efforts.

The scientific research also shows that besides the sorts of quiet innovations adopted by the growers in this book, some moon shots would be a good insurance policy for a stable climate future.[266] Below are a two moon shots already underway that hold some of the greatest future promise.

> • ‹

One sunny June morning I visited The Land Institute near Salina, Kansas, to learn firsthand about its groundbreaking efforts to reinvent agriculture. Dr. Lee DeHaan led me and other visitors on a tour of the research facility and the Kernza* domestication program he directs. The product of an audacious crop-breeding program, Kernza is just one of several transformational foods emerging from an effort begun in 1976 by The Land Institute's founder, Dr. Wes Jackson, along with his family and a group of supporters.

How audacious is Kernza? The Land Institute was attempting something that had never been done before. They would attempt to perennialize the world's staple grain crops. If they succeeded, crops like wheat, soybeans, and corn could be grown without tilling the soil every year. The crops would require only periodic replanting, in polycultures that more closely mimic natural ecosystems, rather than having to be replanted as annual crops every growing season.

Lee leads this radical, open-source crop-breeding effort that has led to Kernza being planted on thousands of acres on several continents. Kernza grain has found its way into beer, snacks, and breads. Universities around the world have joined the wave of perennial agriculture research begun at The Land Institute, and Kernza is just one of the products of their efforts.

At the time of this writing, an even greater but quieter revolution has emerged from The Land Institute's efforts. Perennial rice crops developed at Yunnan University in China, with support from The Land Institute, have produced crop yields equal to annual rice for four years in a row (two crops per year) on tens of thousands of acres in Southeast Asia. The acreage is expanding exponentially each year. This breakthrough is notable not only because rice feeds more people than any grain, but also because it demonstrates that grain crops can both be perennial and produce good yields—maybe not such a moon shot after all! Perennial sorghum and wheat, along with two new grains called Silflower™[267] (an oilseed) and perennial Baki™[268] bean (a novel and nutritious legume) are making their way through the breeding pipeline headed toward early commercialization in the next decade.[269] Growing these crops combined in diverse polycultures rather than monocultures is a central pillar of The Land Institute's research program.

Carbon-storing, soil-protecting perennial grains are becoming more profitable than unsustainable annual crops, and farmers are taking them up. Growing food in agricultural ecosystems that mimic perennial, diverse natural ecosystems has the potential to reverse problems that have plagued agriculture since its beginnings. Replacing shallow-rooted, annual-crop monocultures that must be planted every year with deep-rooted polycultures that need to be renewed only periodically solves many of the problems described in this book—regular tillage, the loss of deep-soil carbon, and the incessant drive to overfertilize crops.

> • ‹

We can and should also learn from the practice of the Indigenous peoples around the world in growing more food on trees. Contemporary almonds, walnuts, pecans, and hazelnuts are the outcome of millennia of breeding efforts by people well before industrial agriculture began. But modern agriculture has largely replaced the diverse, carbon-rich food forests that produced these

Madeline DuBois selects perennial Kernza® seeds with desirable traits on a research plot at The Land Institute, a nonprofit scientific research organization based in Salina, Kansas. *The Land Institute*

nutritious foods with annual-grain monocultures, bleeding away the carbon those forests once held.

The American Chestnut Foundation[270] and the Arbor Day Foundation[271] are two organizations building upon that legacy of wise agricultural ancestors. Their new nut- and fruit-tree varieties, including hybrid chestnuts, hazelnuts, walnuts, hickories, pecans, and acorns, are expanding throughout temperate regions. These new varieties growing outside the confines of the limited range of other commercial nut varieties produce yields comparable to soybeans and wheat, but in permaculture food forests that support grazing livestock or grain crops grown beneath the tree canopy. They could pull billions of tons of carbon from the atmosphere back to the land at levels that spectacular forests once held across multiple continents.

> • <

These transformative initiatives and others like them have tremendous potential to bring delicious, nutritious, low-carbon foods to our tables, while re-creating agriculture as ecosystems more closely aligned with how natural ecosystems work.

Whereas these stories will have to play out over decades, the stories of the innovators described in this book are happening right now. In Curtis Sayles's field, I felt like we stood at the far end of a continuously evolving experiment that began when the first person intentionally cleared some ground and planted the first rice seed in far Asia. It is an audacious idea for a person to cut, clear, burn, and plow one ecosystem and replace it with a completely fabricated, human-engineered ecosystem constructed to bend uncountable millions of years of evolutionary processes to one's will. Doing such a thing takes a certain amount of arrogance. Agriculture itself may be humanity's longest-running experiment. Have we taken a long enough view of history, informed anew by the climate crisis, to argue that agriculture has succeeded?

If we ponder that question with a dose of humility, I don't believe we can label agriculture as an unqualified success. To be clear, conventional agriculture did make civilized society possible. Fabulous technological, medical, and artistic innovations came about because agriculture improved food security throughout the world. That said, it appears very likely that agriculture created the heated platform from which the fossil fuel catapult is hurling us into climatic terra incognita, an unknown region on the climate map that ought to be labeled "Here be Dragons."

Farmers like my great-grandmother Neva and her cohort arrived on the western edge of the Great Plains, an ecosystem they had never seen before, and made fateful decisions that haunt us a century later. They ran steel through soil that had never been plowed, scattered seed from plants that had never before grown in that ecosystem, in soil and a climate with which they had no experience. Within six generations the ecosystem hit rock bottom. It utterly failed as cropland and as prairie.

By working with nature, rather than against it, the growers in this book and others like them have bent the arc of history toward sustainability and regeneration. That gives me hope.

But is hope enough? As a scientist, I chafe at a world bounded by hope on the one hand and rational truth on the other. In the face of seemingly intractable problems, I continually hope that carbon farming becomes the new normal in the world's farm-lands. But the progress feels painfully slow. Sometimes I find myself irrationally wishing the problems would just disappear. Daytime fantasies have me awakening from this fevered dream to find that the climate is still stable, that our food supply is not threatened, and that millions of environmental refugees are not fleeing coastlines on a near-term trajectory to be underwater, with inland desert cities facing Death Valley–like temperatures within our children's lifetimes. Then I discover that no, there was no fevered dream, only a fully fevered reality. I am fully, ratio-nally, terribly awake.

Perhaps you are like me in this regard, and like me, you retreat to the things that give you comfort. For me it is family, my clos-est friends, colleagues, and the land. In those moments spent in retreat and comfort—and even despair—there is often food. We make our grandmother's fried chicken, our favorite aunt's rhu-barb crisp, our best friend's pesto lasagna, our uncle's cinnamon rolls. Or we step into our favorite taco shop or ice cream parlor. We pour a glass of lemonade, pop a beer, accept a glass of wine (or something stronger), and sit down to a meal with the people we love while we try to work through our troubles, or at least for-get them. In those moments of retreat and comfort, food brokers the relationship. Food becomes the organizing principle for the relationships that give us strength. Food protects us, even saves us, for just a little while.

Somewhere between hope and scientific truth is the fact that the way we grow, process, ship, and eat that food, and deal with the waste, is already reducing the threat of the looming climate catastrophe. Not only can the food system help, but it is already bending the curve toward progress. The least expensive, most straightforward methods known to science to strip the extra carbon pollution from the atmosphere are directly under our feet and all around us, in the soil and the plants the ecosystem supports. No apparent downsides to carbon sequestration and reducing emissions have emerged in decades of research into carbon farming. Food provides the mechanisms through which people around the globe can help transform their hometowns into low- and zero-carbon communities.

But can we actually eat our way out of the climate crisis? The answer is a partial yes, but I'd like to reframe the question.

Yes, carbon farming will help. It is mandatory, a required step in the path to our low-carbon future. But—and this is a very big but—we cannot depend upon agriculture and the food system to completely erase today's astronomically high fossil fuel emissions. The agricultural transformations described in this book, combined with reductions in fossil fuel emissions, are the least costly, most efficient, and most effective way currently known to pull carbon out of the atmosphere.[272] They are already being leveraged on millions of acres worldwide and are expanding at double-digit rates annually. The words "low carbon" and "climate friendly" are starting to appear on restaurant menus and grocers' shelves, reflecting growing societal demand.

The best we appear likely to achieve through these farming practices, however, is to offset between one-sixth and one-third of today's annual worldwide carbon footprint, if low-carbon farming practices were widely adopted over the next three decades.[273,274,275]

I'll be honest with you, those numbers make my heart sink a little, and perhaps they do for you as well. I'd rather it was more. I want a stronger answer. What makes that seemingly small percentage feel a little pitiful is not that the mitigation potential of carbon farming is so small, but that fossil fuel emissions remain so incredibly high. We must stop burning fossil fuels completely, and as quickly as possible, and the responsibility to accomplish that goal must not just be placed upon the individual consumer. The ethicist and writer Kathleen Dean Moore laid out this reality in an essay in Salon,[276] where she wrote:

> Let us focus full attention on the real issue here, which is, how can we stop the fossil-fuel industry from destroying the life-sustaining systems of the planet in their seemingly endless, and certainly shameless, quest for profit?

Plant-based foods have the lowest carbon footprint overall. Farmed shellfish have the lowest carbon footprint of any animal food product. Tree nuts are the only net carbon-negative food because of the carbon sequestration in the tree wood, but they consume prohibitive amounts of water in some locations. Note that the emissions from foods grown in particular locations can vary significantly. Individual practices such as growing livestock feeds with regenerative methods, reducing tillage, and utilizing waste-to-compost programs to fertilize crops can significantly reduce emissions. Practices that produce high emissions from burning fossil fuels (like relying on trans-basin, pumped-water irrigation projects such as in California) can add greatly to emissions and substantially reduce the carbon benefits of other regenerative practices.

Carbon Footprint of Common Foods

Pound of CO$_2$e per pound of food

Tree Nuts	-1.3 lbs
Citrus Fruit	0.3 lbs
Most Vegetables	0.4 lbs
Apples	0.4 lbs
Tomatoes	0.7 lbs
Stonefruit	0.7 lbs
Shellfish (farmed)	0.8 lbs
Berries & Grapes	1.4 lbs
Dried Beans/Lentils/Peas	1.4 lbs
Bread (regenerative)	0.8 lbs
Bread (conventional)	1.6 lbs
Tofu	2.6 lbs
Milk	2.7 lbs
Peanuts	3.3 lbs
Salmon (wild)	3.5 lbs
Salmon (farmed)	3.6 lbs
Rice	3.7 lbs
Eggs	4.2 lbs
Tuna	4.5 lbs
Trout (farmed)	6.4 lbs
Poultry	7.5 lbs
Coffee	8.2 lbs
Pork	10.6 lbs
Cheese	12.4 lbs
Shrimp (farmed)	25.45 lbs
Beef (dairy herd)	34.1 lbs
Lamb	40.6 lbs
Beef (meat herd)	60.7 lbs

The choices we make and actions we take cannot be simply individual and personal if we are to succeed. They must propagate through society and government policy so that society, culture, and institutions are aligned to transform both agriculture and our energy and transportation systems to a sustainable future.

How then do we try to eat our way out of the climate crisis?

Ending the practice of slicing steel through soil allows carbon to accumulate in the earth and restores health to the soil, cleans rivers and oceans, and clears the air of the omnipresent agricultural dust that dominates so much of the world's skies today. We must aspire at the same time to solve our age-old dependence on tillage in ways that do not depend upon herbicides.

By bringing our vegetable and fruit farms closer to home, rather than relying on far-flung farms in fragile desert landscapes irrigated from river-destroying, methane-emitting reservoirs behind towering dams, we can dramatically reduce the climate burden in the vegetables we eat. By doing this we also are restoring the estuaries and fisheries once sustained by the rivers that water those farms.

Keeping our native fisheries healthy, and the ecosystems that support them, while restoring the shellfish beds that once dominated our coastlines to the powerful food engines they once were has benefits beyond measure. Responsibly packaging and transporting the seafood they produce will reduce the transportation burden held by seafood currently transported by air.

Pulling animals out of the factory and returning them to the farm, and recycling their manure back into the soil, is critical to growing low-carbon fruits, vegetables, and grains alongside livestock partners with a lower meat and dairy carbon footprint. Besides helping to cool the planet, the practice appeals to a broad spectrum of society, from consumers to nutritionists, animal welfare advocates, scientists, climate activists, and the farmers and ranchers themselves.

Perhaps one of the greatest truths the climate crisis has shown us is that our planet is small, and there is no *away*. Throwing our food and yard waste into landfills is an ignoble waste. **Composting programs designed to cycle the products** of our ecosystems back into the ecosystems themselves will go a long way to curing our climate ills.

That is the view from thirty thousand feet. What can we do as individuals in our daily lives? Here are some guidelines for a cooler planet:

Eat food. Not too much. Mostly plants.[277]

Thank you, Michael Pollan, for that concise and helpful dictum.

Like oysters, mussels do not have to be fed directly, they remove carbon dioxide from the oceans to build their shells, and they clean the waters in which they grow. The coast of Galicia, Spain. *Ken Etzel*

Meat and dairy eaters can reduce their meat- and dairy-dominated meals, and **consider pastured poultry and regeneratively grown grazing animals and dairy products** as lower-carbon alternatives to factory-farmed beef, lamb, pork, and goat. When eating red meat, try to obtain grass-finished meats from growers leveraging regenerative grazing practices. Support transforming the livestock industry from the CAFO model to a system with animals raised and finished out on the land.

Keep your food and yard waste out of the landfill. Sign up with your trash hauler for a compost bucket if they offer that service. If no such services are available, contact your local city council or county commission and ask them to build a waste-to-compost-to-farm program to keep all organic waste out of the landfill and recycle the nutrients back to farmland. Or compost your food and yard waste yourself and use it to grow your own vegetables or contribute it to a neighbor's garden.

Seafood eaters can explore the low-carbon joys of farmed shellfish such as mussels, oysters, clams, and scallops, and other foods recommended by the Monterey Bay Aquarium Seafood Watch program and their Seafood Carbon Emissions Tool.[278] Support policies for sustainably managed, wild-caught fisheries and the wild ecosystems that feed them. Support the continued improvement of aquaculture to sustainably produce foods the wild fisheries cannot supply.

As reliable, verifiable carbon-farming or regenerative-farming food labels emerge, buy foods certified under those labels. Until then, continue to ask the bakers, restaurateurs, grocers, and farmers and ranchers you know for foods grown with regenerative, carbon-farming practices.

Avoid foods that travel by air.

These hopeful, concrete steps will help reduce the greenhouse gases in the Earth's atmosphere, ensuring a safer future in this lovely blue marble floating in space that is our home. Rather than consuming our planet, we can restore and sustain it.

> • <

During our visit to the Hog Island Oyster Company, shellfish grower Terry Sawyer really caught my colleague Amy's and my attention when he told us the company had extended their work into the watershed above their oyster and mussel beds.

"We bought 250 acres of ranchland in the watershed above our oyster and mussel beds, and we are putting the land to work storing carbon and improving water quality in the creeks feeding the estuary," he'd said.

He scanned the ranks of oaks and conifers clustered throughout the grassland on the hillside above where we stood. His eyes softened a little, and I followed his gaze uphill. The breeze off Tomales Bay pushed through the trees and grasses flanking the steep hill. A seemingly infinite number of shades of green stippled the landscape as sunlight flashed off the leaves. Terry described in an optimistic tone some of the efforts from their initiative. They were revegetating degraded stream banks, planting trees, planning to spread compost on portions of the grazing land, and changing the grazing cycles to help restore native perennial grasses to degraded soils. The Carbon Cycle Institute was helping them write the carbon-farming plan for the property, and the watershed above the shellfish beds already showed improvements.

Depending upon the project's successes, the company hoped to buy more land and extend the efforts further. It struck me as not just a hopeful experiment, but also a smart business move for an enterprise relying on clean water, and a strong net positive for the climate and ecosystem. But it was not necessarily an obvious choice. It was exactly the kind of innovative systems thinking I'd heard from regenerative growers presented throughout this book.

"It only makes sense to link the land and sea in an operation like ours," Terry had said. "We will store more carbon upstream while protecting the water quality in our oyster and mussel beds. But as incredibly busy as we already are, it's kind of crazy that we would take this on, really. But we felt like we needed to do it, and so far it seems to be working out."

Then he turned back to Amy and me with a wry grin.

"The problem is, we like to farm. And we periodically need to have our heads examined because of it. But ultimately, we really just like to eat."

Acknowledgments

I'm grateful to the farmers, ranchers, scientists, activists, and others who dedicated their time, energy, and their stories for this book, including Amy Yackel Adams, Rod Adams, Shawn Archibeque, Adrian Card, Regan Choi, Jeff Creque, Steve DelGrosso, Dan DeSutter, Tanya Dideriksen, Steve Ela, Terry Engle, Pete Falloon, Jeff Jermunson, Lynne Kesel, Dan Matsch, Tony Maxwell, Jim Moseley, Chris Myrick, Lynette Niebrugge, Calla Rose Ostrander, Loren Poncia, Stephen Reichley, Ken Rulon, Rodney Rulon, Terry Sawyer, Curtis Sayles, Pete Smith, Julie Stadelman, Albert Straus, Amy Swan, Steve Tucker, Ray Tyler, John Wick, and Bob Yost.

John Calderazzo and Laura Pritchett supported me through hours of conversations, reviewed countless drafts, motivated me with pep talks, and encouraged me to find a home for this project.

A peer review of the draft manuscript by Tim Crews tightened the science presented in this book.

Friends, colleagues, and family who read manuscript drafts or engaged in conversations that helped to develop the stories told

Previous spread: Growers, processors, and businesses come together to learn more about Kernza® and its environmental benefits and economic opportunities. Madison, Minnesota. *Amy Kumler*

here supported this effort in many ways. They include Jill Baron, Leslie Brown, SueEllen Campbell, Hans Cole, Francesca Cotrufo, Dorn Cox, Scott Denning, Jeff Easter, Jim Easter, Maria Fernandez-Gimenez, Edward Heilman, Elaine Hollen, Janet Hood, Dona Horan, Tom McKinnon, Cara Mathers, Jan Moraczewski, Susan Moran, Haley Nagle, Devin Odell, Keith Paustian, Todd Simmons, Meagan Schipanski, Kerri Steenwerth, Matt Stoecker, Crystal Toureene, Tim Vaughan, and Gary Wockner. There are so many people to thank, and I apologize if I inadvertently missed any of you.

Much of this manuscript was written while on retreat at Casita Pura Vida outside Fruita, Colorado. I'm grateful to Dan Birch and Laurie Rink for their kind support. Kathleen Dean Moore and the Summer Fishtrap Gathering of Writers provided a wonderful opportunity to develop concepts for the book.

The Colorado State University School of Global Environmental Sustainability (SoGES) supported the development, reporting, and writing of this book with a yearlong SoGES fellowship.

I am grateful to my agent, Jessica Papin at Dystel, Goderich & Bourret, for ably representing me and for her kind, thoughtful, and helpful advice. Thank you, Michelle Nijhuis, for connecting me with Jessica.

Unending thanks go to my wife, Leslie Brown, for lending her editorial skills, love, and encouragement through the years of this project, and to my family for their patient support. My parents, Jo Ann Heilman Easter and James Arthur Easter, and my brother, Jeff Easter, instilled in me a deep love for food, gardening, and wild places.

Thank you, Karla and John at Patagonia Books, for believing in this project.

Carbon Footprint Disclosure

The following greenhouse gas emissions were estimated to have been produced in the research for and writing of *The Blue Plate: A Food Lover's Guide to Climate Chaos*. All units are in metric tons of CO_2e.

Air Travel:	5.84[279]
Automobile Travel:	1.55[280]
Train Travel:	0.04[281]
Hotel Rooms:	0.34[282]
Electricity Use:	1.54[283]
Estimated total:	**9.31**

Approximately 1.24 kg (2.7 lbs) of CO_2e were produced by the printing of each paper book purchased.[284] Reading or listening to

Previous spread: High-altitude farming is all about avoiding the late and early frosts. Jessie Maza harvests tomatoes at Rugged Roots Farm, a nonprofit created to provide fresh and sustainable produce to communities of the Lost Sierra. Quincy, California. *Ken Etzel*

books on portable electronic devices can have approximately the same carbon footprint as printed books; however, one must read or listen to several dozen books on the device to overcome its carbon footprint from manufacturing.[285] Mike Berners-Lee, the author of *The Carbon Footprint of Everything*, writes, "E-readers are better than paper books if used many times so the paper saving outweighs the device's embodied emissions."[286]

You can reduce this book's carbon footprint by sharing your copy with others or donating it to a library when you're finished reading it. When this book reaches the end of its useful life, you can significantly reduce its carbon footprint by recycling it rather than throwing it into your trash bin, after which it would most likely end up in a landfill where it would generate climate-heating methane emissions.

For More Information

Scan this QR code to access the endnotes, a reader's guide, a teacher's guide, and other resources. You will also find a link to the ebook and the audiobook.

Index

Previous spread: A fisherman pulls in mackerel caught on *anzuelos* hooks—individual hooks wrapped with red wool to resemble tiny crustaceans. This results in live bait being unnecessary, reduces bycatch, and protects the quality of the meat. Santoña, Spain. *Amy Kumler*

Next spread: Donna Kausen harvests end-of-season produce grown by her and her neighbors to store for the winter. Addison, Maine. *Greta Rybus*